T. S. ELIOT:
THE LONGER POEMS

T. S. ELIOT: THE LONGER POEMS

The Waste Land · Ash Wednesday
Four Quartets

DEREK TRAVERSI

Harcourt Brace Jovanovich
New York and London

Printed in the United States of America

Excerpts from the poetry of T. S. Eliot and from his
play, *Murder in the Cathedral,* are reprinted by
permission of Harcourt Brace Jovanovich, Inc.;
copyright, 1935, 1936, by Harcourt Brace
Jovanovich, Inc.; copyright, 1943, 1963, 1964, by
T. S. Eliot; copyright, 1971, by Esme Valerie Eliot.

Library of Congress Cataloging in Publication Data
Traversi, Derek Antona, date
T. S. Eliot : the longer poems.
Bibliography: p.
1. Eliot, Thomas Stearns, 1888–1965—Criticism and
interpretation.
I. Title.
PS3509.L43Z8815   821'.9'12   76-18793
ISBN 0-15-191380-3
ISBN 0-15-692020-4 pbk.

First edition
A B C D E F G H I J

CONTENTS

Author's Note

The studies which make up this book began as an attempt to provide a serious contribution to discussion of the later poetry of T. S. Eliot, and notably of the *Four Quartets*. A review of what has been written on these poems reveals very considerable disagreement on their nature and even more on their merits. Much of the discussion seems to have been rendered nugatory by the propensity of many critics, whether sympathetic or otherwise to Eliot's work, to introduce into the discussion religious prejudices which have little or nothing to do with the poetry *qua* poetry. This applies both to those who advance a Christian or religious view of life, and to those who strenuously oppose it or simply find it incomprehensible. The result has been to divide a remarkably continuous and coherent body of work, in which each new poem of any importance both derives from those which preceded it and looks forward to what was to follow, into parts, which the critics then proceed to exalt or to decry in accordance with their own prejudice. I hope that this study will in some measure have succeeded in avoiding this pitfall and thereby in contributing to a reasonable assessment of the poetry as such.

However greatly critics may differ over the relative importance of the earlier and the later works, most of them have been obliged by the sheer evidence of what is now literary history to recognize the importance of *The Waste Land*. That poem was, indeed, when it first appeared a turning-point both in Eliot's own poetic development and in that of English literature in our time. Only *Ulysses*, perhaps, has in this respect the same kind of importance. In view of this, and since it seemed important to establish the essential continuity of Eliot's work, it soon became apparent that the original intention of dealing only with the later poetry would have to be extended to cover the earlier poem. Ideally speaking, it would have been desirable to discuss work earlier than *The Waste Land*, and notably such poems as *The Love Song of J. Alfred Prufrock*, *A Portrait of a Lady*, and *Gerontion*, in which important aspects of Eliot's achievement first became apparent; but to have done this would have resulted in extending the present study beyond a convenient length. Again, the shorter works, both early and late, are relevant to any full discussion of Eliot's poetry; but I have chosen to confine my attention to three long poems, and to see *Ash Wednesday* as an interim stage, not wholly successful, in the development which led from *The Waste Land* to the *Quartets*, because I believe that the longer poem, or sequence of poems, as distinct from the shorter pieces or the plays (which seem to me to represent a mistake, though sometimes an interesting and — maybe — a necessary one on the poet's part), constitute the form towards which his talents were naturally directed.

In writing this study, I have been aware that Eliot's reputation as a poet has in some measure declined in recent years, especially among younger readers. This is to some extent, no doubt, a natural reaction against the sometimes excessive and uncritical admiration which his work enjoyed among many readers thirty years ago or more. Eliot's poetry certainly has its weaknesses, of which readers of the future are likely to continue to be aware. It is also a fact, however, that almost all the important writers of our time have suffered a temporary decline in their reputation in the years immediately following their deaths, and I have written in the belief that there is in the body of Eliot's work enough integrity, truth to experience, and skill in the poet's craft to ensure him a place in the literary tradition which he hoped in some measure to enrich and to modify by the fact of his own participation in it.

Much of the argument in the following pages was first developed in class teaching and discussion at Swarthmore College, and the actual writing was greatly advanced by a grant from the Andrew Mellon Foundation administered by the College. Without these favourable circumstances the book might well not have been written, and would certainly be less adequate to its subject than it is.

DEREK TRAVERSI
Swarthmore — Rome, 1973–5.

I
THE
WASTE LAND

THE WASTE LAND

[1]
Introduction

The year 1922 can be seen in retrospect as one of major importance in the development of English literature in the twentieth century. It saw the publication of James Joyce's *Ulysses* and of a poem by Eliot—*The Waste Land*—more ambitious in scope and intent than anything he had so far written. The two works, indeed, have between them exercised more influence upon the future than anything published in English in the years between the two World Wars. Both had in common, among other things, the search for a new way of structuring experience, of projecting emotional material by definition fragmented, without obvious connection of a causal kind, on to a containing framework. Both sought the solution of their problem in what Eliot, in a review of *Ulysses* published in 1923 in *The Dial*, called the 'mythical method'.

It is interesting, indeed, with a reading of *The Waste Land* in mind, to recall Eliot's expression of this idea:

I hold this book [*Ulysses*] to be the most important expression which the present age has found ... In using the myth, in manipulating a continuous parallel between contemporaneity and antiquity, Mr. Joyce is pursuing a method which others must pursue after him. They will not be imitators, any more than the scientist who uses the discoveries of an Einstein in pursuing his own, independent, further investigations. It is simply a way of controlling, of ordering, of giving a shape and significance to the immense panorama of futility and anarchy which is contemporary history ... Psychology, ethnology, and *The Golden Bough* have concurred to make possible what was impossible even a few years ago. Instead of a narrative method, we may use the mythical method. It is, I sincerely believe, a step towards making the modern world possible for art, towards order and form, and only those who have won their own discipline in secret and without aid, in a world which offers very little assistance to that end, can be of any use in furthering this advance.[1]

The passage is interesting for various reasons. Eliot is clearly writing with his own work—and notably the recently published *Waste Land*—very much in mind. He is both associating himself as a fellow pioneer and differentiating his own effort from that of Joyce. Both face a common problem, and react to it in ways which can be seen as parallel but neither is an 'imitator' of the other. Indeed, between Joyce's essentially comic genius and Eliot's sense of 'the immense panorama of futility and anarchy which is contemporary history' there is a fundamental difference of outlook. Joyce might have concurred in Eliot's judgement of the world around him, but he would have been less inclined, given his own temperament, to react with the same sense of repudiation and disgust. The difference is one which we shall need to examine further in relation to Eliot's own poetry. Meanwhile, the problem which is being advanced here and which, in one sense or another, concerns both writers is that of the artist's relation to *tradition*. The writer of a long 'narrative' work in English, from Chaucer to Wordsworth, from Defoe to Dickens and beyond, was able to assume that the laws which governed the telling of a story, and the purposes for which the story was told, were a matter for substantial agreement as between himself and his readers. To that extent at least, the poems and novels produced by these writers expressed the outlook of their society and their creative activity involved an element of collaboration.

To come to the second and third decades of the present century is to contemplate a situation essentially different. The problem of the 'modern' poet, as seen by Eliot or Joyce, differs from that of any of the writers of the past who operated, consciously or otherwise, within a recognized tradition. Such writers were able to assume that they shared with their society certain basic attitudes. These normally included a common ground of beliefs about the nature and sense of life, what we might call, in the broadest terms, a given set of 'religious' assumptions: assumptions, let us add at once, which need not have been, and often were not, the object of personal belief, but which were available for use and could be shared as a relevant background. Indeed, most art up to the present time has assumed, with varying degrees of conviction, that man has a distinctive 'spiritual' or moral dimension, though not by any means or necessarily in all cases a 'religious' destination. From this heritage there have derived a number of common, shared convictions about the nature of the universe and about man's place in it: agreed conventions about the nature of time, about such matters as freedom of choice and 'personality', all of which are involved in any poem or novel that sets out to 'tell' some kind of story. The artist is not by the nature of his activities either a moralist or a 'philosopher', and his work is apt to evade, or even to run counter to, the kind of certainty which these activities tend to generate; but his concern, as artist, with human experience is likely to involve him in these matters, and in his recognition of his involvement much of the essential quality of his achievement is likely to emerge.

The poet who was able to assume the existence of this kind of common ground between himself and his public enjoyed certain advantages in his own creative endeavour. He was free to concentrate upon what, in such a situation, he was apt to consider as his *craft*; most obviously, he was not called upon to create his own forms or to invent his own personal *symbols* to convey his sense of reality. Perhaps something of this is what Eliot had partly in mind when he dedicated *The Waste Land* to Ezra Pound and called him, in the phrase used by Dante of Arnaud Daniel in Canto XXVI of the *Purgatorio*, 'the best of craftsmen', *il miglior fabbro*.[2] The example of Dante, indeed, is particularly relevant to Eliot's work. Here was a poet who was able to project his own experience (as man, lover, politician, and exile) and that of his time (its political reality and thought, its metaphysics) into the symbolic device of a journey through Hell, Purgatory, and Paradise: all 'symbols' generally recognized in his society which the poet was able to play off, to set in meaningful relationship against an intensely personal experience. It is not necessary, for this purpose, that we should ask ourselves in what sense, or how literally, Dante *believed* in the objective reality of this framework. In theory at least, he need not have done so in any literal or absolute sense, any more than we can believe in the objective reality of the picture of the universe presented in the *Commedia*, whatever our own beliefs may be, and even if these are covered by the same name as we apply to those of Dante; and yet we can give the poem enough imaginative assent to confer on it an appropriate degree of 'reality'. It is enough to say that the Aristotelian-Christian scheme was there, available for the poet's use, and that on it he was able to project his imaginative conception of a 'journey' that was in effect both a voyage of individual discovery and a representation, a *figura*, of that undertaken by all men in the fulfilment of their individual and collective destinies: a voyage in which each stage is, as it were, *checked* by reference to a scale of values assumed, at least for the purpose of the poem, to be 'objective' and which the poet was conscious of sharing with his readers. The release of creative energy for other tasks which this situation made possible has been an important factor in the creation of many of the greatest artistic achievements.

Eliot (like Joyce) was aware that the artist of his own time had no such resource behind him and that it would have been dishonest for him to pretend otherwise. He had, in other words, to create his own symbolic structures, rather as though Milton had needed to invent the story of the Fall before writing *Paradise Lost* or Dante to work out the details of his cosmic scheme before writing his poem. Having created the equivalent of these symbolic devices out of his own resources, or those which his own time offered him in fragmentary form, the modern artist had to set the result against his own actual, *lived* experience, to see if, and, if so, to what degree, it fitted; for such coincidence could not be assumed or taken for granted, but had—at best—to emerge in the actual process of expression. This was in part because such symbols as are available to modern man are subjective, private in nature; they are not seen as a reflection of *outside* reality (as would have been generally assumed in Europe up to, say, the sixteenth century and —on the whole—recognized for practical purposes long after that), but as a condition shaping our interpretation of what we see or feel. What we see and feel is, in other words, a *construction* based on the forms of our perception; so that we can see, not what used to be held to exist independently of ourselves, but what our mental and emotional structures have conditioned us to see.

Eliot, having studied philosophy at Harvard and in Europe, had become aware of the view that the notion of pure objectivity (or of the supposedly real existence of things independently of our perception of them) is at best ambiguous. When Descartes, in his search for a firmly incontrovertible proposition, formulated his famous 'I think, therefore I am', he found, indeed, what served him as a foundation for his own speculations; but he also opened the way for what became in a great part of subsequent philosophy an impossible separation between 'thought' and its 'object'. The truth seems to be that we can only 'think' in relation to 'objects of thought' and that the two are in reality inseparable parts of a single process, only conceptually separable. Eliot had learnt from his study of F. H. Bradley (on whose philosophy he wrote a doctoral thesis[3]) that there appears to be an important sense in which every human experience of the *self* can be considered as essentially *private*, and that any concept of the so-called 'objective' world rests finally on *symbol*, on a kind of accepted *fiction*. Bradley's formulation of this view is quoted by Eliot in the Notes to *The Waste Land*:

> My external sensations are no less private to myself than are my thoughts or my feelings. In either case my experience falls within my own circle, a circle closed on the outside; and, with all its elements alike, every sphere is opaque to the others which surround it ... In brief, regarded as an existence which appears in a soul, the whole world for each is peculiar and private to that soul.[4]

Two extracts from Eliot's own prose writings show how this view affected his own way of thinking. The first is a comment on Bradley's view of the self as defined in the passage already quoted:

> A self is an ideal and largely practical construction, one's own self as much as others. [The self remains] 'intimately one thing with that finite centre within which my universe appears. Other selves on the contrary are for me ideal objects.'[5]

The second passage takes the form of a comment by the poet on Bradley's view of objects and their supposedly 'real' existence:

> For Bradley, I take it, an object is a common intention of several souls, cut out from immediate experience. The genesis of the common world can only be described by admitted fictions ... on the one hand our experiences are similar because they are of the same objects, and on the other hand

the objects are only 'intellectual constructions' out of varied and quite independent experiences. So, on the one hand, my experience is in principle essentially public ... And, on the other, everything, the whole world is private to myself. Internal and external are thus not adjectives applied to different contents within the same world; they are different points of view.[6]

The two passages, though occasioned by a different concern, are in fact considering the same problem—the nature and limitation of what we call, proceeding in part from the need to make experience intelligible, the 'self'—and have similar implications for the creative activity of the artist. The self is taken to be an assumed identity in space and time, and, like the other activities in which it seeks to express itself, poetry is a 'practical construction' based on this assumption. The phrase defines very adequately the relationship that unites *The Golden Bough* and Miss Weston's study of the Grail myth to Eliot's own poem. These works provide *The Waste Land* with the equivalent of what Dante, Milton, and other traditional poets were able to derive from the accepted 'mythologies' of their own times.

Eliot's interest in these matters is of concern to us, as it was very primarily to him, in relation to his problems as a poet writing in the twentieth century. By his nature as a thinking and feeling being, a centre of consciousness, the poet is moved to *structure* reality, to see it in relation to certain assumptions of a formal nature. For the writers of the past, normally involved as they were in a common tradition, these assumptions amount—as we have suggested—to a world picture, which provided them with a framework on which the poet could build; it served for what Eliot, using a phrase which has achieved perhaps more notoriety than he can have foreseen, called an 'objective correlative' for his own emotions. The passage in question runs as follows:

The only way of expressing emotion in the form of art is by finding an 'objective correlative', in other words, a set of objects, a situation, a chain of events which shall be the formula of that particular emotion; such that when the external facts, which must terminate in sensory experience, are given, the emotion is immediately evoked.[7]

This 'objective correlative' is, briefly, the unifying principle which every artist requires if he is to impose *form*, shape, on the apparent chaos of his initial experience: and Eliot would have agreed with nearly all the great writers of the past that this is what the artist is called upon to do. His way of doing it is conditioned by the kind of experience which his age offers him, and which Eliot saw as being marked in the twentieth century by certain special characteristics. As he put it in another essay:

> when a poet's mind is perfectly equipped for its work, it is constantly amalgamating disparate experiences; the ordinary man's experience is chaotic, irregular, fragmentary. The latter falls in love, or reads Spinoza, and these experiences have nothing to do with each other, or with the noise of the type-writer or the smell of cooking; in the mind of the poet these experiences are always forming new wholes.[8]

This bringing together of disparate experiences or impressions, shaping them round an elusive but indispensable 'centre of awareness', is something that the poets of every age have done. It is, perhaps, the essential impulse behind *all* poetry; but in the twentieth century, at least as Eliot saw it, it is carried out under special conditions which are those notably reflected in much of his own early poetry. This builds, most characteristically, on a fragmented, discontinuous perception of the 'real'. The early Eliot differed from most of his contemporaries in this clear perception of the facts and in his readiness to accept the consequences. He was a *modern* poet precisely in being unable to derive the structuring principle, the 'correlative' which, like all poets, he needed from assumptions and ideas that he could share with his society and assume, for the purpose at least of writing his poems, to be *true*. The most he could do, as he came to see increasingly clearly in the course of his efforts to transcend the merely fragmentary or episodic, was to set a deliberately chosen framework side by side with broken, discontinuous experience. He did this, *not* assuming 'truth' or 'objective' validity of any kind as existing in the framework, but in readiness to wait to see whether, in the process of working out the original creative impulse, it would be found to *fit* and whether the sense of some unifying principle would emerge. It must be stressed that there was, for Eliot as for his readers, no short cut to success in this endeavour. The reader, like the poet, could only tell if the poem constituted a unity, or had achieved form, at the end of the creative effort, after the poem itself had been experienced stage by stage and in its totality.

All this throws light upon the 'method', so to call it, followed by the poet in *The Waste Land*. The poem was thought by many of its first readers to be a chaos; but in fact Eliot, not less than other poets, was out to create a *shape*, a *form* from the material provided by his experience. This implied a projection, an *objectivizing*, of the original private impulse: for it was just in this that the urge to creation, to self-expression, was held by the poet to consist. The special problem of *The Waste Land* rose largely from the fact that it was far more ambitious in scope and intention than any of the preceding poems in which Eliot had followed more or less the same procedure. Its aim was to convey, beyond one man's personal intuition, nothing less than the state of a civilization. To achieve this the poem needed something more than a single, personal centre of awareness, a Prufrock or a *Gerontion* figure of the kind used by Eliot in his early development of the dramatic monologue. His way of conveying the picture which now concerned him turned, we might say, on two guiding principles. The first was an acceptance of the need, which—as we have seen—he felt that his situation imposed upon him, to work through what he called in the poem 'a heap of broken images'. He accepted this need because it was, in reality, a world of *fragments* he was setting out to explore, because he had nothing else on which he could honestly build. The various 'characters', or 'voices', who succeed one another in the course of the poem and who tend, as the poet has told us in his note, to merge into the shadowy central figure of the blind prophet Tiresias, are as 'broken', as shifting as the images which convey such identity—or lack of it—as they possess. Presented by a method not unlike that of 'cutting' in a film—*Ulysses* also makes notable use of this technique—they merge almost imperceptibly into one another, are not individually definable for any length of time. The aim, however, is *not* to create a final impression of chaos. It is simply that the 'shape' of the poem, if it is to come at all, can only emerge gradually, can only be achieved in the process of expression.

The situation of the poet as creator, indeed, can obviously be contrasted in this respect with that of Dante, whose shape and structure were, even to an unusual degree, *given* to him, implicit in the very nature of his symbols. Eliot recognized the disadvantage in which this comparison placed him; but he also saw certain compensations, possibilities for the development of true and important insights, in his own situation. If the modern writer could not share certain advantages enjoyed by his great predecessors, he was more free than they were to develop other important implications of his art. As he was to write, at a rather later date, in *The Use of Poetry and the Use of Criticism*:

> Poetry may effect revolutions in sensibility such as are periodically needed; may help to break up the conventional modes of perception and valuation which are perpetually forming, and make people see the world afresh, or some new part of it. It may make us from time to time a little more aware of the deeper, unnamed feelings which form the substratum of our being, to which we rarely penetrate; for our lives are mostly a continual evasion of ourselves, and an evasion of the visible and sensible world.[9]

Here, as clearly stated as anywhere, is Eliot's sense of the social importance of poetry, of the function fulfilled by himself and such fellow-explorers as Joyce in extending, renewing the range and content of available human emotions. All considerable poetry exercises this function of reshaping the customary forms of human experience, and Eliot would certainly not have denied this to Dante, to Milton, and to the other great writers of the past. He might also have argued, however, as he seems to imply here, that the poet who can best do this for his own age is the one who shares its problems and is ready to build, without simplification or evasion, upon what it has to offer.

The 'heap of broken images' represents, in any case, only one of the two pillars of the construction upon which *The Waste Land* rests. Against them the poet aims to set an awareness of what is left, still available to us, of the continuity of significant tradition. Here we must be more than usually careful not to simplify. It is *not*—as many critics of his work have asserted—that Eliot is setting a nostalgically conceived past against a sordid present, or urging the rejection of what is actually before us in the name of an imaginary, or at any rate inaccessible, past perfection. A good deal of his later criticism *does* tend to do this, directly or by implication, and is the poorer for it; but the poetry—or that part of it which matters—rarely falls into this delusion. In his poetry, as in his best criticism, Eliot knew as well as anyone that elements of life and death, vitality and decay, are simultaneously present in any individual life and at any moment in human experience. The past offers no ready way of escape from the 'immense panorama of futility and anarchy which is contemporary history': for the simple reason that elements of 'futility and anarchy' are present, together with contrary intimations of living significance, at practically any historical moment we choose to contemplate.

There is, in short, and to put the matter in rather different terms, no honest and realistic way of avoiding the recognition of death as an inescapable element in the processes of life, individual and general. This Eliot certainly, and perhaps not unrealistically believed; but he also held that there is a sense in which we, each one of us, and each human society, *are*, quite simply and inescapably, our past, that our lives can be seen as the sum of our past experiences—our own, those of our society, and those of the human race to which we belong—concentrated on the elusive, intangible reality we call the present and projected towards the future. It is in this sense that Eliot, again in 1917, stressed in his famous essay on *Tradition and the Individual Talent* the importance to a poet of the historical sense, which involves

> a perception, not only of the pastness of the past, but of its presence: the historical sense compels a man to write not merely with his own generation in his bones, but with a feeling that the whole literature of Europe from Homer and within it the whole of the literature of his own country has a simultaneous existence and comprises a simultaneous order.[10]

Every writer—whether he is aware of it or not—has become what he is through the operation of a past which, by the very fact of living, has become actually and inescapably his; and it may be that the writers—or the human beings—with the greatest living range are those to whom this reality is most consciously and freely available. Here—to return to our immediate argument—we have the purpose of the quotations which so scandalized early readers of *The Waste Land* and which are far from being the merely frivolous interpolations that Eliot's own notes occasionally prompt his readers to feel they are. They are the still available fragments of a great and constantly enriched tradition which, even in the broken form in which they are offered to a contemporary poet, may yet serve, by the end of the poem (and not before), to give meaning to what otherwise presents itself as broken, fragmentary chaos.

In other words, the poem is built on two great themes, represented by the 'broken' pieces which constitute human experience as it is offered to us in the present and the significant tradition of the past, itself seen in 'broken' form from a standpoint which can only be that of the present. The two 'themes', so to call them, begin apart, like two initially separate subjects in a musical composition; but the hope, the *method*, is that they will be seen to converge upon an emerging principle of unity.

It would seem that this necessary principle can only be arrived at by subjecting the parts, the fragments, to some kind of unifying concept. Since, as we have seen, Eliot cannot share this with his society as the great traditional poets have done, he needs to find an external, a personally significant structuring principle which he can apply to his poem with a view to seeing if it can do the job. This is the substance of the 'mythical' method referred to, in speaking of Joyce's *Ulysses*, in Eliot's remarks already quoted. Joyce, in *Ulysses*, had structured his protagonist's day round the successive episodes of the *Odyssey*. Bloom is Ulysses and Stephen Dedalus Telemachus, and 'father' and 'son' move erratically towards their inconclusive meeting through the various stages of a June day in Dublin. The corresponding device which seeks to impose some measure of continuity on *The Waste Land* rests, as the notes tell us, on two twentieth-century studies of myth. The first was, of course, Sir James Frazer's famous *Golden Bough*,[11] a study of primitive rites of regeneration, of the reproducing in many different human societies of the death of winter through what was originally the annual 'symbolic' sacrifice of the king-priest in order to ensure for his society the 'resurrection' of life in the renewal of spring. This is the principle which Frazer saw reflected in the stories of Osiris, of Orpheus, of Pluto and Persephone, and in the Greek Mysteries.

Side by side with *The Golden Bough* Eliot points to the influence upon his poem of Miss Jessie L. Weston's book *From Ritual to Romance*.[12] This is a study based on methods and ideas largely derived from Frazer of the Quest for the Holy Grail, which relates its supposed symbols to survivals in the Tarot pack of cards and elsewhere. We have accordingly, for the purposes of Eliot's poem, the symbols in the cards of the cup, the lance, and others, which

Miss Weston connects with the Grail legend and sees as sexual symbols connected with the ancient fertility rites and possessing phallic significance.[13] More importantly still for our purposes, we have the legend—prominent in *The Waste Land*—of the Fisher King, who became impotent as the result of an inflicted wound and whose impotence is associated with the failure of fertility in the land over which he rules. This legend is connected with the use in the poem of the symbols of water, as a sign of regeneration, and of fishing; we recall, in the latter connection, the use by the early Christians of the Fish as a symbol of the resurrected Christ. Finally, Eliot's poem takes from Miss Weston's book the idea that the maimed Fisher King can be restored to full life and potency by a knight undertaking a pilgrimage to the Chapel Perilous, where the Grail symbols are supposedly hidden. This 'pilgrimage' is held, in Miss Weston's book, to reflect the trial and initiation processes of the Greek mysteries, which in turn are seen as referring to other and older rites.

Such, then, are the chief symbols which Eliot sought in his poem to impose on his 'broken' material, in the absence of an accepted and common tradition. The *hope*—and it can, initially, be no more —is that the imposition may be found to *work*, that it may serve effectively to give unity to the 'panorama of death and futility' with which the body of the poem is so obsessively concerned. It may be that the main critical problem presented by *The Waste Land* is to decide whether this idea functions in the poem, if in fact a sense of meaning and unity leading to an enhanced awareness of life, even under its aspect of desolation, *is* actually conveyed. The answer cannot, of its very nature, be an absolute one, but has to proceed— like all good reading of poetry, in the last analysis—from a complete submission to the poetic process, the exposure of each individual reader to the successive stages of the experience which the poem actually, and within its own terms of reference, offers.[14]

[2]
The Poem

I

We begin our reading of *The Waste Land*, accordingly, not expecting to find either the traditional forms of structure, those provided by a single speaking voice representing a point of view consistently developed through the poem, or a series of events arranged in temporal or logical sequence and pointing to a foreseen conclusion. As we have seen, these structural elements are, by definition, excluded. What we are given to take their place is, as again we have seen, a set of 'broken', disconnected images, set against the persistent evocation, itself in fragmentary form, of past tradition as seen from one individual perspective in the present. Beyond these fragments, serving *possibly*—and no more—as a tentative unifying principle, we are offered a 'mythical' framework based on concepts of spring and winter, life and death, drawn mainly from the works of Frazer and Miss Weston.

Having in this way grasped that beneath the fragmentary surface of *The Waste Land* there does indeed exist a 'method', a recognizable plan, it is time to see how that unity emerges in the elaboration of the poem. The opening section, *The Burial of the Dead*, brings into play the various themes of the whole conception: themes at this stage apparently separate and incoherent, but possibly destined—though *not* before the end, if then—to assume 'meaning' through repetition and development as parts of what may emerge as a unified creation. Significant is the emergence, for the first time in Eliot's work, of what we might call a 'musical' conception of poetic exposition.

The first lines, elaborating the association of apparently contradictory impressions, at once state the peculiar nature of the creative impulses which produced *The Waste Land* and point forward to the main preoccupation of the whole poem:

> April is the cruellest month, breeding
> Lilacs out of the dead land, mixing
> Memory and desire, stirring
> Dull roots with spring rain.

It is instructive to compare this opening with another famous evocation of spring, that which opens Chaucer's *Canterbury Tales*.[1] Chaucer's spring is a season of life renewed, joyfully and un-ambiguously, after the 'death' of winter. The associations are largely conventional, drawn from familiar topical allusions and developed in accordance with established stylistic practices, but a sense of life breathes through them with a vigour that is more than literary. The 'sweet showers' of April have 'pierced to the root' the 'draught of March', acting with revived, fecundating power on the dormant sources of life; the season is one in which all created things, men and birds alike, are impelled to resume their vital activities — 'So priketh hem nature in hir corages' — and in which men, in particular, are moved to undertake 'pilgrimages' which are a reflection both of their natural and their supernatural destinies. 'Nature' and 'grace', in fact, not seen as separate or contradictory realities but as different aspects of a single, vital process, are here brought together in the common image of life as a journey, a move-ment — whether spiritually directed or humanly wayward — towards a final and necessary goal.

In Eliot's opening there is, of course, nothing of this. April, normally the month of rebirth, has become 'the cruellest month', the month which produces in men momentary flowerings of intui-tive life in a soil which has no nourishing qualities. 'Memory' of a past which is no longer there mingles with the pressures of an ambiguous 'desire', which may be either an irreflexive impulse dedicated to no goal beyond that of its immediate satisfaction or a wish for something difficult to define and, apparently, impossible to attain. The 'dull roots' of winter death are 'stirred', moved to a kind of renewed life, but to what end remains to be seen. The 'lilacs', with their associations of romantic nostalgia, so strong in Eliot's poetry from the time of *A Portrait of a Lady* onwards,[2] are indeed 'bred', born, but born out of death. Winter, beneath the appearance of desolation, the annual laying waste of all that has lived and grown, has indeed maintained a kind of life beneath the barren soil of the 'dead land'. It has even 'kept us warm', induced in those who dwell in the Waste Land and have been subjected to its desolation a certain sense of relief, of release from the intolerable obligation of *choosing* to continue to live. Covered 'in forgetful snow', maintaining 'a little life' in the form of desiccated roots — 'dried tubers' — the dead season has preserved a faint underground

stirring, a suggestion of vitality which may or may not be the pre-
lude to revival. It may be that this is the only kind of life which the
dwellers in the Waste Land desire, or can contemplate.

However this may be, the time for attempting a more definite or
positive statement has yet to come. Meanwhile, a few of the intui-
tions which the revival of spring has induced are recalled, without
any attempt at uniting them, in the lines that immediately follow.
The 'voices' of the poem—those of its 'characters', so to say—
begin to speak: they speak, appropriately, in disconnected, recalled
fragments of conversation. No 'character' in this poem—the poet
tells us in his notes—exists as a separate and self-sufficient entity.
All of them *merge* imperceptibly into one another, until they
eventually concentrate, in the third and central section of the poem,
on the figure of Tiresias, the blind prophet who, though he is
unable to use his experience to modify or change the endless series
of repetitive events of which he is the forewarned spectator, in
effect *sees* what we are told is 'the substance of the poem'.[3] A cer-
tain hour of conversation in Central Europe, remembered against
a spring background of alternating sun and rain; scraps and frag-
ments of the old, established order of what was thought to be a
civilized life; a child's memories of an adventure on a sled, in which
fear ('I was frightened') was inextricably mingled with the sense of
exhilaration which a surrender to life provokes and which is re-
placed in the adult by a retreat into a safe, but meaningless,
routine:

> In the mountains, there you feel *free*.
> I read, much of the night, and go south in the winter:

all these are reflections of an ambivalent state in which the memory
of past glimpses of integrity and confidence—'freedom', involving
in its exercise *risk*, accepted commitment, as a condition of life—
is 'mixed', cruelly because inconclusively, with the 'desire' that the
state in which they were conceived may once more regain reality,
may again, as formerly, indicate the possibility of a purposeful and
integrated life.

Once the prevailing sense of uneasiness has been stated and
illustrated, the poem returns once more to reflect on and extend
the image of the 'dead land' with which it began. The passage
which follows is notably more extended, more continuous in its
effect, than anything that has preceded it. It is, in fact, a first

general statement of the 'waste land' theme and will be taken up again later, more particularly in the concluding section of the poem.[4] Remembering the 'dull roots' that were so disquietingly stirred by the spring rain in the opening lines, the poem returns to 'the roots that clutch' and adds a reference to the 'branches', which in their persistent tendency to 'grow' illustrate the strength of the vital impulse even in the unfavourable environment of 'stony rubbish', the adverse conditions with which *The Waste Land* is so concerned.

The fact is that, even at this early stage, the mood of the poem is undergoing an important development. The prevailing impression is still one of monotony, death, repetition, absence of the life-giving water; and yet there is an indication, tenuous, even ambiguous, indeed, but still present, of change. The 'voice', still afflicted by its sense of perceiving nothing real beyond the 'heap of broken images', fragmentary impressions, the meaning of which we have already discussed, indicates for the first time a sense of possible relief when it refers to 'the shadow under the red rock' in the desert. This relief we are not yet in a position to understand other than vaguely—it may even be an illusion, the product of a wish to step out of the Waste Land, and by so doing to renounce a share in the universal, the *only* human situation—but it is clearly associated even at this stage with a possible breaking of the grip of monotony through the acceptance of the reality of death:

> And I will show you something different from either
> Your shadow at morning striding behind you
> Or your shadow at evening rising to meet you;
> I will show you fear in a handful of dust.

The cumulative rhythm of the passage, with its insistence on the contrast between 'shadow' past and 'shadow' future, what is 'behind' and what is 'rising to meet you', leads up to the direct challenge of the last line and—by so doing—obliges the reader to respond to a new element in the poem. It is not too much to describe this as the emergence of what is to become a dominating idea of the whole work: the idea that to live is, in the first instance, to confront the 'shadow', that the acceptance of death in its tragic reality could imply an understanding that not everything in life is simply repetition and vanity.

The suggestion is that of something 'different' from the unending

succession of 'shadows' at morning and evening, something to
which the designation of 'shadow' cannot—for better or worse—
apply. The recognition of *death* as a reality, a challenge to life, *may*
imply something beyond vain repetition. In the fear of death,
which seems to be the most powerful emotion open to those who
dwell in the Waste Land, there may be the beginning of a more
positive awareness of what it means to be human, alive. The whole
passage, it should be noted, has behind it echoes of the Old Testa-
ment prophets, and more especially of Ezekiel and Ecclesiastes:[5]
messengers, one might say, of doom for the people of Israel, but
messengers who also bore with them the promise of a renewal of
life.

It is worth noting that when the poem, after this passage, returns
to the evocation of fragments of intense experience, its intuition—
this time of beauty perceived through a remembered moment of
something akin to love—is of a profounder and more living kind
than anything indicated in the opening passage. For the first time
there is the sense of a possible relationship, the desire—however
frustrated—of one person to *give* himself, positively and unre-
servedly, to another:

> 'You gave me hyacinths first a year ago;
> 'They called me the hyacinth girl.'
> —Yet when we came back, late, from the hyacinth
>   garden,
> Your arms full, and your hair wet, I could not
> Speak, and my eyes failed, I was neither
> Living nor dead, and I knew nothing,
> Looking into the heart of light, the silence.

Among the human emotions involved in the Waste Land, and there
apparently threatened with reduction to insignificance or decep-
tion, is *love*: love which can be seen as a source of life, or—alter-
natively—as leading only to death. The experience of the 'hyacinth
girl', recalling ambiguous emotions of a kind already present in
earlier poems, and notably in *La Figlia che Piange*, where the poet
seems to be engaged in an effort to master, by distancing it, the
intolerable, is both intense and deceiving.[6] The vision of the
speaker—that conveyed by his 'eyes'—seems to have failed: we
hardly know, in the first instance, whether in fulfilment, in a kind
of recognition of the limits of the expressible, or in disappointment.

The key to the 'vision', indeed, lies in its ambiguity. To be led by an intensely personal experience to look for a moment into the 'heart of light' is also, by a necessary sequel, to contemplate the possibility that at the centre of the 'silence' which follows the 'vision' is—what may follow the 'silence',[7] what the 'silence' may in fact represent at the last: in other words, 'nothing'. At the 'heart' of the experience there may in fact be, emerging from and surviving it, 'nothing', a sense that any 'meaning' it may have has simply escaped our understanding and our definition.

There *may*, however, also be something more. In this glimpse, restored through memory, of the 'hyacinth girl' returning from the garden, 'late', 'with her arms full and her hair wet', we are aware of looking, like the speaker (whether he be the poet himself or a dramatic projection of personal feeling) into 'the heart of light, the silence' of an emotion that is felt to have a barely glimpsed but possible significance. Upon glimpses of this kind, tenuous and passing but at the same time profoundly real, much of Eliot's best poetry will insistently play. Only here, since we are after all in the Waste Land, the moment of intuition—whatever its ultimate sense may be—is significantly framed between two fragments of quotation from Wagner's great romantic opera of love and death, *Tristan and Isolde*. The first (*Frisch weht der Wind . . .*) is hopeful, spontaneous, and forward-looking in tone, the second (*Oed' und leer das Meer . . .*) expressive of a sense of desolation and emptiness which it seems that love itself cannot, in the prevailing circumstances, escape.

After this interlude the 'religious' theme—its entry prepared for by the suggestion of the possible significance of death—enters the poem explicitly for the first time. It enters in a form debased, or at least ambiguous, in accordance with the spirit prevailing in the contemporary Waste Land, which leads those who have no faith, but who still feel the need for it in the light of their sense of their own impermanence, to approach the clairvoyante Madame Sosostris. She, at least, appears to offer a means of foretelling, and thereby of dominating, the future.[8] To the Tarot pack of cards which she manipulates—and which is associated in Miss Weston's argument, the truth or otherwise of which need not concern us, with the rebirth of life that follows the seasonal rising of the waters in the fertility rites of the East—are attached many of the most significant episodes in the poem. The card of the 'drowned Phoenician sailor' introduces the theme of death by drowning which recurs under various forms and finds its most explicit development in the short elegy on Phlebas the Phoenician. 'Belladonna, the lady of the rocks' — 'the lady of situations', as she is also called — is clearly related to the women whose 'situations', in a world where lust has come to be divorced from any redeeming or humanizing conception of love, are the main theme of the second and third sections. The 'Wheel', too, reappears in the fourth poem and, by implication, elsewhere; it introduces the conception of life as circular, repetitive, and directionless. The 'one-eyed merchant' prepares us for Mr. Eugenides, who makes a fugitive appearance in the third section as the embodiment of a particularly sterile form of 'desire', and — beyond him — looks forward once again to the drowned sailor, who is also a Phoenician and also engaged in trade, of the *Death by Water* elegy. The Hanged Man, as Eliot has himself told us,[9] is to be associated with the Hanged God of Frazer, and so with all the sacrificial deities of the fertility rites and, beyond these, with their fulfilment in the Christ. This is possibly the most significant of all the symbols, but we shall not be in a position to assess its importance until the last section of the poem, where it will receive more explicit development.

All we know at present is that Madame Sosostris, the purveyor of false or at least ambivalent 'certainties', is not in a position to find him among the cards she is dealing. The prevailing vision, as seen through her eyes, is still one of 'crowds of people, walking round in a ring': one more expression, if we will, of the concept of the Wheel to which human life seems to be bound by its attachment to unattainable, or illusory, desires. To be noted, finally, as significant for the later development, are the contrasted references in this part of the poem to the theme of death by drowning: death seen either as an end to be shunned — 'Fear death by water' — or as imaginatively transformed, for the first of several occasions in the poem, in the light of Shakespeare's *Tempest* symbolism: 'Those are pearls that were his eyes. Look!' This double concept of death, as tragically meaningless and conceivably redeeming, will be one of the poem's most persistently recurring themes.

The last lines of *The Burial of the Dead* bring us back to the spiritual desolation of the Waste Land, seen now as the 'Unreal City', which is at once the poet's own commuter London and a symbol of the state of his society. 'The brown fog of a winter dawn' brings with it persistent echoes from Eliot's early poetry: this is the city of *Preludes*, of *A Portrait of a Lady*, and of *Prufrock*.[10] It is also, however, in a very real sense, Hell. The preoccupation with spiritual significance is kept alive by the references, underlined in the notes, to Dante's *Inferno* ('I had not thought death had undone so many', and the vision of the morning crowds 'flowing' to their daily work across London Bridge) and to Baudelaire: to Dante who was able to see human life in terms of judgement and in accordance with a clearly established scheme of values, and to Baudelaire—in the last line of the section—for whom the possibility of moral choice was the only thing that could save human life from unutterable tedium.[11]

The final, brief episode which rounds off this introductory stage of the poem is an enigmatic meeting with one of the 'shades' that cross the bridge on the way to their infernal destination. 'Stetson' is, of course, a commonplace name, with twentieth-century and— more specifically—American associations; but the voice which greets him, in something of the tone of Dante's recognition of Brunetto Latini,[12] refers to the battle of Mylae, a decisive moment in the history of Western civilization. The salutation, couched in terms of a peculiar irony, takes up once again the underlying themes of the poem as we have already seen them developed:

> 'That corpse you planted last year in your garden,
> 'Has it begun to sprout? Will it bloom this year?
> 'Or has the sudden frost disturbed its bed?

The lines refer—but in a spirit which is clearly ironic—to the possible 'sprouting' of the buried corpse as symbol of the resurrection rites practised by primitive man in his efforts to ensure, and to associate himself with, the annual rebirth after the apparent death of winter.

The 'resurrection', however, if it is to take place, will now spring from the bottom of a suburban garden, and the following quotation of the dirge from Webster's *White Devil*[13] deliberately confers upon it a sense of parody: Webster's 'wolf' has become the domestic 'dog', beloved of suburban householders, and man's wild 'foe' has been transformed into his ingratiating 'friend'. The 'resurrection' has become a 'digging up' of the corpse, partly sinister, even ghoulish, and partly absurd; and the final quotation from Baudelaire's *Fleurs du Mal* involves the poet and his reader in a common accusation of 'hypocrisy'.

The final question with which we are left is one that can only be advanced ironically in the Waste Land; but its underlying implications are as serious as life itself. Can the modern 'corpse', or death, produce the miracle of life renewed? Will it 'bloom' in this, or any year? The answer can only emerge, if at all, at a later stage in the development of the sequence. In the meantime, by the end of *The Burial of the Dead*, all the main threads of the poem have been introduced and the way is clear for their possible development towards a problematic harmony. That development is the work of the sections which follow.

II

In the second section of *The Waste Land — A Game of Chess —* the development narrows, in accordance with the governing plan of the poem, from the general towards the particular, from a panorama of universal death to two parallel sketches of boredom and vacancy, mainly related to sexual desire, in very different stations of life. What we are shown under both forms is the reality of 'Belladonna, the lady of situations': 'beautiful woman' and poison plant, reflecting in her own 'situation', which is also the outcome of her own deliberate contrivances, what life has become in a world where 'desire', or lust, operates with no relation to any saving concept of love or personal relationship. The title of this section, we recall, is taken from a play by Shakespeare's contemporary Thomas Middleton, *Women Beware Women*, in the course of which a mother is distracted from the seduction of her daughter, which is taking place in a room above, by a scheme to make her absorbed in the progress of 'a game of chess'.[14] The successive 'situations' of the game correspond on the one level to the tragedy of base and sordid betrayal that is being enacted on the other.

The section is divided into two parts — two episodes which are intended to be seen as parallel to one another — at line 138. The first shows us a sophisticated woman alone with her thoughts before her dressing table and carries with it persistent and relevant literary echoes: echoes, more particularly, of Enobarbus' account of Cleopatra on her barge in Shakespeare's *Antony and Cleopatra*,[15] but also — though less directly — of Iachimo's deception of Imogen in *Cymbeline*[16] and of Pope's *Rape of the Lock*.[17] The latter are significant, because each carries in its own way — ostensibly 'romantic' in Shakespeare, mock-heroic in Pope—an implication of betrayal leading finally to the threat or actuality of 'rape'. In a world like that of *The Waste Land*, where love, divorced from any conception of mutual or life-giving relationship between the sexes, has become nothing more than a name for the satisfaction of a physical need, the stronger party inevitably asserts its will at the expense of the weaker, imposes itself in what is ultimately an act of loveless and sterile violence.

This is the sense which is variously conveyed in the first of the two episodes. The reference to Cleopatra's royal progress to meet Mark Antony on the Cydnus serves both to support the prevailing impression of deadness and to point a contrast. On the one hand, the overblown magnificence of Enobarbus' description suggests a civilization which, for all its opulence and splendour, has lost its moral fibre; on the other, the play contains, side by side with other and deliberately contrasted impressions, moments in which triumphant passion seems to find supreme expression. Whatever its limitations may be (and Shakespeare develops them implacably and often to superb comic effect) the quality of the poetry which expresses this passion at its moments of greatest conviction contrasts forcibly with the more obvious and unremitting sterility of the Waste Land; though this is not to deny that there is a very real Waste Land—even more real, perhaps, than Eliot's—in *Antony and Cleopatra* too.[18] As Eliot develops his description of the modern lady, heiress to all the material advantages of a luxurious civilization and unable to put them to any significant use, he contrives to convey beneath the surface of rich sensual variety an impression of artificiality and sterile pointlessness. The 'burnished throne' of the modern heroine glows not, like Cleopatra's barge, on the living, shifting water which is the Egyptian queen's element, but by reflection on a polished surface of dead, unyielding 'marble'. The reflected 'glitter' of her jewels is somehow harsh, artificial, and the perfumes in the unstoppered 'vials of ivory and coloured glass' are explicitly described as 'synthetic'.

The general movement of the passage is from opulently overcharged deadness to a growing intimation of the sinister. If the evocation of Cleopatra suggests the artificial and the sterile as well as the magnificent, that of Iachimo emerging from his hiding-place as Imogen sleeps in her bedroom points to cynicism, betrayal, and a kind of rape. The physical setting of the scene, which partly derives from these parallels, answers to a similar effect. The very description of the dark room, candle-lit and enclosed, increasingly claustrophobic in its effect, points in the same direction. From the 'fruited vines' which hold up the mirror in a gilded parody of fertility there peeps out a 'golden Cupidon' whilst another—as though foreboding or ashamed—'hid his eyes behind his wings'. The 'synthetic' perfumes on the glittering, brittle dressing-table 'troubled, confused/And drowned the sense in odours;' whilst the air 'freshened from the window', reminding us of a world of light and life outside, the heavy perfumes 'fatten' the prolonged candle-flames, recalling the smoke which rose from the offerings in the 'laquearia', the ceremonial bowls of the Roman sacrifices. Exotic flames—'green and orange'—cast shadows, 'Stirring the pattern on the coffered ceiling,' in a heavy, enclosed imitation of Renaissance splendour. In the flickering, 'sad' light so cast, a 'carved dolphin' —a symbol for the classical world of immortality and resurrection —is displayed on the 'antique mantel': displayed, too, is a 'sylvan scene', reminiscent of the pastoral nostalgia of a different world, but here charged with sinister, loveless associations of desire.

For at this point, more precisely, the impression of luxury divorced from life shades off into the first open suggestion of a more bitter reality: a 'rape' more tragic in its implications than that contemplated by Pope in his mock-epic, but not altogether frivolous, poem. Among the elements of the sumptuous decoration is a carving which represents the rape of the legendary Greek heroine and her subsequent transformation: 'The change of Philomel, by the barbarous king/So rudely forced.' 'Rudely' and 'barbarous' reflect the entry of a new and deliberate brutality into the poem. The legend, though it comes from the distant past, has its meaning for a world in which love and lust are on the way to becoming indistinguishable, for the tragedy is in its essence an eternal one. This the poet indicates by a significant change of tense. 'And *still* she *cried*, and *still* the world *pursues*'; the only change is that the poignant tragedy of the 'inviolable voice'—the voice of the nightin-gale, perhaps, which Keats heard when he wrote in his Ode 'No hungry generations tread thee down'[19]—has lost its meaning for the world contemplated in this poem, has come to be no more than a mere ' "Jug-jug" to dirty ears'. *Love* and *lust* have become one, and *love* itself no more than a *rape* forced by the stronger party on

33

an unwilling or (at best) indifferent partner, conceived as an *object* for the satisfaction of ephemeral desire.

After this passing, incomplete evocation of tragedy, which will be taken up more explicitly in the central third section, the rich decoration of the earlier part of the passage becomes more explicitly 'withered stumps of time', the representation of fragments surviving from the past but now divorced of meaning for the indifferent, loveless present: mere inanimate background for a reality in which a sinister element increasingly prevails:

> staring forms
> Leaned out, leaning, hushing the room enclosed.
> Footsteps shuffled on the stair.
> Under the firelight, under the brush, her hair
> Spread out in fiery points
> Glowed into words, then would be savagely still.

In the deep hush of the 'enclosed', now more than ever claustrophobic room, the 'staring forms' lean out in reiteration looking into the fire-reflected shadows. The footsteps, which may be those of an approaching 'lover' (we cannot be sure) 'shuffle', with a muted suggestion of the sinister and the bestial, on the stair; and, as the lady awaits this eruption of a kind of reality from the world outside, the 'fiery points' of her brushed hair 'glow into words' — her own words, expressive of an anxiety barely definable — to be lost, as the sustained passage draws to its close, 'savagely', resentfully 'still'.

These 'words' form, together with the parallel episode in this section, one of the most successfully dramatic passages in Eliot's writing. They take the shape of an extremely subtle interweaving of the woman's spoken anxieties with the main underlying threads of the poem. 'My nerves are bad to-night. Yes, bad. Stay with me.' Four lines of intensely staccato rhythm, expressive of persistent preoccupation and a sense of impenetrable isolation, weave 'Think' and 'Speak' into a superbly evocative pattern of obsessive anxiety. They are broken by the reference to 'rats' alley', to the vision of sordid and hopeless death which is one of the obsessing features of the Waste Land. This, though not 'by water', is one aspect of the death of Madame Sosostris' earlier warning, which the poem is now concerned to bring into focus. It leads to a passage of central importance for the emerging development:

'What is that noise?'
                    The wind under the door.
'What is that noise now? What is the wind doing?'
                    Nothing again nothing.
                                                    'Do
'You know nothing? Do you see nothing? Do you
    remember
'Nothing?'
              I remember
Those are pearls that were his eyes.
'Are you alive, or not? Is there nothing in your head?'

It is worth noting that this passage is not, properly speaking, a dialogue between the protagonist of this part of the poem and her companion. Dialogue, in any proper sense, is not a possibility in the Waste Land. The companion *may* be there, physically present, but his replies—if this is what they are—are not given explicitly as such, isolated in quotation marks. They belong rather to the speaker's own thoughts, project her intimate fears, and answer rather to the main development of the poem than to any of its 'characters'. The point is that in the Waste Land each experience is inexorably enclosed in its own isolation, incapable of breaking the 'prison'—which will be spoken of in the concluding section[20]— which is its normal environment.

Under these circumstances, and in the light of the evocation of unredeemed death in 'rats' alley', the speaker's fear returns and the exchange—which may be with her visitor but seems, as we have said, to be rather a projection of her own thought—gathers new force in a series of shorter, more direct—and less answerable— questions, 'What is that noise now? What is the wind doing?' and in the answer to which these reiterations lead: 'Nothing again nothing'. With the word 'nothing' obsessively repeated and isolated by its position in the rhythmic development, the true motive for fear, which is a sense of impenetrable vacancy, sheer emptiness, comes to the surface: 'Do/You know *nothing*? Do you see *nothing*? Do you remember/*Nothing*?' At this point, with the obsession of emptiness and unreality at the height of its tension, the reference to death returns, but in a form transformed and one more reminiscent of one of the themes stated in *The Burial of the Dead*. This is the theme of death by water, already associated by Madame Sosostris with a key-phrase from *The Tempest*: 'I remember/Those are pearls that were his eyes.' The two possible attitudes to death—that conveyed in 'rats' alley' and that persisting in the memory from Shakespeare's play—frame between them the passage—dialogue or uneasy meditation, as the case may be—which we have been considering. Brought together within these few lines they are balanced against one another in a way which will be fundamental to the structure of the whole poem. They occur repeatedly from this moment, and their relation to one another will not be definable, even in part, until the end of the poem. Indeed, the definition of this relationship—which will in any case be in poetic terms, terms of experience and expression and not those of doctrine and abstraction—will be the end towards which the whole work may be said to move.

For the moment, the fresh tone in this second reference to death remains no more than a suggestion. It is overwhelmed almost at once in the question that fellows: 'Are you alive or not? Is there nothing in your head?' In the light of this persistent sense of emptiness the echo from *The Tempest* dissolves ironically into the jazzed notes of 'that Shakespeherian Rag', and the answer to the insistent, the obsessive question:

'What shall I do now? What shall I do?' . . .
What shall we do tomorrow?
'What shall we ever do?'—

remains the mere continuation of an existence so sheltered from reality as to be without meaning. 'The hot water at ten', 'a closed car at four' if it should rain; this is the daily round of an existence cushioned against the actual and devoted to the elaboration of meaningless 'situations' in the abstract 'game of chess' to which Eliot—giving a personal echo to the dispassionate unfolding of intrigue in Middleton's play—reduces the relationship of the sexes in the society with which he is concerned. The game, in fact, is being played by those who are sharers in death—'Pressing lidless eyes'—and who await only the final 'knock upon the door'. The 'knock' which brings this first episode to a close at once represents the culminating moment in the sexual pattern—the arrival of the rapist-lover, which will be confirmed, in a different social key, in the central episode of the third section—and suggests, in the background, the disturbing shadow of death which will come sooner or later to bring the whole intrigue, the 'situation', to an end.

The second part of *A Game of Chess* offers a parallel case of the tragedy hidden in less sophisticated circles by the operation of sexual passion in the absence of a redeeming vision of purpose or value. The main intentions are sufficiently clear. Through the narrow, embittered comments of her companions in a London pub, we are shown a working-class woman in the desolate post-war world in the process of losing her hold at once on her husband and on life. Beneath the different social setting, it is the same game that is being played: the game in which fear of *betrayal* can only express itself in fear of *death* and in which, in fact, the two realities are in the process of becoming one. Those who are out of sympathy with Eliot's poetry sometimes say that there is an element of condescension, even of distaste, in his portrayal of 'lower-class' life. This may on occasions be true; but here, at least, the charge is implicitly refuted by the presence of the preceding passage, which surely establishes that the Waste Land situation is not one of class or social background, that the roots — and the occasions — for a pity which is *not* aloof or condescending belong, by their very nature, to quite a different order of reality. At all events, Eliot — who could fail in these matters, as his acceptance of the prose passages in his most unfortunate work, *The Rock*, will show — never came closer than here to picking up, and turning to 'dramatic' use, the rhythms of ordinary, 'working-class' English speech and producing from it a genuinely human effect. Much of what he was later to write in his ostensibly dramatic production is, by contrast, affected and dead.

The husband in question has, we are told, just been demobilized, and has come home with the intention of seeking in the sexual act no more than the 'good time' which, he feels, has been denied him during the years of war service. His desire is in the process of being translated into reality in terms of unwanted children who bring with them, in the circumstances, no more for the woman than the shadow of a life of sordid drudgery always liable to terminate in a painful and meaningless death. 'She's had five already, and nearly died of young George.' There is, in the comments of the speaker, a notable element of cruelty and perverse satisfaction; as though she were seeking compensation for troubles of her own in contemplating those of someone who, she feels, has more of them and thereby is rendered in some sense more *abject* than herself. Woven through the entire passage is the closing time

call—'Hurry up please it's time'—carrying with it an intimation
of death, the equivalent of the 'knock upon the door' which
brought the previous episode to a close.

The whole passage is skilfully worked round these themes. The
woman reporting and the one whose situation is under discussion
face one another in remembered conversation as barely disguised
rivals for the same man. Mutual jealousy is, in the Waste Land,
the other face of the betrayal of trust, and its expression is at once
mean and pathetic:

> He's been in the army four years, he wants a good
>   time,
> And if you don't give it him, there's others will, I
>   said.
> Oh, is there, she said. Something o' that, I said.
> Then I'll know who to thank, she said, and gave me a
>   straight look.

The speaker at this point is conscious of possessing the upper
hand, and ready to let her victim know it: for behind the latter's
protest there lies the shadow of betrayal by the husband in the
name of the Waste Land's prevailing desire—that for 'a good time'—
which is in reality itself yet another cover for the sense of emptiness.

Against this background of unwanted children, confirmed in the
reference to the abortion pill, and in the face of a fear of senseless
and painful death, the question of the *end*, the purpose of marriage
is raised with brutal directness. 'What you get married for if you
don't want children?': 'Albert won't leave you alone': in the Waste
Land the sexual drive is pursued without compassion or con-
sideration for the victimized partner; pursued without reference
to human feeling or for the furthering of a creative purpose. Life
in this desert, on all levels of society, reduces itself to an attempt
to evade responsibility, to undertake actions without any thought
of the consequences to which they are likely to lead; and it is only
death that, by persistently throwing its shadow across the human
scene, affirms that ultimately there is a limit to this too, that
responsibility cannot be shunned without depriving existence of
all meaning. This marriage, like so many in the Waste Land, was
born in accident and a triviality not in itself unworthy—'Well,
that Sunday Albert was home, they had a hot gammon'—but its
end, as in the companion episode, is the menace of death echoed

in the barman's insistently repeated call which runs like a *crescendo* theme through the whole monologue and which concludes on the last words of the betrayed Ophelia: 'Good night, ladies, good night, sweet ladies, good night, good night.' At the end of this section, there are already signs that the various themes, episodes and echoes first announced in *The Burial of the Dead* are in the process of being gathered together into something like a coherent and resolving vision.

III

In this process of integration, the third section, *The Fire Sermon*, has a central part to play. Carrying a stage further the presentation of sexual relationships in the Waste Land initiated in *A Game of Chess* it introduces a more specific note of tragedy and prepares the way for a tentative statement of such positive attitudes as the poem is prepared to contemplate. The timeless vision of Tiresias, linking the various isolated episodes into a repetitive unity is, in Eliot's own words, 'the substance of the poem'. The vision emerges from the episodes, is not in any sense imposed upon them; the method is that of meaning achieved through a process of cohering intuitions, never through the statement of an externally valid point of view.

The section opens with a return to the 'water' symbol which runs—as we have seen—through the whole poem with its double association of death and restoration. It is now taken up in a vision, itself 'double', of the river Thames—'London river', the river of the 'Unreal City'—at once polluted and commerce-stained in the present and recalled in its literary associations of vanished splendour. Once again it would be too simple to say that these two aspects of the one river are seen in terms of a straight contrast, the supposed splendour of the past set against the stressed ignominy of the present. The contrast is more subtle, the interlocking of past and present at once closer and less clearly differentiated than such a view would imply.

The two aspects—today's river, bearing its empty bottles, sandwich papers, and cigarette ends, spectator of the amours of the modern 'nymphs' and their friends, 'the loitering heirs of City directors', and the river of Spenser's *Prothalamion* which serves as background and contrast—are woven together in a passage in which the note of desolation prevails. Today's 'nymphs' have 'departed' with their swains, as—in a different way—have those conceived by Spenser before them. It is Autumn, 'the last fingers of leaf' fall, 'sink into the wet bank', and the wind that bears them comes from the 'brown', the bare land. The sense of desolation is conveyed through the words of the Psalm expressing the grief of the people of Israel in their exile. 'By the waters of Leman I sat down and wept': the substitution of 'Leman' for 'Sion' reminds us that Eliot wrote at least part of this poem when recuperating from illness and mental stress in Switzerland. At the end of the opening block of lines, the Spenserian refrain returns more irresistibly and is linked with an ironic parody of Marvell's lines on the imminence of death in *The Coy Mistress*.[21]

Once more, as the meditation proceeds, the thought of death imposes itself and the vision of 'rats' alley', carried over from the preceding section, is more explicitly developed. As in *A Game of Chess*, however, it brings with it a contrasted reference to *The Tempest*; the glimpse of the rat 'Dragging its slimy belly on the bank' behind the gas house near the 'dull canal' is broken by a repetition of Ferdinand's lines on death by drowning, with their hint of a richer, finer conception of death:

> Musing upon the king my brother's wreck
> And on the king my father's death before him.

No doubt the fact that the speaker at this point shades, through the line 'While I was fishing in the dull canal', into the Fisher King, whose restoration by Parsifal at the end of the quest for the Grail was accompanied by the lifting of the curse upon his kingdom, is of significance for the 'mythical' symbolism of the poem; but, though the theme is repeated at the end of this introductory passage in the quotation from Verlaine's poem recalling the voices of the choir at the Holy Thursday ceremony which preceded the healing of the wounded Amfortas, it remains necessarily tenuous and indefinite. More immediate at this point, and more closely related to the prevailing mood, is the renewed evocation, after the *Tempest* reference, of death and desolation, the background to the amours of Sweeney and Mrs. Porter, set here by ironic contrast against a further echo of Marvell's great lines and the romantic associations of the passage, quoted in the notes, from Day's *Parliament of Bees*.

Here again, with the nostalgic purity of Verlaine's *Parsifal* line
—'Et O ces voix d'enfants, chantant dans la coupole'—still present
in our minds, the course of the poem, the flow of the river, as we
might say, is interrupted by yet another echo from the preceding
section, another indication of the growth in complexity and cohe-
rence which accompanies the unfolding of the pattern. The song
of the nightingale after the rape of Philomel —'So rudely forced'—
is evoked once more in its double manifestation of bird cry and
classical legend. 'Twit twit twit . . . Tereu': Tereus, we remember,
was the name of the assailant, here echoed in the sound of the
bird's lamentation, itself set in contrast to the 'jug jug' which,
already in *A Game of Chess*, it evoked in the sordid indifference of
the Waste Land. The subject is again the central one of rape, and
as such anticipates what we are about to see in the central episode
of this section and, indeed, of the whole poem; and the contrast is
between the 'inviolable' voice of tragedy and its reception in a
bored and callous present.

This broken but significant interlude serves as an introduction
to the central part of *The Fire Sermon* which is concerned with
two episodes of life in the 'Unreal City', to which we now return.
'Under the brown fog of a winter noon': a sense of the passage of
time, corresponding to the development of the poem, is conveyed
by the substitution of 'noon' for 'dawn' in a line otherwise repeated
from the conclusion of *The Burial of the Dead*.[22] The first of these
two episodes, that of Mr. Eugenides the seller of currants, is
barely touched on, but reminds us once more of the theme of 'the
one-eyed merchant' announced by Madame Sosostris. It also pre-
pares the way for the drowned and transformed Phoenician sailor
of *Death by Water*.

The second and much longer incident, which shows the London
typist whose consent to seduction reflects rather boredom than
any positive pleasure (her first half-formed reaction to the depar-
ture of her 'lover' is, 'Well now that's done: and I'm glad it's over'),
is given a universal significance by being seen through the eyes of
Tiresias, and so becomes the turning-point of the whole poem.
The 'old man with wrinkled female breasts' (developed following
a hint taken from Ovid) shares the detachment of the poet as
spectator and is, like him, divided 'between two lives', between his
sense of the futility of a temporal order conceived as an end in
itself and an intuition, itself unrelentingly tragic in its implications,

of possible value. His stated bi-sexuality, moreover, and the old
age which has made him a spectator, rather than an agent, in
regard to the importunities of desire, make Tiresias uniquely
placed to convey what is becoming the central vision of the entire
work. As Eliot tells us, what he *sees* is the substance of the poem.
All the previous 'characters', or 'voices', merge into this observer,
whom we may also see as either a 'character' or as a 'voice'.

In the figure of this spectator, whom nothing however sordid
can surprise and nothing however complex deceive, the permanent
and the accidental aspects of love—already suggested in the refer-
ences to Philomel and implicitly present, though unrealized, in the
scene now presented under his contemplation—are openly brought
together for the first time:

> And I Tiresias have foresuffered all
> Enacted on this same divan or bed;
> I who have sat by Thebes below the wall
> And walked among the lowest of the dead.

It is hardly an exaggeration to see in this explicit relation of
immediate futility to a sense of permanent tragic content the
beginning of a transformation which affects the whole poem.[23] Its
episodes, hitherto separate and presented as devoid of meaning,
now begin to assume the likeness of a distinctive shape or pattern;
if, thus far, the fragmentary and meaningless seem to have pre-
dominated, from now on we shall be increasingly concerned with
the difficult and gradual exploration of what *may* emerge—one
should not say more—as elements of permanent value in human
experience.

The detailed working out of this general concept is worth a little
consideration. The setting of the scene is the evening, 'violet'
hour, a deliberate displacement of the familiar romantic setting for
sentimental experience. The adjective has about it something un-
expected, at once lucid and vaguely synthetic, which makes a
fitting setting for the desolate incident we are about to witness.
'The human engine' throbs 'like a taxi throbbing waiting'; we are
reminded of the essay in which Eliot insisted that one of the tasks
of a modern poet is to give expression to the contemporary rhythms
incorporated in his experience.[24] Tiresias, the timeless spectator,
is involved in this atmosphere, is aware of the faintly unnatural
twist given to romance by the 'violet' hour, himself 'throbs'—in

his own way, transcending the limitations of sex and time—
'between two lives'. What he sees is framed in a romantic parody
of the 'evening hour' 'that strives/Homeward, bringing the sailor
home from sea,' and bringing also the typist home at tea-time; and,
as he watches her making her unromantic preparations for her
assignation, we are made aware through his eyes of the sense of
what, yet again, he is about to see—the endless repetition of the
course of loveless desire:

> I Tiresias, old man with wrinkled dugs
> Perceived the scene, and foretold the rest—
> I too awaited the expected guest.

What follows down to the end of the episode (lines 235 to 248,
and 249 to 262) is cast, not without significance, in the form of a
pair of sonnets. The unprepossessing seducer, 'the young man
carbuncular', arrives, and is received. He has the confidence, the
'assurance' of one in whom desire is not complicated by any trace
of personal regard for the object of its satisfaction; and the victim,
so approached, is aware in her boredom of no valid motive which
might lead her to offer resistance:

> The time is now propitious, as he guesses,
> The meal is ended, she is bored and tired,
> Endeavours to engage her in caresses
> Which still are unreproved, if undesired.

The seducer's action, under these circumstances, can only con-
stitute the grotesque parody of an act of love. It is, in fact, an
'assault', a rape, that is being committed; this is 'desire', when
divorced from any human conception of love, in the Waste Land.
The 'assailant' requires no response. Indeed, he makes 'a welcome
of indifference', because he feels himself thereby absolved of
responsibility for what he has done. The incident once completed
in a way that confirms Tiresias' sense of unending, tragic repeti-
tion, he makes his departure,

> Bestows one final patronizing kiss,
> And gropes his way, finding the stairs unlit.

The 'victim', on her side, is hardly aware of what has happened to
her: only relieved that the meaningless episode has come to an end.
Her attitude is summed up in the parody of Goldsmith's 'romantic'

lines from *The Vicar of Wakefield* which rounds off the entire
incident.

The first effect of the change of emphasis in this part of the
poem is an indirect one. The episode of the typist has just been
'framed', in a way characteristic of this poem, by references to its
setting in the 'Unreal City', which is, in the last analysis, Hell, by
definition the heart of unreality. To the city we now return, but in
a manner notably transformed. A further echo of the water-music
of *The Tempest* — 'This music crept by me upon the waters' —
brings us to a new vision of London, one strikingly unlike that of
The Burial of the Dead:

> . . . along the Strand, up Queen Victoria Street.
> O City, city, I can sometimes hear
> Beside a public bar in Lower Thames Street,
> The pleasant whining of a mandoline
> And a clatter and a chatter from within
> Where fishmen lounge at noon: where the walls
> Of Magnus Martyr hold
> Inexplicable splendour of Ionian white and gold.

The riverside London that now emerges is human in its associa-
tions and beautiful in its buildings. It is not an accident that,
instead of the crowd of 'dead' souls crossing the bridge in 'the
brown fog of a winter dawn', we hear now the sociable sound of
the music with which the 'fishmen' of Billingsgate pass their
leisure in the companionship of a riverside bar, and that the sinister
reference to the 'dead' sound of the clock striking at St. Mary
Woolnoth[25] is replaced by a glimpse of 'splendour' on the walls of
another of the City churches. For a moment, at least, the city has
ceased to be 'unreal' or to suggest hell. The contrast with what has
gone before does not amount, in rational terms, to a reversal of
what has been the almost unrelievedly sombre tone of the poem,
but it does introduce a new element into it and hints, however
tenuously, at the possibility of a shift in the prevailing mood.

The following passage, introducing the song of the three
'Thames daughters', is surely rhythmically one of the most satis-
fying in all Eliot's poetry. The contrast is once again between the
modern and the Elizabethan river; but, as we read it, we shall
once more do well not to over-emphasize the contrast in any
simple nostalgic or 'romantic' sense. The commerce-stained

Thames of today is given, on the one hand, a peculiar beauty by the power with which its oily surface and drifting barges are evoked; and, on the other, not all the splendour—itself so equivocal in Shakespeare's play—of the setting of the Cleopatra-like Elizabeth can conceal the reality of the dubious and finally sterile 'game of situations' which she played with her lover Leicester.

Against the background of these lyrical lines the Thames-daughters speak in succession, echoing the song of the Rhine-maidens in Wagner's *Götterdämmerung*. What is shown is, indeed, a new 'twilight of the gods', reflecting in fragmentary utterance the section's main theme of meaningless seduction:

> 'On Margate Sands.
> I can connect
> Nothing with nothing.

Once more the key-word 'Nothing', so intensely introduced into the meditations of the 'lady of situations' at her dressing-table in the preceding section of the poem, is given stressed prominence. In the absence of a coherent attitude to give it meaning, all experience of personal relationships reduces itself to a series of isolated impressions, in which fugitive glimpses of 'the broken finger-nails of dirty hands' replace what should have been the moment of ecstasy, and disillusionment achieves pathos—tragedy is beyond its scope—in the anonymous resignation of the poor: 'My people humble people who expect/Nothing.' The first Thames-daughter echoes Dante's La Pia, whose betrayal by her husband ended in violent death: both are 'supine', accept their situation with a resignation which recognizes the inevitability of the cruel and the meaningless in their lives. The second is left, after her seduction, with her heart 'under her feet', realistically aware of the emptiness of the seducer's expressions of remorse—'After the event/He wept. He promised "a new start" '—and offering no comment: 'What should I resent?' In a world where *nothing* is real, or counts, any expression of hope or illusion for the future is simply and inescapably vain.

It is in the light of this repeated insistence on nullity that the closing lines of *The Fire Sermon* present for the first time references to representatives of the ascetic tradition both in East and West, and introduce the fire-symbol which gives its name to the section. St. Augustine and the Buddha both saw in fire a symbol of lust or desire, but also of purification. For that reason here, at the turning-point of the poem, we are offered the vision of a fire which at once consumes and, when refined into prayer, purifies. 'O Lord Thou pluckest me out': the redeeming idea of prayer has made its first explicit appearance, admittedly in a broken fashion which corresponds—as we have seen—to the 'method' of the poem, but which also indicates the entry of the tragic and religious vision with its suggestion of redemption. Impermanent and inconclusive as it is, apt to be swept away and to leave nothing more substantial than a broken memory, this is also a part of the total life of the poem. In this manner, the way is prepared for the concluding section, in which the themes so far developed will be taken up once more and integrated, as far as may be, into the artistic reflection of something which resembles a positive sense of life.

IV

What the Thunder Said is preceded, however, in a way that foreshadows Eliot's use of a similar device in each of the *Four Quartets*, by the short interlude *Death by Water*, which has a place of its own in the architecture of the poem. Explicitly connected with the use of the title-phrase in Madame Sosostris' manipulation of the cards, it has also an evident link with the repeated use as a key-theme of the 'death', also by water, of Ferdinand's father in *The Tempest*. The idea of death is now associated with glimpses, sensed rather than clearly defined, of a more spiritual vision of reality; though it would evidently be a mistake to look for new thematic development when the connections with the rest of the poem are clearly to be experienced in terms of mood and contrast rather than in explicit statements. It is in the *mood* which these lines convey—one of elegy tinged by an underlying irony—that we must seek the contribution which they make to the complete effect.

Among the things forgotten by Phlebas, 'a fortnight dead', is 'the profit and loss', the commercial preoccupation so sordidly embodied in Mr. Eugenides. These obvious deceptions need to be renounced in the face of death, which will in any case make them irrelevant; so, perhaps, and more subtly, does an undue concern with the immediate fruits of all human actions and decisions, the 'profit' and 'loss' to which men short-sightedly look in undertaking them. In the moment of death the details of past life seem to acquire significance—'He passed the stages of his age and youth'—in a way which has a lesson, of a kind, to convey. Gentile and Jew alike are exhorted to consider seriously the spectacle of the drowned Phoenician sailor and the subjection to mortality which it implies and which is common to all men. Not immediately comforting, the realization may yet have a certain purifying effect, rather similar to that of the sea which picks the bones of the dead man 'in whispers', cleaning and leaving them free of the contamination of flesh.[26] The contemplation of death by water points, in its own way, to the same possible liberation from triviality, from the wheel of desire, as was previously indicated in the transformation of the fire of lust into the purgatorial flame of Christian and Buddhist tradition.

V

In the last section (*What the Thunder Said*) the time has come for a drawing together of the various threads of the poem and for their gathering up, as far as may be, into a coherent pattern. The opening is a passage in which impressions of the Waste Land are interwoven with evocations of the incidents surrounding the Passion of Christ; such are the references to the 'silence in the gardens', and to the 'agony'—felt, be it noted, in the 'stony places'—which we may connect at once, in the spirit of double vision which characterizes so much of this poem, with Gethsemane and the Waste Land. Once more, as in the opening lines of *The Burial of the Dead*, there is a reference to 'spring', but this time associated not only with the Easter drama, but with a suggestion of impending—or at least possible—relief in the mention of thunder, still for the moment distant and menacing but due to break before the poem has come to a close.

Easter, however, has still to come—may, indeed, never come, may only be the expression, for us, of a pathetic and impossible illusion. The death which concluded the Passion, at least in the eyes of the disciples who were present as onlookers—'He who was living is now dead'—is associated with our own death as individuals and with the collective death of our civilization:

> We who were living are now dying
> With a little patience.

It is significant that, in the moment of desolation, we return once more to the opening vision of the desert. To the passage in the first section beginning 'What are the roots that clutch . . .?' corresponds the evocation of the rocky, waterless road among the mountains, where once again the hint of thunder occurs, but still conceived as menacing: 'dry', 'sterile', with no promise of relief.

Mere repetition of the theme of the Waste Land is not, however, the true purpose of a passage which aims at the integration of that theme into the developing resolution of the complete poem. By a subtle development of the prevailing imagery of drouth, we are led to a sense of delirium which is the basis of the next stage in the unfolding of the conception. Water, absent in reality from the desert, becomes so intensely present in the imagination that the longing for it merges with the recollected 'drip drop' of the hermit thrush's note to produce an impression in which reality and the over-wrought imagination are inextricably fused together. The passage is one of those in which Eliot uses short lines and an un-erring sense for the rhythmic development of their connections to intensely evocative effect:

> If there were water
> And no rock
> If there were rock
> And also water
> And water
> A spring
> A pool among the rock
> If there were the sound of water only
> Not the cicada
> And dry grass singing
> But sound of water over a rock
> Where the hermit-thrush sings in the pine trees
> Drip drop drip drop drop drop drop
> But there is no water.

It is in this state, poised between reality and hallucination, that there appears the vision of 'the third who walks always beside you': an appearance which may be that of the risen Christ as he appeared to his stricken followers on the road to Emmaus, but which may also — by an association referred to in Eliot's own notes — answer to the impression reported by Antarctic explorers at the extremity of their strength that a mysterious extra person is walking at their side. The peculiar quality of this vision answers to the state in which the poem is conceived and which remains relevant to the last. The experience of the Apostles was, in terms of the Gospel narrative, a reality, a proof of resurrection; that of the explorers is, quite simply, an illusion. The state of those who live in the desert, the Waste Land, is somewhere between the two. The Christian affirmation serves in some measure as a focal point for the constructive forces which are now making their presence felt in the poem; but the time to affirm its reality, to state that its evocation is a reflection of its validity and not of the plight of a civilization clinging to illusion in its despair, has not yet come.

Indeed, in *The Waste Land*, it never comes. Any attempt to impose on this poem a reading in a distinctively Christian key must end finally in failure to match up with what we are actually given. After the brief moment of ambiguous 'vision', the poem returns once more to the impression, also conceived in delirium, of universal ruin in the desert which is envisaged as the end of our, and every, civilization. The barbarian hordes swarming over the 'endless plains', advancing over the 'cracked earth', are a reflection —so the poet tells us in a note—of the post-revolutionary chaos and civil war which dominated Eastern Europe at the time when the poem was written and which—it is insinuated—could well advance to overwhelm the traditional centres of Western culture. Here, perhaps more than usually, the poem simply *dates*, shows signs of its having been conceived at a special, and limited, moment in time. We, it may be, have become in the intervening years less one-sidedly convinced of the unique value of our Western 'civilization', more aware of the fact that all civilizations are involved in death and that such death is not necessarily final. The significance of the lines, however, it is fair to add, transcends any single situation. The note quotes a work by Hermann Hesse, *Look into Chaos* (*Blick ins Chaos*) and the impression is just that—a foreboding of *universal*, not merely 'Western' ruin. The 'city' which has been the supreme symbol of man's ability to live together in a reasonable and spiritual *society* is in danger of becoming no more than a mirage, an unreal illusion. The impression is one of 'falling towers' in which the urban centres of the civilized world are, like the city in *The Burial of the Dead*, fundamentally 'unreal'. The bells 'toll' in reminiscence of what was once, but is no longer, alive, and such voices as remain to express what formerly lived sing out of 'empty cisterns' and 'exhausted wells'. The sources of our civilization seem to be finally and irremediably dried up, exhausted.

A brief reference follows to one of the main unifying symbols which Miss Weston's book has bequeathed to the poem: the Chapel Perilous, the object of the Grail Quest, which has now brought the seeker to what is at once an empty, deserted shrine and a place of testing. The *emptiness* is perhaps the most significant feature of the Chapel, constitutes the essence of the ordeal; for it is vacancy, the mere absence of all belief or content, that contemporary man—so the poet would seem to be saying—is called upon to face. The test is connected with death, with the presence of 'tumbled graves', almost romantically evoked in the 'faint moonlight', and with the grass 'singing' around a ruin which is only 'the wind's home'. Perhaps, the poet may seem to imply, ours is the first human generation which finds death neither tragic nor repellent, neither to be accepted as a necessary aspect of the life which is its contrary nor rejected in pursuit of the will to live, but —like the life which it concludes—simply pointless. What the seeker has to face, what may be in effect his supreme test in the Waste Land, is that the Chapel he set out to find is 'empty', like the shrines of our once-living tradition: that the idea of death itself has been emptied of real terror ('Dry bones can harm no one'), has become, neither frightening nor in any way challenging, but just senseless.

This, the recognition of the 'nothing' that has run like a menacing under-theme through the entire course of the poem, may either lead to the indifference of futility or imply—when faced as the supreme ordeal and with the resolve to go further—the beginning of a certain restoration of confidence. We do not know, and perhaps are not meant to know, which of these alternatives can prevail. What is certain is that something of the nature of a decisive change is introduced at this point by the voice of the cock —'Co co rico co co rico'—a voice, so the note tells us, which has been regarded by many primitive peoples as having the power to drive away the forces of evil. The crow is a signal for the contemplated break in the weather, for the distant flash of lightning and the sense of the first 'damp gust' bringing rain—or the possibility of rain, for we are never made quite certain of what, if anything, has actually changed—to the parched desert soil. The voice of the thunder, spoken to a world 'waiting for rain', uttered from the 'black clouds' gathered in menace over the 'far-distant' mountains and above a jungle threateningly 'crouched, humped in silence', brings none the less an indication of possible relief. Its message, heard alike in the Chapel Perilous of Western tradition and in the jungle of the East, concludes the poem and brings as much restoring vision as can be obtained in the Waste Land.

'Then spoke the thunder.' Its message is summed up in the three traditional Sanskrit words *Datta, Dayadhvam, Damyata*; 'Give, sympathize, control'. Each of these three words, leading as it does into its successor, needs a moment's consideration, because it is by relating them to the fragments of possibly significant experience which have emerged from our exploration of the Waste Land that some suggestion of positive content may appear.

Give. What we have given—and the poet here answers his own question—is, in spite of timidity and lack of faith, the moment's surrender to instinct which is the necessary prelude to any experience of value: the surrender, we remember, which Mr. Prufrock in Eliot's earlier poem had never dared to make,[27] but by virtue of which alone our lives may aspire to amount to something more than thin memories and obscure obituaries:

> By this, and this only, we have existed.

To live is to *give* and to accept the risk implied in giving: to make, in other words, an act of faith, not necessarily in any specifically religious sense (which may, indeed, well be impossible), but in life itself as rewarding and sustaining beyond our possible anticipation.

From *Give* we pass, naturally, to *Sympathize*; for the instinctive acceptance of our fundamental impulse to live brings with it logically a desire to surpass the isolation which seems to be built in to our Waste Land condition, and to relate our own situation to that of humanity as a whole. Sympathy is required, therefore, with the chief elements in that situation as the poet sees them: in the first place with the sense of isolation that characterizes the modern intellectual, enclosed in the private world of his own experience and unable to extend to any meaningful connection with external reality (like Dante's Ugolino in the solitude of his tower, hearing the key turn inexorably in the lock of his prison door[28]), and, in the second, with the dim intuitions of a state of heroic integrity, the 'aethereal rumours' that 'revive for a moment' the 'broken

Coriolanus', whom reason has exposed in what it sees as his egoistic weakness without, however, entirely destroying the sense we retain—however illogically—of his nobility. The reference, it may be, is poised, in a way which would be deeply characteristic of Eliot, somewhere between Shakespeare's strangely unnatural, adolescent hero[29] and the more heroic suggestions of Beethoven's *Coriolan* overture.

By accepting tragedy in this way we may arrive, finally, at something like a human and spiritual reading of our lives. After *give* and *sympathize* comes *control*; for to sympathy, the acceptance which must precede creation in the artistic as in the moral order (and Eliot always held that the two orders, though each governed by its own laws, were finally connected), corresponds the control by which existence is given meaning. Only by accepting the challenge which life offers to each of us can we hope to affirm some measure of significant *control* over its course; only so may experience, once accepted in a spirit of risking, 'giving' sympathy, be given *meaning*. To convey a sense of the possibility of such control the poet returns once more to one of his images from *The Burial of the Dead*. The boat from *Tristan* which bore the lovers happily forward under the impulse of a favourable wind[30] returns once more. 'Gaily' it responds to the 'hand expert with sail and oar', and 'gaily' the heart of the loved one '*would* have responded' in identification with a control based on the principle of sympathy. The passage ends on a note which is purposely vague, deliberately conditional, as if in recognition of the 'shadow' that, in Eliot's own *Hollow Men*, separates 'potency' from 'act', the desire from its fulfilment.[31] The conditional may, indeed, point to the presence of a deeply personal stress derived from the poet's own private circumstance;[32] but it is not necessary, for a reading of the poem, to assert this. Although the moment for more precise definition has yet to come, and does not, indeed, come at all in this poem, there is suggested here an initial act of possible acceptance and a conceivable line of development. Indeed, it could be said that the exploration of the terms on which such acceptance can become actual is the theme of all Eliot's later work.

The final lines may be taken as a summary of the position reached by the poet as a result of this particular creative effort. Like the Fisher King of Miss Weston's legends, the protagonist is seen sitting, in the past ('I *sat* upon the shore': the exploration with which this poem is concerned is over and done with), on the far side of this ordeal. He is still in sight of the 'arid plain'—the Waste Land through which we have passed with him—but it is now *behind* him, in a sense overpassed. His vision of the state of civilization is still what it was at the beginning, a picture—expressed in the words of the nursery rhyme, 'London Bridge is falling down'—of collapse and disintegration. But we know now that the individual can at least aspire to some measure of control over his own existence, and that it is his human obligation, even in a time of desolation, to achieve such degree of personal order as lies within his reach. 'Shall I at least set my lands in order?' This is perhaps the question, the challenge, which the Waste Land leaves to humanity, and to each human being, in an age deprived of all accepted certainties.

To this end the protagonist, identified in his situation with the Fisher King, has 'shored', stored up, certain 'fragments', scraps of the ideally integrated traditions of humanity, against the threat of ruin. Such scraps are those which record Arnaud Daniel's acceptance of the purifying fire in Dante's *Purgatorio* (this takes up again the theme announced at the end of *The Fire Sermon*), and the quotation from the *Pervigilium Veneris* with its suggestion of life renewed and of the return, with the spring, of the swallow to its summer breeding places: 'When shall my spring come? When shall I be as the swallow?' Yet, since the serenity so indicated is precarious, less a reality than an aspiration, and since it is still liable to be interrupted as no more than a moment of delirium, the last lines of the poem alternate these tentatively positive references with others, to the madness of Hieronimo in Kyd's *Spanish Tragedy*, and to the hero of Gerard de Nerval's *Desdichado* who—like educated Western man—has lost his inheritance and finds himself as a result rejected, unfortunate. With this final acceptance of contrasts, recognized to be necessary though not yet understood—Eliot himself in his notes refers to 'the peace that passeth understanding'—the poem is brought to an end.

If the foregoing analysis is sound at least in its general direction it would appear that *The Waste Land* is something more than the poem of despair and disillusionment it was so commonly assumed to be when it first appeared. Eliot himself, indeed, made this clear in a published comment on the first reception of his work.[33] It is, in fact, a poem which stands in a close relationship to both his earlier and his later verse, summing up the positions reached in the 1917 and 1920 volumes and anticipating—though not entering upon—the aim of the later work, which is the creation of poetry at once fully contemporary and genuinely 'religious'. It is important not to simplify in this matter, and more especially not to read the poem for what it is not, an explicit statement of belief. The gap between a modern secular experience, honestly accepted as the only starting point available to a poet who recognizes the obligation to reflect his time as it is, and traditional religious forms is not of the kind that a true poet can bridge by mere assertions of *belief*. The attempt to do so can only lead to a kind of rhetoric and abstraction that is of its nature unpoetical and that has always been contrary to everything that Eliot admired in the literature of the past and sought to express in his own poems.

The true importance of *The Waste Land* lies precisely in the refusal to simplify, to produce a final statement of belief which was not adequately based on experience as given in the course of the poem. In so far as the inspiration of the work includes Christian elements—and this is clearly not so in the same sense as in *Ash Wednesday* or the *Four Quartets*—its 'Christianity' not only co-exists with other, and non-Christian aspects which are in no sense subjected to a religious 'message' or conclusion, but is seen to emerge from a development which is thoroughly and without prejudice contemporary. There can be no question of calling in the tradition of the past as a *deus ex machina* to resolve all difficulties and to lead the reader to a foreseen or contrived conclusion. It is the sense of this scrupulous integrity in the conception and execution of *The Waste Land* which not infrequently seemed to fail Eliot in his later prose writing, but which he succeeded in affirming—and the fact stands greatly to his credit—in the best verse of his later years.

II
ASH
WEDNESDAY

ASH
WEDNESDAY

[I]
Introduction

T. S. Eliot's *Ash Wednesday* series of poems, which was published
in its final form in 1930, offers perhaps the most ready approach
to the later poetry. Notably tentative and exploratory in kind, it
pulls together and gives the form of a sequence to a set of short
poems originally published separately in some cases and not quite
in the order in which they finally appeared. The first part of the
sequence to be published, in December 1927 under the title of
Salutation, answers to the second poem in the final order. It was
followed, in the Spring of 1928, by *Perch'io non spero* ('Because I
do not hope'), which eventually became the first of the *Ash
Wednesday* poems, and—in the Autumn of 1929—by *Som de
l'Escalina*, which is the third poem in the final version. The pro-
cess of building a series of originally separate lyrics into a sequence,
by providing links to answer to a sense of personal development
and by expanding into new matter, already tells us something
about the poet's intention in shaping the series.

The sequence as it stands is the fruit of a period of pause and
meditation which had marked Eliot's development as a poet since
the publication of *The Waste Land* eight years earlier. Most of his
effort during this time had gone into critical writing; of the few
poems produced during this period one—*The Hollow Men*, com-
pleted in 1924–5—represents a development of the mood of *The
Waste Land* and indeed includes verses originally intended for
that poem and only excluded from it at the suggestion of Ezra
Pound. The only other poems of importance produced between
1922 and 1930 were *The Journey of the Magi* (1927) and *Marina*
(1929), both of which anticipate in certain respects the longer
poems to come.

Coming at the end of this period of recollection and stock-
taking *Ash Wednesday* is also, if we except *The Journey of the*

57

Magi, Eliot's first poem of distinctively Christian inspiration. The title, it is hardly necessary to say, has penitential implications, though these are not necessarily such as to imply a 'personal' or biographical content. The 'I' of these poems need not be taken to be the poet speaking in his own voice, though it is clear that, whatever he may be, his experience is related to that of the author. What we have is the poem as a self-sufficient and self-explaining creation, and in the case of Eliot it is more than usually inappropriate to seek to go beyond this and to search for the 'man' personally revealing himself through the poem.

What the poems do convey very notably is a sense of the continuity which is so marked a feature of all Eliot's important poetry. Implicit in the sequence is the intention of taking up again the theme of death, already explored in *The Waste Land*, with a view to making of it the point of departure for something which, in the earlier poem, is at best only dimly foreshadowed: a process of growth into acceptance, reflecting what could be called—again in a very special sense—a *conversion*. The result is a poem at once religious in feeling and contemporary in intention: at once thoroughly personal and without concession to sentiment. The main theme is an acceptance of *conversion* as a necessary and irretrievable act of decision following from man's distinctive privilege, and obligation, of *choice*: an act which brings with it dangers and difficulties of its own, which *may* even turn out to be a false path or a deception, but the necessity of which needs to be acknowledged, in a spirit of recognized risk, if life is to have meaning at all. The answer to the question posed nearly twenty years earlier by Prufrock in his monologue—'Do I dare disturb the universe?' —clearly lies in the poet's use of the opening phrase of Guido Cavalcanti's *balletetta*, *Perch'io non spero di tornar giammai*, transcribed as 'Because I do not hope to turn again'. The answer is to be an embarkation, dangerous but decisive, upon the adventure of faith.

[2]
The Poem

I

The decision not 'to turn again', not to evade the challenge of the present by returning to the more comfortable routine of past years, is stated accordingly in the opening line of the first poem in the sequence. It is relevant that whereas Cavalcanti, thinking of his exile and the mistress he had left behind in Florence, wrote *tornar* in the sense of 'return', Eliot—with a more ample and universal theme in mind—writes only 'turn'. The poet is concerned here not with the content of choice, the specific position chosen, but with the irreversible and initially disturbing nature of choice itself. The decision not to turn back is not one easily made; the second line, by breaking short at 'I do not hope', involves a renunciation of the customary forms of relief, a recognition of the irretrievable nature of every responsible decision. The renunciation is to be that of all the comforting possibilities which life seems —but perhaps only *seems*—to offer of falling back upon the safe, the familiar and the known, in evasion of the perpetually renovating challenge of the present. 'Hope' of this kind would be, as the *Quartets* will affirm more clearly, 'hope for the wrong thing',[1] for that which—whatever it may have been in the past—can no longer be a source of life in the present.

Among the things to be so renounced are those mentioned in Shakespeare's Sonnet XXIX: the desire to emulate 'this man's gift and that man's scope', to follow paths which seem attractive when glimpsed in the lives and work of others but which are seen —in the light of a maturing experience—to be either irrelevant to one's own needs or unattainable in the consciousness of one's own limitations. The image of the 'aged eagle'[2] answers to the protagonist's present estimate of his situation, which involves a rejection of vain effort—'I no longer *strive to strive* towards such things': the repetition of the verb conveys the difficulty, the sense of accumulated strain, which even such a renouncing, 'negative' decision implies—and an acceptance of the need to build, with whatever difficulty, upon what is actually *there.*

Not everything in this act of renunciation is limited or dis-
spiriting, though an element of disappointment is certainly part of
the complete effect: 'Why should I mourn/The vanished power of
the usual reign?' This 'power' has in any case 'vanished', has come
to be seen as irrelevant to the needs of the present; so that to seek
to cling to it would be—at this stage—no more than a comforting
illusion of life, an escape from the constantly fresh challenge of the
present. From now on, indeed, this becomes a central feature of
the poet's thought, marking the separation of such 'religious' atti-
tudes as the poem develops, or postulates, from all nostalgic
attachment to the dead and vanished past. We may well believe,
indeed, that for Eliot such attachment amounted to a temptation
of marked attraction, which had to be consciously and deliberately
renounced if he was to 'live' as a poet. If 'the usual reign', the
world of safe, unexamined assumptions handed down from pre-
vious generations or developed from past experiences, was ever
able to impart life, either to the poet or—in the long run—to any
man, its power to do this in the present is over, irretrievably
vanished, and can never be revived.

What the poet is stating, accordingly, is not merely a personal
impression, but what he has come to see as an inescapable law of
life. It is necessary to *renounce*, deliberately and consciously, in
what amounts to an act of affirmed *choice*, the things that had once
been regarded—neither wrongly nor unnaturally at the time—as a
source of 'hope': the very things which had formerly presented
themselves as life, as 'glory', as imparting a sense of meaning and
achievement to each man's involvement in the temporal process:

> Because I do not hope to know again
> The infirm glory of the positive hour
> Because I do not think
> Because I know I shall not know
> The one veritable transitory power
> Because I cannot drink
> There, where trees flower, and springs flow,
> for there is nothing again.

The hard way to the future—and it *is* hard, as implied even in the
repetition of 'know' ('Because I know I shall not know')—lies
through the renouncing even of the things which, in an earlier
stage, seemed 'positive', but which are now seen to represent an

'*infirm* glory' tied to what has become an irrelevant moment of past time. The poet, in short, now 'knows'—the word carries a sense of affirmation, of conscious and deliberate choice, against the nostalgic implications of 'hope'—that he cannot, in his present situation, find satisfaction in what was once indeed a 'veritable' but 'transitory power': 'veritable' because its former attraction cannot be denied, because it lives still, if only in the memory, but evidently 'transitory', as being no more relevant to the needs of the present time. These needs demand *new* choices (and do so at every moment) as an inescapable condition of continuing to live. It is no longer possible to 'drink', 'where trees flower, and springs flow', in the places where life seemed formerly to dwell, but where there is now 'nothing' again. The reference to 'springs', or to their absence, seems to be taking us once again into a desert, or 'Waste Land' situation, but one which is now approached in a new and largely transformed mood.

Behind these affirmations of the necessity and the difficulty of *choice* there lies, as compared with *The Waste Land*, a new kind of preoccupation with the temporal process. As a first step in realizing his present situation the protagonist asserts his understanding of the limitations which *time*, the very fact of our temporal nature, imposes upon him:

> Because I know that time is always time
> And place is always and only place
> And what is actual is actual only for one time
> And only for one place
> I rejoice that things are as they are . . .

At each moment we are, as human beings, called upon to *choose*, or to *accept*; but each choice and each acceptance, limited as they are by the chooser's situation in *time* and *place*, refers only to the 'time' and 'place' in which it is made. Sound choice in the present implies, as an indispensable condition, a recognition of things as they are, and with it a *renunciation* of all premature hope for illumination, of any continuing dependence *in the present* upon intimate experiences —'the blessed face'—which had once brought with them a sense of beatitude.

It is not that the *past* moments of illumination were in any way worthless or illusory in themselves. On the contrary, they may have been—were—intensely moving, even genuinely transforming; but it is part of the nature of such things—and of *our* nature—that the moment of illumination which continues to live only in the memory cannot serve as a source of life in what is at every moment an essentially new situation. A renunciation, accordingly, needs to be made, at the appropriate moment in time and in full consciousness; and so

> I renounce the blessèd face
> And renounce the voice
> Because I cannot hope to turn again
> Consequently I rejoice, having to construct something
> Upon which to rejoice.

The renunciation implies—to repeat the essential point—a recognition that there is no *true* 'hope' to be found in retreating into sources of comfort that now belong quite irretrievably to the past. The beginning of wisdom lies in recognizing that no valid comfort is to be obtained in seeking to regard the past as present. The past needs continually to be renounced, not because it did not once, in its own time, offer genuine fulfilment, but simply because it *is* past, and as such finished, not to be confused with the elusive but living present. 'I cannot' (and therefore I do not) 'hope to turn again.' By a seeming paradox, this renunciation of easy consolation leads the poet—or, rather, the 'I' of the poem—to 'rejoice', to find motives for rejoicing in the hard obligation 'to *construct* something/Upon which to rejoice,' to build out of his personal effort, unsupported by past sources of comfort which are no longer there, 'something' of personal value, upon which true, as distinct from merely sentimental, rejoicing may be built. Once this has been done, once the 'past', considered *as past*, has been deliberately, responsibly renounced, what was alive and valuable in it may be seen as continuing to contribute to, to *live* in, the present; but whether this is so cannot be affirmed in isolation, can only be verified through the complete development of the poetic experience.

This effort of construction, which makes use of personal and inherited symbols in the attempt to build a new structure of poetic meaning, is to be the aim of the sequence as a whole. Meanwhile, the immediate result of the new meditation, finally positive beneath all the stressed difficulty, is seen as a setting aside of excessive preoccupation, of fruitless self-analysis and useless self-justification: of all 'these matters', in fact, 'that with myself I too much discuss/

Too much explain.' These, too, are things the speaker has now left behind him, and to which he no longer 'hopes' — or desires — 'to turn again'; for renunciation of what he has now learnt to see as false hope is a condition, albeit initially a hard one, of life in the present. In this spirit, he is ready to accept that he may deserve 'judgement' for the faults of the past, but tempers this acceptance with a 'hope' that judgement itself, having now been accepted, may be compatible with a compensating mercy: 'May the judgement not be too heavy upon us'.

The lines which follow return to the image, already introduced, of 'the aged eagle'. Inspiration in the present is recognized to be hard; more than most poets Eliot's career may be seen as a struggle — not the less harshly conducted for itself becoming in due course a condition of the poetry itself — against the possible failure of the capacity to create. The 'air' in which the protagonist is called upon to exercise the wings of his imagination is felt to be — as it might have been in *The Waste Land* — 'thoroughly small and dry'. The 'will' alone is still alive, still capable of asserting itself, but in circumstances which are now felt to be less than favourable, and which need to be accepted as such in a spirit which combines the continuing capacity to feel with a necessary measure of detachment. 'Teach us to care and not to care' has become the burden of the prayer with which this first section concludes: a prayer which is extended to cover a universal human situation.

'Teach us', in other words, the poem goes on to say, to continue to express ourselves with *sympathy* — for without this we are dead, as the conclusion of *The Waste Land* has already recognized — at the same time as we refrain from resting all our being upon the objectives which an indiscriminate 'sympathy' may propose to us and which may, considered as exclusive ends in themselves, be illusory or premature. The point, which is central to the entire sequence, and indeed, from now on, to Eliot's poetic thought, will be made again in the final poem,[3] where the need for detachment will be seen in the context of a larger and more positive design. Already, in the meantime, we are told that true wisdom consists, given the necessarily incomplete pattern of our temporal existence, in the ability to 'sit still', not to seek the illusion of consolation in mere surrender to the endlessly changing present, but to wait on an illumination which cannot be forced or brought into premature existence, but which only the fullness of time can bring into being.

The first poem, like all those which follow, ends on a liturgical phrase appropriate to the present state of the developing argument: at this time on a phrase from the prayer of the Angelus[4] joining the personal recognition of sin to the acceptance of death as a necessary stage in any conceivable progress or enlightenment.

II

In considering the next two sections (poems II and III) of the *Ash Wednesday* sequence, it will be well to remember that these parts of the complete work were originally published separately, and that they were in all probability the first to be written. They are also the sections in which the poet is most obviously concerned to create a symbol, or—as he might have called it—an 'objective correlative' for the emotional states he aims at conveying. The 'Lady' who is invoked at the opening of the first of these two poems is closely related, under certain aspects, to Dante's Beatrice, though she has little of the complex intellectual and theological implications of the earlier, and greater, poet's conception. There are times, indeed, when she seems to have a nineteenth-century 'pre-Raphaelite' air that is foreign to most of Eliot's poetry. She will, however, intercede for the protagonist with the Virgin, much as Beatrice did for Dante, thus opening the way for him to rise to the Vision of God. Eliot's 'Lady' will not take him so far, being the reflection of a more limited, a less comprehensive and less strikingly affirmative purpose; but the parallel remains valid, within its limits, and points to the direction which the sequence is intended to take.

Similarly, the image of the 'juniper-tree' in the desert, drawn from the story of Elijah,[5] is a development to new and different ends of the Waste Land concept. The poet, or his 'voice', associates himself with the despair of the prophet who, mortally threatened by Jezebel, sat under the tree and prayed: 'Now, Lord, take away my life; for I am not better than my fathers'.[6] All these borrowed images, however, are transformed in the use made of them, deprived of their original associations—much as had been the case with the quotation from Cavalcanti that opened the sequence—and related more closely to intimate personal states.

The 'three white leopards' who devour the human remains under the tree in the desert also have their literary connections. They recall the beasts, which were also three, who met Dante at the outset of his journey in the 'dark forest' in the middle point, which was also a turning-point, of his life.[7] There is little sense in these beasts, however, of the overpowering fear[8] which those in Dante's first Canto so intensely inspired. They are on the contrary primarily beneficent in their effect, radiantly, almost heraldically 'white' and associated with 'the cool of the day'. Their picking clean of the bones and of the perishable parts of the remains before them takes up another Waste Land theme, which again they develop to ends finally less desolating, more positive, or at least reassuring, in their effect. The reference appears to be to the mythic hero who is devoured and regenerated, and the pertinent question is that addressed by God to the prophet: 'Shall these bones live? shall these/Bones live?'[9] The emphasis, in fact, is now upon the *life* which may be found even in the Waste Land; and the question is whether the death contemplated there, now accepted in a spirit which may be described as 'purgatorial', can lead to renewed life. The 'bones' are still 'dry', as they had been in the earlier and more desolate poem, and their 'chirping' associates them with the 'cicada' which had there uttered its note of anguished monotony;[10] but there is now even a touch of humour in their reply to the question that God had once addressed to the prophet and which is repeated with a new insistence: 'Shall these bones live?' Can life, in other words, be born out of the accepted experience of death?

In their reply, the bones see the possibility of restoration in the intercession of the Beatrice-like Lady, who is beautiful in her 'goodness' and who 'honours the Virgin in meditation'. As a result of her intercession they are able, even in their recognized and accepted dryness, to 'shine with brightness'. At this point 'that which had been contained/In the bones' becomes, in the continuation of its speech, 'I', an intimate voice which, though aware of being 'dissembled', taken apart, is ready to 'proffer' its 'deeds' — such as they are — to 'oblivion', to accept in a spirit of humility the reality of its condition. The scattering of the old self is now seen, in other words, as the possible prelude to reformation round a new centre of life.

It is here that the matter of the new poem connects with that of its predecessor. Even the 'love' of the self's former days, like the rest of its deeds in the past, has now become matter for renunciation, needs to be bequeathed, in so far as it is over and done with, 'to the posterity of the desert and the fruit of the gourd': to be related, in other words, to the desert fruit which stores nourishment, in the form of life-giving waters, against the dryness of the wilderness. The result of an acceptance of the need to embark upon a new life is next associated with a kind of resurrection of the body, now seen, still playfully, with a touch of irony, as aspiring to 'recover'—in the double sense of 'covering again' and 'finding again'—the former fleshly envelope of the dry bones. To be forgotten, to 'proffer one's deeds to oblivion', in detachment from their significance for the self, may be a prelude to becoming *converted* in purpose.

The Lady, meanwhile, is 'withdrawn' in concentration, in the 'white gown' which is reflected in 'the whiteness of bones'. These —the 'bones'—do not expect any direct attention from the Lady whose intercession is effective precisely because it is directed to other ends:

> Let the whiteness of bones atone to forgetfulness.
> There is no life in them. As I am forgotten
> And would be forgotten, so I would forget
> Thus devoted, concentrated in purpose. And God said
> Prophesy to the wind, to the wind for only
> The wind will listen.

The 'bones' are, in fact, ready to accept their own necessary death, ready to 'forget' a past which is now seen to be irrelevant to their present condition; but if they are now prepared to be forgotten, it is as a means to an end—the end of being 'concentrated' in a new purpose, of being 'devoted', following the example of the Lady, in contemplation. The aim of the poem is now seen, in short, to be that of entering into a new aspect of love, unlimited by restriction to desire, and essentially expansive beyond the limitations of the self, finally and completely life-giving. As in the case of the prophets of the Old Testament, all expressions of the personal voice seem to lose themselves, in so much as they are heard only by the 'wind'; but we are now ready to suspect that this appearance of neglect and indifference was also part of the complete purpose. The *cost* of the new vision, in other words, is the forgetting of the old. In this new consciousness the life symbolized in the bones is ready to 'sing', recognizing the limitations of its mortality in the Waste Land condition, newly aware that, in the light of death, even remembered desire, considered as an end in itself, needs to be renounced. (The lines recall *Ecclesiastes*: 'the grasshopper shall be a burden and

desire shall fail: because man goeth to his long home'.[11]) In renun-
ciation, acceptance of the inevitable death of a 'desire' which is
conditioned and limited by time, the key to possible life is now seen
to lie.

The 'song' of the bones, which follows, takes the form of a
prayer, or litany, to the 'Lady of silences'. It combines memories
of the Catholic Litany of Our Lady with Dante's hymn to the
Virgin Mary in the last Canto of the *Paradiso*.[12] Put into the mouth
of the contemplative Saint Bernard of Clairvaux Dante's lines cor-
respond to the point in the *Commedia* where the poet has finally
reached the vision in which 'desire' is fulfilled,[13] his 'love' on all
its human levels achieved in grace, sublimated in the Vision of God
for which, according to Christian theology, man was created: for
the end of man, we are told, is 'to serve God in this life and to
enjoy him for ever after death in the next'.[14]

In Eliot's conception, the litany becomes a reconciling of oppo-
sites through the 'silence' of contemplation, and the action of the
Lady is seen as a mediation between carnal and spiritual love. The
image of the 'rose', traditionally applied to the Lady, the object of
love in the medieval world of *amour courtois*, is now in the process
of taking its place in the Garden, where love itself may find fulfil-
ment in a still greater good, where temporal opposites may be
reconciled through the necessary, and now life-giving, acceptance
of the need to renounce. In 'the Garden/Where all loves end,' the
Lady 'Torn and most whole', after being glimpsed under the aspect
of the 'rose' of 'memory' and 'forgetfulness' — 'Exhausted and life-
giving/Worried reposeful' — becomes the 'single Rose', the point
of possible unity upon which all human contradiction finally
converges:

> Terminate torment
> Of love unsatisfied
> The greater torment
> Of love satisfied.

All temporal love is revealed as containing an element of 'tor-
ment':[15] 'unsatisfied' love obviously so, while 'satisfied' love perhaps
contains an even greater element, in so far as it seems to postulate
an eternity which it cannot, under its temporal aspect, achieve.
What is born in time, inevitably dies in time: only through renun-
ciation, dedication to an end beyond the temporal, can 'love' be

maintained, be conceived as triumphant over the action of time and the 'torment' to which its apparent frustration leads.

The end of the 'litany' finds the poet struggling, as he will so often do from now to the end of his career, with the problem of finding words to express ideas, states of being, that hover on the edge of the inexpressible. Paradox becomes a means, not to evade the challenge to achieve meaning (as is often the case in lesser writers), but to express what is seen, within the limitations of our temporal vision, as a unifying of contradictions:

> End of the endless
> Journey to no end
> Conclusion of all that
> Is inconclusible
> Speech without word and
> Word of no speech
> Grace to the Mother
> For the Garden
> Where all love ends.

Life in time is seen as an 'endless journey' to 'no end': 'endless' because it can never be seen as complete during human existence in time, since *in time* we are subject at each moment to new and transforming influences; and 'to no end' because, in time, every moment is replaced by its successor, so that no moment, while the time of each individual life lasts, can be conceived as offering the sense of a final, unsurpassable goal. The 'conclusion' of what presents itself to us, under the temporal aspect, as 'inconclusible' can only lie through a renunciation, *as final* (not altogether or in itself) of temporal experience: or, to put the same point in another way, the 'word', the instrument of the poet's craft, can only have final validity in relation to 'the Word', the creative action of God entering our experience from a point of vantage *outside* time and acting in transformation upon the temporal process.

In this way the Lady, through her contemplative dedication, has introduced into the poem the completing, integrating concept of 'Grace'. We have been brought to the Garden, which throughout the 'litany' has gathered up into itself a variety of associations: the Rose Garden of the *Roman de la Rose*, at the heart of which, inaccessible and intensely desirable, the object of love dwells; the Garden of Eden, where God walked in the cool of the day and where Adam enjoyed, and lost, his state of innocence;[16] the Earthly Paradise where Dante found Beatrice and, in the process of returning to her, himself, at the summit of the Mount of Purgatory;[17] the *Hortus Conclusus* of the Song of Songs, the setting for an intensity of sensual experience and at the same time, as seen by the commentators of the Middle Ages, a figure applied to the Womb of Mary as Mother of the incarnate God. All these associations are now drawn together in a conception of the 'place' where all love ends and towards which the universal search for it is directed: *ends* under its purely temporal aspect which, precisely because it is time-conditioned and limited, needs to be renounced, and *is directed*, finds its consummation beyond and through the act of renunciation which its very nature imposes. The concept which underlies the 'litany', and indeed gives its sense to the whole of this 'conversion'-sequence, is one of life as receiving its meaning from the end to which it is dedicated and which is achieved through an acceptance, as necessary and appropriate, of the death in which all human experience in time ends.

The song of the bones, 'scattered and shining', has now become one of happy acceptance, a common recognition of the futility of their self-conditioned and self-limited past: 'We are *glad* to be scattered, we did little good to each other'. It is a song sung in the desert which recalls the Waste Land, but sung now under the tree of the opening line and 'in the cool of the day': we may note that this phrase also echoes the beginning. Above all it is a song sung *in community*, in the recognition of a common limitation and the aspiration to a common destiny. The 'sand' is capable, in the light of the new development, of being associated with 'blessing'. The 'blessing', in turn, is obtained in a new state of forgetfulness of self, a deliberate renunciation of the trivial, the distracting, and the premature; and it leads to the affirmation of a spirit of unity in the 'quiet' fulfilment of the wilderness:

> Forgetting themselves and each other, united
> In the quiet of the desert.

The 'desert', in other words, has now come to be seen, not as a symbol of waste and futility, but as in some sense God-given, the rightful and natural 'inheritance' of the soul which has renounced all premature concern with 'division' and 'unity', with the former opposition between carnal and spiritual love, or between 'love' and 'desire'. The good implicit in the concept of unity will come, in due course, not through the individual grasping for what he is not yet in a condition to receive, but as the generous gift of God offered in the natural fullness of time. This is what is implied in the use made at this point of Ezekiel's life-giving prophecy in the valley of bones —'I will cause breath to enter into you, and you shall live'[18]—and in the uniting of the divided nations of Joseph and Judah,[19] which is achieved precisely when the fact of division ceases to be important:

> This is the land which ye
> Shall divide by lot. And neither division nor unity
> Matters. This is the land. We have our inheritance.

III

The third poem of the sequence, which—like the preceding one— was originally written and published separately, seems to record a struggle against various forms of personal temptation. It is structured, though rather indefinitely, in the traditional spiritual image of the *stair*. We remember the seven steps into which the Mount of Purgatory is divided in Dante's poem,[20] where they correspond to the seven Mortal Sins, and also, perhaps, the three steps of the ante-Purgatory,[21] answering to contrition, confession, and restitution, in the same poem. Relevant too are various equally traditional visions—those contained in the writings of St. Bonaventure and St. John of the Cross, among others—of the ascent of the soul in its contemplative journey. It must be realized, however, that the symbols are used throughout in a personal sense, and that it would be out of place to look for detailed points of coincidence.

It would be wrong, in other words, following the same line of argument, to try to ascribe any 'step' in the manner sanctioned by tradition to any single, well-defined temptation. Each 'step' answers to a personal state; and, if it is true that we are back in the spiritual darkness of the first poem, it is also true that the lesson of humility in acceptance, conveyed by the 'Lady' in the second poem, is also present. The first temptation, glimpsed from above, 'At the first turning of the second stair,' and associated with 'deceitful' appearances of hope and despair, may perhaps be identified with what Eliot in a study of Pascal called 'the demon of doubt which is inseparable from the spirit of belief'[22] and which stands in the same relation to faith as self-absorption to the abandonment of selfish and self-centred motivation.

It is associated with a sense of intimate disgust, conveyed by the vision of the 'twisted' shape on the banister and by the presence of 'fetid' air; and it leads to a further temptation, 'At the second turning of the second stair,' which is that involved in the surrender to emptiness, to negation and despair:

> There were no more faces and the stair was dark,
> Damp, jaggèd, like an old man's mouth drivelling,
> beyond repair,
> Or the toothed gullet of an agèd shark.

This stage of the ascent is 'dark', and the images associated with it are similar to those which we find in *Gerontion* and *The Waste Land:* the 'Dead mountain mouth of carious teeth that cannot spit.'[23] Here, however, they seem to be intensified, to be more intimately related to what emerges as an obscure personal state. The old man's mouth 'drivelling', the 'toothed gullet' of the 'aged shark': these are images of self-disgust and vain old age which appear to proceed from deep and hidden places in the writer's consciousness and which pursue the imagination as intimations of final emptiness. It should be noted, however, that these 'temptations' are once again seen from above, as in some sense over-passed. 'I *left them* twisting, *turning below*'; and beyond this it would be a mistake to make the images more concrete, more definite than in fact they are. They represent 'states' or conditions of moral being, rather than the clearly defined or objective 'sins' dealt with in the schematic treatises on the spiritual life.

The third, and last temptation, which recalls the voice of the First Tempter in *Murder in the Cathedral*,[24] is very noticeably more *alive* than the preceding ones, and implies a reflection of 'the *infirm glory* of the *positive* hour', already mentioned in the poem which opens the sequence. It is, in fact, a return to the 'sensuous' temptation, there prematurely renounced:

> At the first turning of the third stair
> Was a slotted window bellied like the fig's fruit
> And beyond the hawthorn blossom and a pasture scene
> The broadbacked figure drest in blue and green
> Enchanted the maytime with an antique flute.

Blown hair is sweet, brown hair over the mouth blown,
Lilac and brown hair;
Distraction, music of the flute, stops and steps of the
    mind over the third stair,
Fading, fading; strength beyond hope and despair
Climbing the third stair.

A colourful 'medieval' scene, which we need not confuse unduly
with pre-Raphaelite artistry, is evoked, seen through a 'slotted
window' on the stair. 'Bellied like the fig's fruit', it seems to embody
a sense of life which is in itself positive, because fruitful, but which
is now seen as no longer relevant to the speaker's present condi-
tion. The prevailing intimations are those of spring and early sum-
mer, and there is a 'romantic', almost a deliberately literary quality
about such things as the reference to the 'antique flute'. To confuse
'literature' with reality and to seek refuge in the confusion may
indeed be an aspect of this temptation.

The lines which follow, lingering over the sweetness of the
remembered 'brown hair', and associating these memories with the
haunting deception of the spring 'lilac', recalls Eliot's obsessive
image of the 'hyacinth girl', in *The Waste Land*[25] and in some of his
earlier poems. These things too have eventually to be renounced,
not as in themselves evil (for they are tender and humanly sweet),
but in as much as they have become motives of 'distraction', reali-
ties no longer there and which serve now only to impede the soul
engaged on an ascent towards the purity of motive which is to be
found, perhaps, at the top of 'the third stair'. Meanwhile, at all
events, they are 'fading' temptations, losing actuality in the pres-
ent, unable finally to affirm themselves in a new and different
situation. The condition of a truly spiritual ascent of the 'stair' is
now seen to be renunciation of 'hope', considered as a final emo-
tion on which the soul may be tempted to rest, in order to gain a
strength which may be solid, precisely because it is 'beyond hope'
and the 'despair' which is its insuperable companion: beyond, in
other words, the deceitful appearances evoked in the form of the
first temptation at the opening of the poem.

Behind this renunciation of 'temptations' which are seen as be-
longing to the past, to an order of things once conceived as desirable
but now surpassed, there lies a vital paradox in what is emerging as
the poem's present line of thought. To 'hope', in the state of time-

conditioned and time-limited existence, is necessarily to be led to 'despair', for 'hope' is conditioned by the time which inevitably ruins it. This is because hope needs to preserve itself from illusion, to look beyond the merely temporal aspiration to a world of 'values' in which the temporal, the past and finished experience, may find their place and justification. As we saw earlier, what was born in time, time necessarily and inevitably destroys. To recognize this reality is not to reject the creations of time as valueless or insignificant; but it does lead to a renunciation of the *finality* of all merely time-based consolations in the hope that such renunciation may lead to an intuition of permanence.

The strength we need to acquire must lie, if it is to be convincing, 'beyond hope and despair' considered as final and self-sufficient states.[26] It must lie therefore outside our normally time-conditioned selves: but only, on the other hand, through an initial acceptance of time (since we are what we are) can this be achieved. The theme is one which will become central to Eliot's thought as developed in the *Quartets*.[27] At all events, the impulse to defeat the 'distractions' and to continue the climbing of the stair-way must come finally from outside or beyond the self: so that this part of the sequence ends appropriately on a recognition of unworthiness and dependence, in the words—once more—of the liturgy: *Domine, non sum dignus . . . sed tantum dic verbo et sanabitur anima mea*.[28] 'Speak the word only': to live is seen to be to look beyond the limitations of the self and to be ready to receive the 'word' which cannot, in the nature of things, come from within the self, but which the self, conscious now of its inevitable incompleteness, needs for its justification.

IV

The fourth poem in the sequence, opening on the pronoun 'Who', takes up and develops the theme of the Lady, a Beatrice-like figure, never forgotten from the past. The figure is now being developed in accordance with the poet's present, sublimating purpose. To be noted is the stress laid, throughout the poem, on the word 'between':

> Who walked *between*
> The various ranks of varied green . . .

Here are the years that walk *between*, bearing
Away the fiddles and the flutes . . .

The silent sister veiled in white and blue
Between the yews.

The lady appears to 'walk' *between* remembered reality and imaginative vision, *between* Dante and the poet's own experience as relived or projected into a state of dream, *between* the garden flowers which seem to recall tangible moments of possible happiness in real life (or the colours of the temptation on 'the third stair' in the previous poem?) and the liturgical colours of the Church.

Similarly, she is seen as moving in daily life, 'talking of trivial things', suspended *between* the normal state of imperfect human awareness—'in ignorance'—and yet sharing an insight beyond the normally human into the reality of suffering, of 'eternal dolour'. Moving among the 'others', like Dante's still-living Beatrice in the early chapters of the *Vita Nuova*,[29] remembered as having lived in the real world of every day, she is also now approached as a source of the life symbolized in the 'fountains' and 'springs' of the garden: symbols 'made strong', brought to renewed life in the light of her transformed and transforming memory. It is she who, as the speaker now recreates her in his own recollection, made 'cool the dry rock' of the desert—the Waste Land—and 'firm' its sand. Under her influence the desert blooms into what is at once natural, living colour and the 'blue of Mary's colour': in other words, she fulfils for the poem something of the function that Beatrice (also a memory from another poet's past life) fulfilled in Dante's great work.

Memory, indeed, is of the essence of this intense, intangible experience, in Eliot as it had once been in Dante. What is remembered lives again and is in the process transformed by what has happened in the time between. Appropriately, therefore, the poet, as he considers his own condition, is moved to echo what were perhaps, for Eliot, the most consistently evocative lines in all poetry, those which convey Arnaud Daniel's prayer at the end of Canto XXVI of the *Purgatorio*: 'Sovegna vos.' 'Be mindful': a prayer that, it should be remembered, is almost immediately followed in Dante's poem by the renewed vision of a transformed Beatrice, one of whose purposes is to lead the poet, after he has passed through the flames which separate him from her and from the Earthly

Paradise,[30] to reconsider the aberrations of his own past life as a prelude to entry into a new state.

The relationship upon which this vision is based is, indeed, recalled intensely in the lines immediately following:

> Here are the years that walk between, bearing
> Away the fiddles and the flutes, restoring
> One who moves in the time between sleep and waking, wearing
> White light folded, sheathed about her, folded.
> The new years walk, restoring
> Through a bright cloud of tears, the years, restoring
> With a new verse the ancient rhyme. Redeem
> The time. Redeem
> The unread vision in the higher dream
> While jewelled unicorns draw by the gilded hearse.

The experience, it should be noted, is again recalled as *past*; for 'between' the reality of the former time and the present dream there stand, still alive and still relevant, 'the years that walk between'. They bear away 'the fiddles and the flutes' that sounded so evocatively in the preceding poem. They carry these things away in the act of 'restoring', recreating the original experience in the time of dreams, 'between sleep and waking'. They 'restore' it, however, in a new, an essentially transformed aspect, and in 'symbolic' form: half-dream and half a recreation of the medieval symbol, 'folded', 'sheathed' in 'white light', much as Beatrice appeared to Dante in the Earthly Paradise[31] and throughout the following ascent into the spheres. The influence makes itself felt immediately through a sense of personal loss—'a cloud of tears', as the poem puts it—beyond which, however, it is now recreated, 'restored', to use the word on which the poem now insists, with its implications of renewed life, to become a great deal more than a nostalgic memory of what has been irreparably removed. Like the sorrow felt by Dante at the death of Beatrice, according to his account at the end of the *Vita Nuova*,[32] this dream has the power not merely to recall but to 'restore', to bring back with an added significance 'the years': the power to give a new content to existence—for the *new* years now walk in the garden of the poet's life—and new meaning, even in terms of his activity as a writer ('the new verse' transforming the 'ancient rhyme') to the forms used by former generations.

This recovery of life through the transforming operation of

memory has, however, a condition. For it to be possible, the 'time' in which the experience has been developed needs to be 'redeemed', both brought back — 'restored' — and fulfilled in the light of the present. To the double emphasis on 'restoring' in the passage quoted, there immediately corresponds the equally double injunction to 'redeem' the time by making it live again, under a renewed aspect, in the light of the sublimating vision. The time 'restored' needs to be 'redeemed', given a new fullness of meaning in the light of the continuing processes of life. In other words, the 'unread vision', implied in Dante's conception which the poet is making his own, and which has so far been neglected or set aside, as being apparently without meaning for the changed present, has to be 'redeemed' through what Eliot in his study of Dante called 'the higher dream'.[33] It has to be subjected to a process of sublimation, in the light of which its meaning for present experience may become apparent. Eliot himself has warned us, in the same essay, not to confuse the effect of this kind of symbolic, ceremonial poetry with the decorative medievalism of nineteenth-century taste.[34] The 'jewelled unicorns' belong, in essence if not in detail, to the 'higher dream' of Dante's Procession of Revelation in the Earthly Paradise:[35] the 'gilded hearse' which takes the place of the chariot on which Beatrice appears, drawn by the double-natured beast (and which may also be the vehicle on which the Sacrament is borne in the Corpus Christi procession), refers in Eliot's scheme to death as a necessary element in the complete experience of living, as well as to the fact that the capacity to experience the 'higher dream' seems to have been lost by the time in which he lives.

The thought of death is, however, by now inextricably intertwined in the poem with intuitions of life. The 'silent sister' is seen, still in the dream, as standing 'between' (again this key-word) 'the yews', which are symbols both of death and immortality.[36] She is also 'behind the garden god' (Priapus or Pan) whose flute has become in a dream-like way 'breathless', suspended in a reality beyond that of time. Like the Lady of *amour courtois*, whose sublimation — among other things — she has now become, the lady 'bent her head' in silent greeting, 'signed but spoke no word'. The gesture, though in itself ambiguous, deliberately unclear, is enough to bring a new life to the symbols associated with the garden and now seen in the light of a temporal process which requires to be 'redeemed', made actual in the new and timeless intuition:

> But the fountain sprang up and the bird sang down
> Redeem the time, redeem the dream
> The token of the word unheard, unspoken.

The 'fountain' and the 'bird', both familiar symbols of life, return. They take up, in an intensified form, the preceding recognition of the need to 'redeem the time' and the 'dream', to restore the vision which is the 'token' of the otherwise 'unheard, unspoken' word which may give a meaning to life. The 'word', however, though intuited in this way, will remain unspoken for us until we finally penetrate the secrets of life and death, of mortality and immortality, at the end of our temporal existence: 'Till the wind shake a thousand whispers from the yew'.

The final liturgical reference is accordingly taken appropriately from the evening prayer *Salve regina*, and is characteristically double in its implications. 'And after this our exile': the words, placed in this way in the poem, may bear either of two meanings. They may imply an inevitable return to 'exile' after the necessary fading of the dream: they may also refer, and perhaps do this more strongly, to the eternal life which is the object of the soul's prayer to Mary, Queen of Heaven, and which may be offered to us after the exile of our present existence, *post hoc exilium*.

V

The opening of the fifth poem leads us from the intensely personal experiences we have been following to more general considerations. We are now to concern ourselves with the present state of the world in which the poet exercises his craft. It is a world which is heedless of the Word, but which yet derives such 'meaning' as it possesses from the 'unseen' reality which its very existence and nature presupposes but which it so signally fails to recognize.[37] The contrast in the opening lines is between unceasing and apparently aimless movement at the surface of things and an intuited central stillness. The 'light' of the opening of St. John's Gospel shone 'in darkness' whilst

> Against the Word the unstilled world still whirled
> About the centre of the silent Word.

Introduced at this point and threaded through the entire development are the words of reproach from the Good Friday liturgy:

Popule meus, quid feci tibi; aut in quo contristavi te;[38] and it should be noted that the intricate initial lines themselves recall a Passion-time sermon by the seventeenth-century Anglican bishop Lancelot Andrewes.[39]

In the lines which follow the 'world' is explored for the possibility of a right response to the Word, the *Logos*, a response not to be found where 'silence', willingness to renounce the immediate and illusory assertion of the self, is lacking:

> Where shall the word be found, where will the word
> Resound? Not here, there is not enough silence
> Not on the sea nor on the islands, not
> On the mainland, in the desert or the rain land.

In the absence of the life-giving Word, which is only to be heard in and through interior silence, abstraction from noisy self-assertion in the individual as in society, the world necessarily walks in the darkness:

> Both in the day time and in the night time
> The right time and the right place are not here
> No place of grace for those who avoid the face
> No time to rejoice for those who walk among noise and
>   deny the voice.

The use of internal rhymes and assonances, so marked in *Murder in the Cathedral* and typical of Eliot's verse at this time, is used to point the central contrast on which this part of the poem rests. Where there is only 'noise', dedication to meaningless self-assertion which amounts to an attempt to evade the real, the 'voice' which conveys a true sense of the human situation is necessarily rejected and with it the acceptance of life-giving 'grace', the possibility of any true or valid 'rejoicing'.

In the next section, the poet—or, more properly, the 'voice' through which he speaks—sees himself as 'torn' in the world between the contrary states of faith and doubt, and as walking therefore in 'darkness'. His dilemma, which he shares with the time in which he lives, is to find himself divided *between* alternatives, to be in the condition of those who can neither pray with conviction nor entirely renounce their need for prayer, who 'choose' and 'oppose' at one and the same time.

Once again the condition the poet has in mind is conveyed through the use of internal rhyme—'Those who are *torn* on the

horn' —and the juxtaposition of a single word —'season' and 'season'
—in significant association. Hope for those who find themselves in
this state must lie in the intercession of the 'Lady', 'the veiled sis-
ter', who is to be apprehended by those who 'wait in darkness', in
the contemplation of death, but who is *not* herself death, though
she is 'veiled' and stands '*between* the slender/Yew trees,' between
the reality of a mortal state and an intimation of eternal life. The
last intercession is asked on behalf of those who are 'terrified' and
who are yet unable to make the 'surrender' which is a necessary
prelude to restoration: who are plunged in contradiction, simul-
taneously affirming and denying, poised between the 'world' and
the 'rocks', the desert, at once craving and refusing the renuncia-
tion of self which might be an initial source of restored life.

The final struggle takes place in the 'last' of many deserts: a
Waste Land which has been modified by the reference, taken up
from the preceding poem, to 'the last blue rocks'. If it is true that
the desert survives, that it continues to project its presence in the
'garden' of the new life—'The desert in the garden, the garden in
the desert', the two seemingly contrary conditions inextricably
intertwined—it is also clear that both 'desert' and 'garden' are in
the process of being reconstituted, transformed in relation to a new
and greater, more embracing reality. If the state of 'drouth' is still
a present reality, and will remain so for as long as life is experienced
under the aspect of time, it is now seen that there may also be a
flowering of the garden in the desert; even in 'drouth', in a state of
spiritual dryness and exhaustion, such as the entire sequence con-
templates, it is possible to assert the positive sources of the life
lived in a state of contrition (as it is called in familiar traditional
terms), by 'spitting' from the mouth in consciously motivated re-
jection the apple-seed—and there is a reference suggested here
to the original temptation in the Garden of Eden[40]—which is now
'withered' by the meaningless passage of time in the speaker's own
life and has accordingly lost its power to attract. With a final broken
reference to the passage already used from the liturgy of the
Passion—'O my people'—this part of the poem is brought to a
close.

VI

With the opening line of the last poem in the sequence, the time has come to return to the affirmation placed at the beginning of the first poem. The line now runs '*Although* I do not hope to turn again'; it is to be noted that 'although' has replaced the original 'because'. The first emphasis had been on the need to renounce 'hope', in so far as this represented a premature, a limiting possibility of relief. Here, in spite of and beyond this renunciation, which has made possible a positive return to the sources of life, the desire to live survives. 'Although' the protagonist has chosen to renounce his initial, instinctive desire to 'turn again', the possibilities before him have been expanded rather than reduced. The new condition is still one of hesitancy between alternatives, of '*Wavering* between the profit and the loss' (we are reminded of Phlebas the Phoenician, who died by water in *The Waste Land*);[41] the setting for the choices that now impose themselves is still the 'brief transit' of a life where 'dreams cross', where the motives of life and death in 'The dreamcrossed twilight *between* birth and dying' are intermingled, much as the new, the spiritual, and the old, the unregenerated life, continue to co-exist in time.

In this transitory condition (and to live in time is, in terms of this poem, to participate in a transitory situation) the entry to resolution lies through a confession of personal inadequacy: 'Bless me father.' This is the first, inescapable choice, a recognition of reality, from which all further choices will follow. Renunciation is required, not for its own sake or in a spirit of rejection of life, but in the interests of a more completely fulfilled existence. When the speaker says 'I do not *wish to wish* these things', he is in fact recalling, translating into terms of personal, willed decision the account of his state given in the opening poem; there the corresponding line had read 'I no longer *strive to strive* towards such things'. The resolution has been made, and is here reaffirmed, though with a proper recognition of its difficulty; for it is part of the sense of the poem that the symbols of a past nostalgically conceived still retain their power, express themselves with evocative force through the reference to 'unbroken wings':

> From the wide window towards the granite shore
> The white sails still fly seaward, seaward flying
> Unbroken wings.

The lines have all the sense of a poignantly recalled image from the poet's own past, perhaps of the Massachusetts landscape of his childhood which will reappear in *The Dry Salvages*. Although the memories need to be in some sense renounced, the 'unbroken wings' also appear to indicate an answer to the mention, again in the first poem, of the 'wings that are no longer wings to fly'. It may be that to renounce the past, deliberately and in a full consciousness of motive, is the only way to ensure that what was valuable, truly living, in it will continue to exercise influence as a positive element in the formation of the present.

The 'wings', in fact, not only continue to live in the imagination, but are felt to lead to other, and even stronger emotions equally derived from recollections of past glory:

> And the lost heart stiffens and rejoices
> In the lost lilac and the lost sea voices
> And the weak spirit quickens to rebel
> For the bent golden-rod and the lost sea smell
> Quickens to recover
> The cry of quail and the whirling plover
> And the blind eye creates
> The empty forms between the ivory gates
> And smell renews the salt savour of the sandy earth.

The 'heart', though now felt to be 'lost', associated with things that are no longer there and which cannot be recovered, responds still — instinctively 'stiffens' — to the sense of 'rejoicing' which comes to it from the remembered presences of nature. As with the vision through the window on the stairs in the third poem,[42] these things have now come to be seen as distractions from the requirements of the present, and as needing therefore — in so far as they are such — to be set aside, renounced. It is not, however, a matter of simple rejection. Though these impressions are disavowed by a poet whose concern is now with the present as leading to the future, the emphasis on *temptation* is significantly diminished in the light of the progress achieved and recorded in the course of the sequence. In spite of their recognized inadequacy as final goals, complete resting-places for the spirit (and no resting-place can properly be regarded as final by those engaged on a time-conditioned journey, if only because incompleteness is of the essence of temporal experience), these remembered intuitions of beauty now stand in significant contrast to the desert, the Waste Land associations of the 'landscape' in the opening poem. They are seen as belonging to the natural life of man and so can give life, causing the 'weak spirit' to 'quicken', in an emotion that carries implications of rebellion indeed (and that is why it has been necessary to contemplate their rejection), but with it a recognition of continuing natural life, a recovery of the real if transitory exaltation of the senses. What is lost can finally be recovered, but only at the cost of recognizing it as lost, as belonging irretrievably to a past that can never replace the need to accept and participate in the present.

This, indeed, as the poem immediately goes on to say, is 'the time of tension' between 'dying and birth' with which the whole sequence has been concerned: between 'dying and birth' now, be it noted, not as earlier 'between birth and dying'.[43] The changed order of the words answers to the development of a rhythmic concept of life which is now seen to underlie the sequence. If 'birth' is the first term in a progression that already implies 'death' as its end, that death—the presence of which is to be recognized at every moment in human life[44]—can be seen, once it has been consciously understood and accepted, as the possible prelude to 'birth', the entry into a new and transformed life.

The point is one which Eliot had already made in *The Journey of the Magi*[45] (dated 1927), and it has behind it, among other things, the lasting impression made upon him by the recognition scene at the end of Shakespeare's mysterious *Pericles*—'Did you not name a tempest,/A birth, and death?'[46]—as well, perhaps, as the Shepherd's phrase in *The Winter's Tale* which represents the pivotal point on which the entire construction of that beautiful and complex play turns: 'thou mettest with things dying, I with things new-born'.[47] In Eliot's poem, the 'place', the setting of the interior drama, is necessarily and justly one of 'solitude': a place 'where three dreams cross', poised between the real and the insubstantial. The experience to which the poem refers is still situated in the desert, the rocks of which, however, are now seen as 'blue', compatible, beyond the difficulty and the drouth, with intimations of a more spiritual reality. The 'voices' which 'drift away', in a line which bears beautiful echoes of insubstantial dream, still speak of mortality, but those which 'reply', which are 'shaken' from 'the other yew', confirm the suggestion of immortality ('birth' set in relation to, and proceeding from, 'death' again) and lead to a final prayer addressed to the 'Blessed sister' who is now merging into the 'holy mother', and who may bring with her the sources of renewed life in the spirit symbolized, in a fusion of pagan and Christian, natural and supernatural elements, under the familiar aspects of the 'fountain' and the 'garden'.

The prayer which concludes the poem, and with it the sequence, amounts to a call to sincerity:

> Suffer us not to mock ourselves with falsehood
> Teach us to care and not to care
> Teach us to sit still.

The prayer is now to be allowed to renounce the temptation 'to mock ourselves with falsehood', denying both the tragedy and the 'glory' which our lives, when lived in a state of complete consciousness, are seen to imply. To respond to the real is to identify ourselves with life, in other words 'to care'; equally, however, this implies a readiness to accept its limitations and to refrain from asking of life more than what life, considered as an ultimate and self-sufficient end, can give:[48] a readiness, in other words, 'not to care', in so far, at least, as to 'care' exclusively for what is transitory and therefore, in one sense, unreal is to diminish our capacity to respond to life as a whole. What is implied here is, in the last analysis, an attitude of moral realism, based upon a balanced view of the human situation, as the poet has now come to see it. In this view, elements of life and death are interwoven and need to be regarded in a spirit of realism, without concession to the permanent human craving for evasion and self-deception.

In the light of these considerations, the object of the final prayer will be a *creative* renunciation of the illusion of completeness, the attainment of a state of detachment which is never to be confused with indifference—for indifference is a confession of failure[49] and, in religious terms, a sin—but which springs from true realism. 'Even among these rocks' we need, having accepted the necessary incompleteness of all our mortal intuitions, to know how 'to sit still': to sit still, however, knowing, in the words of Dante's *Paradiso* here recalled, that 'Our peace is in his will'.[50] Accepted in this spirit as the relevant setting of human life, the 'rocks' are seen to look upon 'the sea',[51] and the final aspiration of the sequence is summed up in an intimately personal, appropriately non-liturgical prayer from the *Anima Christi*. 'Suffer me not to be separated': a prayer which is supported, in the last words of the poem, by its more formal, liturgical equivalent: 'Let my cry come unto Thee'.

III

FOUR
QUARTETS

FOUR QUARTETS

[1]
Introduction

The *Four Quartets* are—if we exclude his plays, the later of which by the common consent of criticism constitute inferior work—the last important poems that Eliot wrote; they represent in fact his last word as a poet. They show most obviously the remarkable continuity of theme and technique which marked all his work, and which is most apparent in the balance between lyrical and reflective passages, and in the division into five sections which had marked *The Waste Land* and, with variations, *Ash Wednesday*. The 'musical' technique which is a feature of earlier poems also persists and becomes indeed more explicitly marked. There is the same sense of originally disparate images finally uniting to produce what we can now agree to call—given the title Eliot himself chose for the sequence—a 'movement'; whilst the 'movement' in turn combines with other, similar 'movements' to produce a 'quartet'.

By the time Eliot came to write his last sequence of poems, these aspects of his earlier work have advanced from a device used among others to a central structural principle of the poetry. His own observation, in an essay published in 1942 and therefore contemporary with the later *Quartets*, is of interest in this respect:

> I believe that the properties in which music concerns the poet most nearly are the sense of rhythm and the sense of structure ... The use of recurrent themes is as natural to poetry as to music. There are possibilities for verse which bear some analogy to the development of a theme by different groups of instruments; there are possibilities of transitions in a poem comparable to the different moments of a symphony or a quartet; there are possibilities of contrapuntal arrangement of subject matter.[1]

All these possibilities may be said to come together to form the

Quartets, a series which aims at taking up the motives explored in the earlier poems, to consolidate the ground there gained, and to arrive—not rhetorically, but by direct communication through words—at the crowning of the poetic process by an act of 'religious' affirmation. The affirmation, however, emerges not as the result of a linear development of argument designed to arrive at a foreseen conclusion, but as a result of the drawing together of a number of initially separate themes until—in the measure that the poem 'works'—they are seen to fit together in the form of a design or 'pattern' of meaning greater than the sum of the separate parts.

Once again, however, our use of the word 'religious' in this connection reminds us, as it did in considering *Ash Wednesday*, that we need to be particularly careful in our choice of terms. Lack of care in this matter, indeed, is perhaps a principal reason why so little that is really useful has been written about these poems. The *Quartets*, more than most poetry, seem to invite us to step out of the normal concerns of criticism and to impose, or at least consider, judgements that have little to do with the creative activity of the poet; and this is a temptation which has, even more than usual, to be resisted. It is essential to understand that here, as in *Ash Wednesday*, we are not dealing with poetry which attempts to induce specifically 'Christian' feelings in readers who may be assumed to share the poet's own supposed way of thinking. On the contrary, the aim is to explore a fully contemporary experience (in which *doubt*, the difficulty of acceptance, has a full part to play) in order to see whether, and if so under what terms, one man's conclusions on these matters can be made to *fit*.

As always for Eliot, the poet is *not* an original philosopher, or one whose business it is to argue the *truth* of any particular set of convictions: 'It is not the poet's job to think: his job is to express the greatest emotional intensity of his time, based on whatever his time happened to think.'[2] The poet's concern with the beliefs he has incorporated into his poems begins to operate, in other words, at the point at which they touch life as lived, and the quality of his choices will be justified (if at all) in so far as he induces his readers to feel, through the vitality of his language and his use of the forms he has chosen, that feeling and thought have been enriched, enhanced, and deepened by them. The criterion by which we, as readers of poetry, may judge his success in doing this is not one of reasoned assent or dissent to a set of propositions which may be said to emerge from the poem, but our feeling of his success—or lack of it—in moulding his emotional material into a shape, or form, which seems to fulfil our instinct for a satisfying, integrating 'pattern' of experience.

The tendency to see poetry in this way is perhaps necessary to the nature of the art, which may be thought of—in so far as it is poetry—as essentially non-moral, non-assertive in its final nature: though, of course, assertions of this kind have played a great part in the creation of many important poems. It is certainly characteristic of much of Eliot's earlier poetry and criticism. There are, however, significant differences as well as similarities between the *Quartets* and even those of the earlier poems which seem to resemble them most. We shall be struck, perhaps, as we read them by the fact that the presence of quotations, so prominent in *The Waste Land*, is no longer felt in quite the same way. The references are still there, almost as numerous as ever, but they no longer stand out or need to be identified by appending notes to elucidate the poetry. They have been, as it were, assimilated into the body of a continuing meditative discourse, made a part of it in a way that simply does not occur in the earlier poem. The sense of the poetry as proceeding from a single voice reflecting a continuous but expanding point of view is central to Eliot's conception in the *Quartets*, in a way which is notably different from the impression we receive from *The Waste Land*.

In the second place, the famous 'objective correlative', provided for *The Waste Land* by Frazer and Miss Weston, and by a combination of the Dantesque 'higher dream' and the Catholic liturgy in *Ash Wednesday*, no longer seems to apply. The poet seems now to be speaking with a voice which can be said to be his own; or, perhaps better, he seems to have found a consistent voice, a voice which utters personal thoughts and feelings more directly and intimately than ever before. The result is a new style, to which we might give the name of 'meditative'. The poet puts forward what are presented as personal thoughts and emotions (some of them very intimate for this apparently least 'personal' of poets) and builds a meditative discourse around them. He introduces them, develops and then drops them, seems to switch to other concepts, apparently unrelated, and then returns to the original themes, which emerge generally enriched, more subtly rendered, in the process. Ideas and feelings exist, in fact, in a constantly shifting and developing web of relationships. They lead by the end of the series to conclusions which we could not have foreseen at the beginning (the first readers of *Burnt Norton* found the poem puzzling, even incomprehensible, and certainly 'unpoetical'), but which are seen, by the time we have finished reading, to belong to a logical and consistent whole. There *are* indeed passages—not, perhaps, very many—in the *Quartets* where the tension seems to drop unduly, which are prosaic or even pedantic in the effect they make on us, and there is also an occasional suspicion of imaginative exhaustion. The critic will give a proper weight to these impressions. They constitute both a real weakness of Eliot's poetry and a problem of which he was conscious and which he wrote, in part, to overcome; but, perhaps, when this has been recognized, we shall conclude that the series, taken in its entirety, remains remarkably self-consistent and alive as the expression of a life-time's developing experience.

When we look more closely at the structure of these poems, we shall find a definite pattern that corresponds, on a superficial level, to the five sections into which each quartet is divided and which, a good deal more obviously than in *The Waste Land*, carries forward the complete development. If each quartet is to be conceived as part of a unity greater than itself, each 'movement' *within* each quartet not only needs to be seen in relation to each other 'movement' in the poem to which it belongs, but refers, back or forward as the case may be, to each corresponding 'movement' in the other three poems. The reader is induced to say to himself, as he reads: 'I've seen that before', and to ask himself 'What's become of it at this stage?' By these means, among others, the exploration of experience is communicated on a number of different levels, giving what we might call a sense of depth or *perspective* to the undertaking and contributing to a rich complexity in the final result.

It is worth looking, briefly, at some of the devices which play their part in producing this effect. In the first place, the two quotations from Heraclitus on the title page, which were originally given to *Burnt Norton* (the first and most ostensibly 'philosophical' of these poems), but which were finally applied to the series as a whole, tell us something about the nature of what we are to read. In translation they read as follows:

Although the law of reason (the *Logos*) is common, the majority of people live as though they had an understanding (or wisdom) of their own.

The way up and the way down are one and the same.

The first quotation asserts, from the point of view of these poems, that a reasonable truth is, or ought to be, the common possession of men, whose lives in fact can only be lived significantly *in common*, in recognition of their essentially social nature; but also that most men arrive at such truth as they may finally hope to possess through their own private and personal efforts. In this respect the poet is like the rest of men. His time and circumstance (as well as his nature as a human being) have imposed upon him the need to make this private, personal effort, which is at once a condition of his humanity and (and in so far as the effort is restricted by being self-contained, isolated) his problem. The necessary uniqueness of each man's experience and its relation to an equally necessary ground in a common humanity, are central themes of the series. They are finally, perhaps, associated with the larger theme, which also dominates these poems, of the relationship of life to death in human experience. Men *live* in a common understanding, and *die* alone; this is perhaps for Eliot, as for many great poets, something like a definition of human life.

The second passage from Heraclitus asserts a notion that will play an equally important part in the thematic development of the series: the idea that the way to understanding, to spiritual fulfilment, may pass *either* through an increased response to the nature of external reality (what some writers on the spiritual life have called the Way of Affirmation) *or* through an equally deliberate and progressive renunciation or elimination of the self, a descent into the darkness and obscurity which our experience can be seen to imply in its temporal limitation when contrasted to the extra-temporal and therefore inapprehensible nature of what we call, rather unsatisfactorily, the 'spiritual'. The second path has affinities to what traditional writers on the life of the soul have sometimes called the Negative Way. In theological terms, which the poems are both aware of and concerned to use in a personal way, God is *life*, and so to participate in life—to *live*, in the proper sense of the term—is to share in some real part of his essence; but since he is also by definition *eternal life* (whatever that may mean: to give the word meaning in terms of actual experience is perhaps a principal concern of the series), and since human experience seems to be inexorably confined to the temporal, we can only speak of him by way of negation, can only hope to define to ourselves something of his nature by establishing what he is *not*.[3]

The Way Up and the Way Down thus related to the phrase attributed to Heraclitus are to be seen, accordingly, as being in a real sense 'the same', as pointing to a common end. The aim of this series of poems will be to hold them together in creative tension, to explore *both* ways in the light of one poet's experience (the limitations of which he fully recognizes), and to show, not theoretically but in terms of language and the living experience which it reflects that they are in fact directed towards the same conclusion. His success in this undertaking will be communicated —we repeat—not as an abstraction, but in so far as the poetry itself conveys this sense of an experience harmonized and achieved.

Other aspects of the *Quartets* which serve to underline their common, developing purpose can be briefly mentioned. Each of them is named after a *place*, which is significant for its understanding, which answers to important associations in the poet's mind. *Burnt Norton* is the name of a seventeenth-century house in Gloucestershire, which the poet envisages as in ruins or deserted and which he associates with a particularly intense, if fugitive, moment of experience. This moment becomes the occasion for a philosophical 'discourse' on the nature of *time* in its relation to 'reality' and to our experiences as human beings. *East Coker*, the title of the second quartet, has stronger personal associations. It is the name of a village in Somerset from which the poet's ancestors set out, again in the seventeenth century, for the New World. Here the poet is concerned not so much with ideas or abstractions as with an effort to return to his own historical roots, the point in time from which his ancestral journey may be said to have derived. This effort leads him, logically enough, to consider the action of time in moulding and transforming the material, and possibly the spiritual conditions of human experience. *The Dry Salvages*, which gives its title to the third quartet, are—as the poet explains in a brief initial note—a group of rocks on the coast of Massachusetts, which he associates with recollections of his childhood. These memories merge, in the course of the poem, with other early American memories—notably that of the river Mississippi, on the banks of which Eliot was born, in St. Louis[4]—and to further consideration of human life in its relation to time, death, and to more explicitly religious formulations. Finally, *Little Gidding* is the name of the English village to which the Anglican priest Nicholas Farrar and certain associates retired (once more in the seventeenth century) to form a religious community at a time of particular stress in the English Civil War. This last quartet is less immediately personal in its implications than a reflection of the spiritual position in relation to tradition which has come to attract the poet in respect of the time and place in which he finds himself. As such it forms the natural and appropriate conclusion to the sequence.

Many other references and points of intersection emerge from any close reading of the *Four Quartets*. A number of them will be mentioned in the process of the discussion which follows. Worth noting at this point, perhaps, is the fact that each of the poems corresponds to one of the four elements in the traditional scheme. *Burnt Norton* stresses the element of *air*, *East Coker* that of *earth*, *The Dry Salvages* turns largely upon images of *water*, and *Little Gidding*, finally, is characterized by the crowning association of *fire*. In each the element in question plays an important part in the development of the poem to which it corresponds and in the moral scheme which it is concerned to develop.

Finally, the interrelationship which we have been discussing between the various sections of each of the *Quartets* is strengthened by a structural pattern of reiterated, if loosely developed themes by which they are further united.[5] The first 'movement' in each poem consists of what might be called, in appropriately musical terms, a *statement* and *counterstatement*: a general proposition and a particular instance, sometimes (though not always) implying a kind of contradiction which the quartet as a whole aims at resolving. The particular instance is in each case related, more or less closely, to the title of the corresponding poem. The second 'movement' in turn opens with a passage in rhyme, which is followed by a more 'colloquial' or discursive commentary in which the idea treated in metaphor or symbol in the first part is expanded and given more directly personal application. The commentary often refers to some aspect of the time-theme, and seeks to relate an understanding of this to the general interpretation which is growing out of the series as a whole.

A similar reiteration of pattern can be detected in the later 'movements' of each quartet. The third 'movement' may be said to form the core of each poem, the theme out of which the corresponding resolution grows in each case. In the process of exploring further the ideas stated in the two preceding 'movements', the poem passes from the 'abstract' to the 'human', or 'moral' aspect of the theme under exploration, dealing with the implications for conduct of the speculative positions established, or at least advanced as illuminating possibilities, in the earlier 'movements'. By contrast, and as though to interrupt this sense of logical progression, and to restore a necessary emotional balance, the short fourth 'movement' is in each case a lyrical 'interlude' which seems to break the preceding line of development but is at the same time related in spirit to the point reached by the main argument. It performs, in short, the function given to the similar 'interlude'— *Death by Water*, also the fourth section of the poem to which it belongs—in *The Waste Land*. The fifth and final 'movement', which follows this interlude, resembles the second in being divided into two parts, but with a significant formal reversal: the 'colloquial', discursive passage now comes first, and is followed by a grave and more 'poetic' close. The 'movement' generally begins by relating the 'philosophical' problems already indicated in the course of the quartet to the artistic and personal ones involved in the poet's own efforts to use words: to the difficulty—more precisely—of defining the issues of any given moment vividly and exactly through means of expression which invariably, in the nature of things, strike the poet as inadequate to his purpose. Starting from this point, which may be thought of as the application to the poet's special concern of the general problem about the nature of time which plays so important a part in the development of the series, this final 'movement' aims at reconciling the general, 'philosophical' exposition, given in the second section of each poem, with the 'human' or 'moral' matter of the third section; and, in so doing, the 'movement' aims at defining the position attained in each poem, and in the series as a whole, by this continuous creative effort.

It needs to be stressed, by way of conclusion, that the 'skeleton' or framework sketched in this way is no substitute for complete and continuous response to the changing texture of the poems. The 'skeleton' is there because it serves the poet's purpose, because the poetry may be built upon it; but is not in itself—and of its nature cannot be—poetry. It needs, as a skeleton, to be filled out by a development of the thematic matter and by interweaving the images which are, so to speak, the living materials of the finished organism. This will be what we shall attempt to do in the detailed discussion which follows.

[2]
Burnt Norton

Any useful reading of the *Quartets* must raise, at some early stage, a question as to the kind of poem we are dealing with. The poet himself has warned us, at least by implication, what *not* to expect. Above all, perhaps, he has taken care to discourage any attempt to appropriate any of his poems in the interests of a narrow, overtly 'Christian' reading. Devotional poetry, he has said in one of his critical essays, commonly expresses not what the poet believes, but what he *wants* to believe.[1] In this sense at least the *Quartets* are clearly not 'devotional' poems, and still less contributions to Christian 'apologetics'. The impulse which went to their making is essentially *exploratory* and, at least initially, *tentative* in its nature. Their concern with beliefs is at the point at which these touch life as lived in the present, and the choices which they explore will be justified (if at all) in so far as the poems make us feel through the viability of their language, the quality of their rhythms, that thought and feeling have been enriched, enhanced, and deepened, in the process of development.

Rejection of the notion that the *Quartets* are in any usual sense 'theological' or 'devotional' writings is apt to bring with it a problem of a rather different kind. It has been argued that the series is concerned with the creation of 'concepts', the formulation of an expressive language appropriate for conveying certain intuitions of a spiritual nature which cannot be projected in the terms established by traditional usage.[2] This way of looking at the poems is certainly nearer to the poet's purposes, and true to the concern with language and its expressive possibilities which is a recurrent theme in the *Quartets*. It carries with it, however, when incautiously or insensitively used, the danger of reading the poetry in an abstract key, and so of finding it finally arid, remote from actual, lived experience. Much criticism of the *Quartets* has arrived, though with varying degrees of emphasis, at this kind of conclusion.[3] To fall into this danger is to deny the quality of the poems *as* poetry, to read them for what is not intended to be there. Eliot insists more than once in his critical writings that the poet is not to be thought of as an original philosopher, whose business it might be to advance

96

the *truth* of his particular conclusions.[4] If the poetry lives, it is not in relation to abstract concepts or general 'truths', but as the expression of a developing experience, a pattern of intuitions which conveys itself through the indispensable poetic medium of image and rhythm and which can only emerge in its full significance (if it is found to have one) at the end of the creative process.

I

With these generalizations in mind, we can turn to the first and most overtly 'philosophical' poem in the sequence, *Burnt Norton*. It opens with the tentative statement of a general proposition about the nature of time and the part it plays in human experience. The point of departure is the familiar philosophical dilemma about the nature of the 'present', conceived of as being at any given moment the indefinable 'point' which separates the no-longer-existing past from a future that is always coming into being. It is not necessary to posit any one philosophical precedent, among the many possible, as being in the poet's mind when he advances this idea of time as involving a concept of simultaneity; but perhaps St. Augustine's treatment of the theme in the Eleventh Book of the *Confessions*[5] is as close to the general intention of the *Quartets* as any:

> Time present and time past
> Are both perhaps present in time future
> And time future contained in time past.

The key-word in this initial proposition is 'perhaps'. The poet is putting forward a hypothesis, not stating a fact: the hypothesis that our experience *may* imply a certain simultaneity and that accordingly, as the lines immediately following go on to suggest, the time that is 'eternally present' may be, by virtue of that very fact, 'unredeemable', impossible to consider as being other than what it in fact is. Our awareness, in time, of alternative possibilities (of 'what might have been') would seem to exist only 'in abstraction', present indeed in our thoughts and feelings, but only in the order of conceptual thinking, the 'world of speculation'.

At this point the poem initiates an essential shift from the deliberate abstraction, the calculated and almost conversational detachment of the opening lines, to preoccupations more directly personal in kind. A distinction is put forward, in terms which begin to approach those of immediate living, between the actual past events which have led to the present moment ('what has been') and the alternative, unrealized possibilities which these events seem to have relegated to the order of the unreal: 'what might have been':

> What might have been and what has been
> Point to one end, which is always present.

The emphasis, conveyed in a barely perceptible quickening of the rhythmic pace, is shifting from abstraction in the direction of the personal. *Both* 'what has been' and 'what might have been' are seen now as forming part of our lives, though only—in view of what has already been said—as regarded from the standpoint of what has been realized (in so far as it *is* realized) in the unique actuality of a moment which, by the very fact of its 'presence', is, as we have already been told, 'unredeemable'. Upon that moment, *both* strands of our experience—'what might have been' and 'what has been'—converge; but the contribution at any given point in time of what is unrealized is actual only in relation to what has actually occurred, to the 'end' which is always, at any given moment in our lives, the actual 'present' reality.

Throughout this opening discussion of the temporal implications of experience, the poet's aim has been tentative, exploratory. Indeed, to give body in terms of actual living to an intuitive conviction that the temporal and the timeless (which *may* turn out to be 'the real') stand in meaningful relationship to one another might be described as the end of the whole series. Meanwhile, 'what might have been' and 'what has been' are clearly phrases loaded with potential implications of personal nostalgia and fulfilment. As such they imply a change from the abstraction of the opening and serve as a transition to a new, a more explicitly 'poetic' phase in the development:

> Footfalls echo in the memory
> Down the passage which we did not take
> Towards the door we never opened
> Into the rose-garden. My words echo
> Thus, in your mind.

The shift towards a more intimate mood makes itself felt at this point—as it must do in poetry—in a more intimate response of rhythm to meaning. The 'memory' of the first line is a personal faculty and the 'footfalls' that 'echo' in it do so not as dismembered abstractions but as experiences that might actually have occurred and been shared—the fact that the poet for the first time uses actual personal pronouns ('my', 'your', 'we') is in itself indicative of a new phase in the poem—in genuine intensity of feeling.

The poignancy of the lines, indeed, derives from their relationship to possibilities that remained only such, that were never translated into actual lived events. Prominent through these verses, and giving them a new force of personal meaning, is the sense of aspirations that remained unfulfilled: the remembered 'passage' was never entered, the 'rose-garden' which might have been the setting of intimate communion never achieved. The 'rose', indeed, is a symbol that will come to play an increasing part in the development of the sequence. Connected, as a symbol, with sexual love (and here we recall the medieval tradition which produced the *Roman de la Rose*), it was also 'spiritualized' by Dante for whom the rose became, at the end of the *Paradiso*,[6] a symbol of the vision of the Divine Reality. These implications, however, remain for the moment deliberately unperceived. A parallel is made with the 'words' that, recalling personal states of emotion, have a definite meaning for the speaker, but which can only 'echo *thus*' (note the deliberate, and beautiful, placing of the word at the beginning of a new line) in an unrealized manner, indicative only of *possibility*, in the mind of a reader who cannot share the original emotion. The following evocative image of the 'dust' which has lain for a long *time* on a bowl of dead, cut rose leaves and which is *disturbed*— as intuitions of possible meaning obscurely disturb our habitual patterns of thought—to an unknown end ('I do not know') serves as a further transition to the central experience of this opening section.

Immediately, indeed, the 'echo' of the preceding lines, which reverberated in the mind, joins the reference to the 'rose-garden' to evoke a definite moment—passing, indeed, but while it lasted luminous and intense—of potentially shared experience: the experience in the deserted garden of the house of the title which the poet, in the act of recreating what 'might have been' in its relation to what actually 'was', feels may have some relation to the problem put forward in the opening general statements:

Other echoes
Inhabit the garden. Shall we follow?
Quick, said the bird, find them, find them,
Round the corner. Through the first gate,
Into our first world, shall we follow
The deception of the thrush? Into our first world.
There they were, dignified, invisible,
Moving without pressure, over the dead leaves,
In the autumn heat, through the vibrant air,
And the bird called, in response to
The unheard music hidden in the shrubbery,
And the unseen eyebeam crossed, for the roses
Had the look of flowers that are looked at.
There they were as our guests, accepted and accepting.
So we moved, and they, in a formal pattern,
Along the empty alley, into the box circle,
To look down into the drained pool.
Dry the pool, dry concrete, brown edged,
And the pool was filled with water out of sunlight,
And the lotos rose, quietly, quietly,
The surface glittered out of heart of light,
And they were behind us, reflected in the pool.
Then a cloud passed, and the pool was empty.
Go, said the bird, for the leaves were full of children,
Hidden excitedly, containing laughter.
Go, go, go, said the bird: human kind
Cannot bear very much reality.
Time past and time future
What might have been and what has been
Point to one end, which is always present.

The experience, or its recalling, has to be caught on the passing moment, like the song of the bird which is associated with it. Perhaps, indeed, it never happened, and is only significant as an intimation of possible, unrealized fulfilment. In any event, it cannot last. 'Quickly', because it is fleeting, like an intimation of original innocence ('through the first gate'), it hovers at best on the limits of our time-conditioned awareness. It exists, in fact, 'round the corner' and may indeed be, as the poet goes on to insinuate, not the hoped-for illumination, but a disappointment, a 'deception'.[7]

What is tenuously recaptured, a glimpse of possibilities opening into 'our first world' (the phrase is repeated and stressed, on the second occasion, by the fall of the rhythm), is left deliberately impalpable. It is, at all events, connected with a ghostly evocation from the past: the evocation, perhaps, of the poet and another person, not as they were in reality, but as they might have been, imaginatively recreated, moving 'without pressure' over the 'dead' leaves of an autumn which answers, beyond the seasons, to a state of being. The air is 'vibrant', charged with intense if unrealized significance, and the song of the bird responds to the 'unheard', 'hidden' music of dream.

What in fact is happening, and what the increasingly urgent rhythms and stresses of the passage beautifully recreate, is the insinuation of a sense that the orders of reality and dream — 'what has been' and 'what might have been' — are felt, for as long as the experience lasts and in the words, once again, of the opening, to be simultaneous, 'always present':

> the unseen eyebeam crossed, for the roses
> Had the look of flowers that are looked at.

Whereas the opening statement had tended to assert that only the present is real, and by so doing had seemed to render *all* time 'unredeemable' (because 'redemption' implies the recovery, and so the continued existence, of something other than the merely, exclusively present), the new experience moving from the field of logic to that of intuition seems to suggest the possibility that the two orders — the present and the potential, 'what might have been' and 'what has been' — can perhaps be seen as converging on an enriched, more *living* awareness of what the 'present' really implies. The worlds of reality and dream are fused into a pattern of mutually supporting significance, 'accepted and accepting', until they 'move' together into the 'formal pattern' which the garden itself reflects.

Responding to the dream-like compulsions of memory, the poem induces us to accompany the ghostly protagonists along the 'empty alley' into the deserted centre of the formal garden, where the vacant, 'drained' pool is circled by 'box': we recall the significance of the 'yew', indicative of both death and resurrection, for the poet of *Ash Wednesday*.[8] The pool itself is at first seen, in its present reality, as 'dry' ('dry', 'dry concrete': the emphasis is deliberate);

but, as it is imaginatively recreated in the light of a past in the process of being restored, 'redeemed', it becomes the heart of a transforming emotion. The transformation expresses itself in terms of 'sunlight' and 'water', the tranquillity of the 'heart of light':

> the lotos rose, quietly, quietly,
> The surface glittered out of heart of light;

it is not an accident that the lotos is associated with the Buddhist experience of contemplation and that the Dantesque symbol of light will be repeatedly evoked in the course of these poems to convey the essence of spiritual reality.

Nor, for that matter, is it an accident that the phrase recalls another, and similarly intense, moment of speechless emotion from Eliot's earlier poetry: the passage from *The Waste Land* when the protagonist of *The Burial of the Dead* returning, in company, 'late', from 'the hyacinth garden', found himself inarticulate in the face of an intense, if ambiguous emotion:

> I could not
> Speak, and my eyes failed, I was neither
> Living nor dead, and I knew nothing,
> Looking into *the heart of light*, the silence.[9]

There the moment of vision ended, for all its intensity, in a 'silence' which the following line from Wagner's *Tristan, Oed' und leer das Meer*, indicates as that of desolation, ultimate betrayal. Here the mood, though equally tenuous and transitory, is capable of a more positive interpretation, and the symbols do not impose themselves as such, remain subsidiary to the intense, sensitive evocation of the fleeting moment of intuitive experience. Their quality is transitory, associated with memories and possibilities glimpsed in the world: memories and possibilities which take us, as it were, unawares, coming from over the shoulder to evoke fleeting moments of intense life before being dissipated, returned to the neutral state of daily reality by the intervention of a passing cloud. 'Then a cloud passed, and the pool was empty': empty as it had been before the intensely recalled emotion seemed to raise a corner of the curtain, and to afford a glimpse into the 'heart' of a possible reality. Held for a moment in a precarious unity, recreated in a kind of transcending of the normal limitations which time imposes, the experience has scarcely been perceived, caught, when it is interrupted by the presence of the outside world and returned to its separate fragments.

The experience in the rose-garden is one of fundamental importance for the design of the *Quartets*. The later poems in the sequence repeatedly return to it, seek to interpret it in the light of the intervening development. It is important, therefore, to be as clear as possible regarding the nature of the experience itself and the claims, if any, which Eliot can be said to make for it. To begin with, it should be said at once that we are evidently *not* being offered any kind of 'mystical' or specifically religious insight. There is no suggestion that the poet felt himself, either at the time or on reflection, in touch with any kind of extra-temporal or supernatural reality outside the self. The experience, in itself, posits the existence of no kind of 'God', makes no statement, direct or indirect, about the possible nature of such a hypothetical Being or about any relationship which might conceivably exist between Him (or It) and a human person. What it *does* seem to offer is rather an increase in *consciousness*, a sense that the normal limitations of time have been for a moment suspended, so that the past is brought to life in relation to the present in a way which suggests that the laws of succession by which we are normally bound can be set aside, replaced—for the duration of the experience—by an intuited simultaneity which *may* indicate something about their true nature.

The experience so offered can be paralleled in the work of other writers of the twentieth century, among them—in England—Eliot's contemporaries E. M. Forster[10] and Virginia Woolf.[11] The most suggestive parallel, however, may be that provided by Marcel Proust who succeeded, in his great novel, in building upon just such moments of intuition nothing less than the whole design of his work. For the greater part of *A la Recherche du Temps Perdu* the full sense of these fugitive moments remains concealed, the moments themselves without obvious development. The first of them, as every reader of Proust will recall, is occasioned by the author's action of dipping the famous 'madeleine' into his tea and being thereby transported into what is to be the central theme of his great undertaking. The unexpected experience is charged, indeed, with illuminating force, causes the author to feel, in his own words, that

at once the vicissitudes of life had become indifferent to me,
its disasters innocuous, its brevity illusory—this new sensa-
tion having had on me the effect which love has of filling me
with a precious essence; or rather this essence was not in me,
it was myself. I had ceased now to feel mediocre, accidental,
mortal.[12]

These are large claims indeed—considerably larger than any
immediately made by Eliot for *his* experience—but it is noteworthy
that Proust is content to let them stand, that he makes no attempt
at this stage to substantiate them by letting us know upon what
precisely they are based. Much the same can be said of the subse-
quent flashes of illuminating insight which are briefly introduced,
raise elusive questions as to their possible meaning, and are then—
or so it seems—set aside to return to the onward progress of the
narrative. There is, for instance, the glimpse of the church spires
at Martinville later in *Du Côté de chez Swann*,[13] and the reaction,
in *A L'Ombre des Jeunes Filles en Fleurs*, to the sight of three trees
in an otherwise featureless landscape.[14]

It is not until the great enterprise has reached its final stages, in
the volume significantly entitled *Le Temps Retrouvé*, that the full
sense of these seemingly fortuitous episodes becomes apparent.
The occasion is a further experience which has notable similarities
to that which Eliot has sought to convey in his poem. The author,
now an elderly and disillusioned man, is once again tired and
depressed, as he had been so long ago at the time of the 'madeleine'
incident. He is making his way to a social gathering—the last of
many such in the novel—offered by the new Princesse de Guer-
mantes. The fact that it is the *new* Princess whom he is about to
greet is, of course, relevant; it confirms his sense of the inexorable
passage of time and of the meaningless caducity of all human
affairs.

In this state, and on the point of entering the house, he stumbles
over an inequality in the pavement, and recovers his balance by
setting one foot on a stone a little higher than the one on which his
other foot is resting. The effect, he tells us, is immediate and
transforming. It is also associated with the elusive glimpses of
illumination evoked, in passing, in previous moments of the novel:

    ... all my discouragement vanished and in its place was that
    same happiness which at various epochs of my life had been

given to me by the sight of trees which I had thought that I had recognised in the course of a drive near Balbec, by the sight of the twin steeples of Martinville, by the flavour of a madeleine dipped in tea, and by all those other sensations of which I have spoken and of which the last works of Vinteuil had seemed to me to combine the quintessential character.[15]

The sense of fulfilment, of plenitude fleetingly achieved, is something with which we are already familiar from the earlier passages, here significantly recalled in succession, which involved, essentially, the same type of transforming experience. What is new is that *now*, at the end of the novel, at the moment in which time is 're-discovered'—Eliot, in the *Quartets* and elsewhere in his poetry, uses the word 'redeem' to express what is essentially the same idea —the sense, the *meaning* of the experience is seen to lie in the bringing together, the rendering simultaneously 'co-existent' (to use Eliot's word again) of moments of illumination widely separated in time and apparently without connection:

... again the dazzling and indistinct vision fluttered near me, as if to say: 'Seize me as I pass if you can, and try to solve the riddle of happiness which I set you.' And almost at once I recognised the vision: it was Venice ...[16]

At this point, the parallels with Eliot—already sufficiently suggestive—can be taken a step further. With the mention of 'Venice', the conjunction that gives life to the apparently separate experiences so far described is finally established. Two moments widely separated in time—the present sensation caused by the involuntary act of stumbling and the memory, hitherto unconscious, of two uneven stones on the floor of the baptistery of St. Mark's— have come together in such a way as to produce a sense of simultaneous existence, of the overcoming of the barriers which temporal sequence normally imposes upon our experience. This is the moment of intuitive illumination which seems to render orderly and significant all that has gone before; and it is one which as Proust recognizes—cannot of its very nature last:

Always, when these resurrections took place, the distant scene engendered around the common sensation had for a moment grappled, like a wrestler, with the actual scene. Always the actual scene had come off victorious, and always

the vanquished one had appeared to me the more beautiful
of the two . . .[17]

The connection with Eliot's discovery, in the light of *his* moment
of revelation, that 'human kind/Cannot bear very much reality',
is clear. For Eliot, as for Proust, it is man's destiny to be expelled
from the state of paradise;[18] for both, the Fall is a universal human,
if not necessarily a theological reality.

For both, moreover, the Fall, conceived in this sense, is a merci-
ful dispensation. Eliot will state this explicitly at a later, more
reflective stage of his first quartet.[19] Proust, meditating on his
experience immediately after describing it, goes on to say

> and if the actual scene had not very quickly been victorious,
> I believe that I should have lost consciousness;

for, as he explains,

> so complete are these resurrections of the past during the
> second that they last, that they not only oblige our eyes to
> cease to see the room which is near them in order to look
> instead at the railway bordered with trees or the rising tide,
> they even force our nostrils to breathe the air of places which
> are in fact a great distance away, and our will to choose
> between the various projects which those distant places sug-
> gest to us, they force our whole self to believe that it is sur-
> rounded by these places where we now are, in a dazed
> uncertainty such as we feel sometimes when an indescribably
> beautiful vision presents itself to us at the moment of our
> falling asleep.[20]

Proust, as befits his much larger canvas, is more explicit, more
analytic in point of detail, than Eliot is, or needs to be; but the
final conclusion is evidently the same. For both writers, the vision
can only be momentary in its duration, for to seek to extend it in
time would be to annihilate the present and so to make human life
impossible.

The two experiences, then, are clearly similar in kind and lead,
in important respects, to similar results. In both the past, appar-
ently lost and irrecoverable, lives again in the present, and in both
each term is seen as a result under a new light and with a new
intensity. Once again Proust's comment can serve to illuminate
Eliot's experience:

The being which had been reborn in me when with a sudden
shudder of happiness I had heard the noise that was common
to the spoon touching the plate and the hammer striking the
wheel, or had felt beneath my feet the unevenness that was
common to the paving stones of the Guermantes courtyard
and to those of the baptistery of St. Mark's, this being is
nourished only by the essences of things, in these alone does
it find its sustenance and delight . . . But let a noise or a scent,
once heard or once smelt, be heard or smelt again in the
present and at the same time in the past, real without being
actual, ideal without being abstract, and immediately the
permanent and habitually concealed essence of things is
liberated and our true self which seemed—had perhaps for
long years seemed—to be dead but was not altogether dead,
is awakened and reanimated as it receives the celestial nour-
ishment that is brought to it. A minute freed from the order
of time has recreated in us, to feel it, the man freed from the
order of time.[21]

Common to both experiences, to Proust's as to Eliot's, is the sense
of contemplating a reality that may throw some light on the nature
of what, for want of a better word, we call the 'eternal'; and com-
mon to both is the fact that each lasts only for a moment. That
moment, however, amounts to what Proust called 'the recovery of
time', the understanding under a new light of the temporal process
itself. 'The only way to savour them more fully,' he says of these
transforming moments, 'was to try to get to know them more
completely in the medium in which they existed, that is to say,
within myself, to try to make them translucid even to their very
depths.'[22]

The last point is important, for Proust as for Eliot. Proust tells
us that the kind of experience he has described has, while it lasts,
the effect of creating a species of new self. What he does *not* say,
and indeed is careful to avoid saying, is that this second self
amounts in any way to an access of 'supernatural' life. What is
created by the experience seems to be the recovery of another,
deeper self, one which had seemed dead and which the impact of
the forgotten past experience has brought back to life; but there is
no reason to believe, in terms of the experience as given, that what
is in this way realized is in any way outside the self, or that any

kind of contact with a transcending reality is necessarily implied. To realize these experiences fully, Proust says, it is necessary 'to know them more completely' and this can be done by directing our attention 'where they are', that is, in ourselves, with a view to clarifying their deepest essence. What these experiences can give is, in other words, an increase of consciousness, a deeper and more extended awareness of what our temporal natures finally imply. This, again, can only be achieved by renouncing any attempt to cling to the experience itself as uniquely significant, by accepting rather the human obligation to return to the normal pattern of daily life and to see, in relation to that pattern, personal and social, what in the experience given survives as illuminating or valuable. What we attain by this exploration in depth may (or may not) have supernatural implications; the experience itself does not, and cannot, tell us. It may be used, as Eliot finally—but *only* finally—uses it to give new life, fresh meaning, to traditional religious concepts; but it may also serve, as in Proust, as the basis for an exploration of human reality which has no necessary or specific religious content.[23] Which path the writer chooses is a matter of his own conviction and temperament. What is common to both is an awareness that the experience which serves as the point of departure for the creative effort is not an end in itself but something to be built on, in a spirit of conscious and continuing reflection, after the moment of illumination has, of its very nature, ceased to exist.[24]

Eliot's passage, then, is to be seen as the point of departure for what may ultimately prove to be a large and positive design. It shares with Proust's description, at all events, a preoccupation with the transitory and the ephemeral. At the moment of greatest intensity, the possibly significant dream is shattered. The leaves, 'full of children', 'hidden excitedly', 'containing laughter', have suggested a fleeting sense of intensified being, which the notable quickening of the expression beautifully and immediately reflects; but the voice of the bird, recalling the initial '*deception* of the thrush', comes back with renewed urgency to expel the dreamers from the 'first world', to assert their normal inability, as time-conditioned creatures living in and limited by 'the present', to hold to what may be, on another, scarcely apprehensible level, 'reality'. The 'time present and time past' of the first line of the poem becomes now 'time past and time future', in an echo of the earlier lines affirming the central relevance of the eternally ungraspable present:

What might have been and what has been
Point to one end, which is always present.

The breaking of the moment of vision, though possibly not final,
is necessary in so far as it answers to the nature of human, if not of
ultimate, reality. It represents, above all, the poet's unwillingness
to arrive at premature conclusions. The very phrase we have just
used—'ultimate reality'—raises the question whether *any* concep-
tion of an 'ultimate' as distinct from a merely 'human' reality can
in fact have meaning. It is a question that can be answered, if at all,
in terms not of abstraction but of actual, lived experience: experi-
ence which, in this particular case, needs to be made actual and
accessible through the poetry. The intuitive illumination just de-
scribed *may*, indeed, correspond to the fragments, as seen by our
partial vision, of a picture in itself complete; but nothing we have
been told so far properly confirms this. The problem, having been
posed in a way appropriate to poetry, in terms of experience
actually lived and remembered, needs to be attacked less directly,
more discursively, in the effort to arrive by a different path at the
same conclusion. Until then, the moment so evocatively described
can be no more than a possible illustration of the general proposi-
tion tentatively put forward in the opening lines of the poem.

II

The transition to discursive exploration is managed, as it will be in
each poem of this series, through a consciously 'poetic', even
literary passage, which turns on the reconciling of opposites in the
time-conditioned processes of nature. The underlying concept is
the Heraclitean idea of reality as perpetual strife eternally resolved,
reconciled into harmony. The 'trilling wire' in the blood 'Sings
below inveterate scars', repairs, 'appeases', the wounds left by
wars once actual but now 'long forgotten'. This is an idea that will
be taken up in more concrete form, later in the series, with refer-
ence to the civil conflict that divided England in the seventeenth
century.[25]

For the moment, however, we are concerned with a universal
pattern rather than with any particular application. The 'dance of
life', 'along the artery' and prefigured in 'the circulation of the
lymph', finds its larger reflection in 'the drift of stars' and in the

annual renewal of life in the budding tree. The imagination moves 'in light', open to the sun, whilst on 'the sodden floor' below, where the fallen leaves rot and lay the foundation of new life in the future, the hunter and the hunted ('the boarhound and the boar') are joined in the 'pattern' which finds its reconciliation, beyond savagery and death—which are also part of the design—in the larger unity of the universal processes. The sense, conveyed through the imagery and rhythm of the passage, of life as a 'dance' of reconciled opposites serves to point the transition from the intuitive content of the opening 'movement' to the more discursive passage which now follows.

What poetry can recreate in 'lyrical' form needs, indeed, if it is to arrive at a more enduring meaning, to be explored in other terms. Since the experience in the garden has vanished beyond recall, and since to attempt to recreate it directly would only be to replace reality by words, the approach which must now replace it has to be more indirect in nature. The purpose is now exploratory, a working out of *concepts* which may prove to be useful to the end the poet has in mind. The concepts, in short, have to be applied, developed, until they can be found to rejoin the original experience. Only if this is the case, if the fusion can be seen as *poetically* valid, confirmed in terms of emotion as expressed through language and rhythm, will it be seen to be truly relevant, in short, *to work*. In Parts II and III of *Burnt Norton* two such concepts are presented as alternatives which seem superficially to be opposites, but which may be found in the event to lead to the same point. These are, respectively, the 'way up' and the 'way down' of the Heraclitean doctrine which has been placed at the head of the poem and which, we are told, lead by different paths to the same end.

The longer part of the second 'movement' of *Burnt Norton* opens, accordingly, with an attempt to define, in terms which we may call relatively 'philosophical', the problem which seems to be involved in any conceivable relationship between experience in time and its possible extra-temporal ground. The point of departure is the scholastic (and Dantesque) vision of eternity 'at the still point of the turning world',[26] motionless source of movement and unchanging first agent of change. The attempt to understand this concept involves us, as beings enmeshed in time, in the use of *negative* categories. We can only begin to grasp the nature of what *is* by saying what it is *not*, by making an effort to free ourselves from our limited categories of thought and speech. The 'still point', 'where past and future are gathered',[27] cannot be conceived in terms of 'fixity', for it is the source of life, necessarily 'fleshless' indeed but assuming the existence and reality of flesh and partaking of the nature, the continual subjection to change, which life in the flesh implies. Neither 'movement' nor 'arrest' can be its final attributes, since only in relation to its 'stillness', as eternal point of reference, can ordered motion be conceived, and only through this motion can our time-conditioned faculties grasp, however precariously, the existence and universal presence of the central 'stillness':

> Except for the point, the still point,
> There would be no dance, and there is only the dance.

It should be stressed once again that these ideas are *not* put forward in the poem as *true*—whatever that may mean—or with a view to establishing any objective validity that they may conceivably have. They are introduced as *concepts*, tools to aid in the organizing of experience, and such validity as they turn out to have will be tested in terms of their successful use for this purpose: tested, in short, as we have already stressed, by the quality of the poetry they produce.

What concerns us at this point, in other words, is an attempt to produce poetry which shall be at once exact and emotionally evocative out of ideas of an abstract or 'metaphysical' nature. Such poetry has necessarily to deny itself some of the qualities which are normally available to writers of verse and, in so doing, to run the risk of a certain rarification of effect which can easily turn, where true emotion or a high degree of expressive skill are lacking, into the pedantic or the prosaic. It calls for a special use of imagery, in which the sensual content of other kinds of verse (even that associated with a poet like Donne, who is often thought of as a 'metaphysical' writer, but who obtained his most striking effects by an unusually intense fusion of analytic exactitude with powerful sensuous feeling)[28] has little part to play. Poetry of the type at which Eliot is aiming, here and in other passages of the *Quartets*, is effective to the degree in which it succeeds in making itself unobtrusive. The images, and the rhythms in which these are incorporated, must strike the reader as existing in function of the dominating idea, which emerges in limpid simplicity from a medium which is felt to have no existence in separation from itself.

The image must appear not so much striking as inevitable, the rhythms answer as closely as possible to virtues which are founded upon those of clear, expressive prose exposition; and the 'poetry' must be felt to lie, not in something added to or imposed upon these virtues by way of decoration or emphasis, but in the satisfying and inescapable propriety of the formulation of the subject in hand.

The image of the 'dance' in the lines we have quoted is conceived with just this kind of 'metaphysical' end in view. It is a figure of our experience in its temporal guise or 'movement', distinguished by the intuitive presence of form, 'pattern', from mere anarchic flow. The 'dance', like the elusive moment of insight in the garden, might be comprehensible as a reflection of the central point of reference in relation to which its successive motions fall into place; but the direct apprehension of the 'point' itself is beyond our grasp, and only in so far as we can identify ourselves with its reflection in the 'dance' of time-conditioned movement can we aspire to understand something of its nature: 'I can only say, *there* we have been: but I cannot say where./And I cannot say, how long, for that is to place it in time'.

Although the way of definition passes necessarily—given the nature of what is to be defined—through 'what is not', the experience with which we are trying to deal is positive and accepting, involves commitment to 'the way up'. As much is conveyed in the lines which now follow. Certain experiences of being 'freed' from the normal limitations of the 'practical desire', from 'action' and 'suffering', bring with them 'release', a sense of sublimation or *Erhebung*,[29] a new 'concentration' in which nothing is lost or 'eliminated': the intuition, in short, of a '*new* world' of experience, in which, however, the '*old* world' is not so much renounced or rejected as 'made explicit', 'understood' under a new light, in some sense fulfilled in the previously misunderstood range of its true possibilities: 'understood', in other words, as the poet puts it,

> In the completion of its partial ecstasy,
> The resolution of its partial horror.

The 'ecstasy' partially glimpsed in the original experience in the rose-garden is felt to be 'completed', and the accompanying 'horror'—partial, like the ecstasy which is seen to be its other face —is given 'resolution' in relation to a new, a larger and more inclusive vision.

These considerations have a bearing on our present experience
as creatures in time, and therefore upon the original intuition in the
garden. At this point, therefore, we return to the consideration of
'time past and time future' with which the poem began, and which
we may now hope to see under a new light. As the poem goes on
to say:

> Time past and time future
> Allow but a little consciousness.
> To be conscious is not to be in time
> But only in time can the moment in the rose-garden,
> The moment in the arbour where the rain beat,
> The moment in the draughty church at smokefall
> Be remembered; involved with past and future.
> Only through time time is conquered.

Once again, it is important to pay attention not only to the prose
sense of the passage, but to the rhythmic development, the way in
which the key-words echo and reinforce one another, are integrated
through their shifting position in the unfolding and counterbalanc-
ing verse structure into a 'meaning' that emerges progressively in
the process of expression. After the initial statement, in the first
two lines quoted, of a prosaic, if essential fact—the limitation which
temporal succession imposes upon the range of what we call 'con-
sciousness', true awareness—the words 'time' and 'moment' are
involved in a development which makes each of their uses signi-
ficant by virtue of its place in the complete statement. Rhythm
underlines and reinforces the sense of an unfolding argument,
building on the virtues of prose statement to produce the kind of
significance which only poetry can fully and appropriately
give.

We are, in fact, approaching what is—for this poet at least—a
central paradox of the human situation. It must finally be true, if
the illumination in the rose-garden is to bear any meaning, that to
be fully 'conscious' is, in some sense, 'not to be in time'. This is
what is asserted in the first three lines just quoted, where the first
phrase builds up, through the double reference to 'time'—'past' and
'future'—to the introduction of the central human concern with
'consciousness'; and where the third line, strongly isolated as a
contrasted affirmation, begins by picking up, in 'conscious', the
preceding key-word and ends by referring once again to 'time', but

under an aspect set in deliberate opposition to the initial statement of succession.

The statement, however, strongly affirmed as it is, does not and cannot exhaust the reality to which it refers. If there is truth in the statement that 'to be conscious is not to be in time', that truth has to be set against another reality: that such 'consciousness' as is accessible to us in time is limited to the 'moment' of intense realization which is, of its very nature, fleeting and impermanent. The lines immediately preceding have already asserted a further truth, moreover, and the examples now given, with their triple repetition of 'the moment' inserted into the rhythmic build-up of the whole towards its conclusion, confirm it: that subjection to the limitations of the temporal serves to protect us 'in the weakness of the changing body' from experiences which would otherwise be, in their undisguised nakedness, simply intolerable.

That, after all, is why the song of the bird in the garden carried the assertion that 'human kind/Cannot bear very much reality'. This truth is now seen to be not only limiting but salutary, protective of our human nature. Only in and through time can we, as mortal beings, grasp something of the eternal intuitions. The paradox to which this assertion of the affirmative way (the way up) leads is the new discovery of this part of the poem. 'To be conscious is not to be in time.' Yes, perhaps; but, on the other hand, 'Only through time time is conquered'. In these two phrases the poet sums up, illustrating his meaning through reference to certain particularly evocative moments, what has now become a central and significant tension at the heart of life. The first step in resolving the problem posed by the illumination in the garden is to realize that time, whilst a necessary condition of experience, is not the whole of it. If we consider the temporal succession of events as a self-sufficient reality our intuitions become finally meaningless; but if we deny the reality of the temporal process we make our very experience inconceivable. Since time and change are the laws of our being, the inescapable framework which conditions *all* our experience, the prolongation of the moments of ecstasy which seem to take us outside the temporal would cost man nothing less than his life. The two elements—the temporal and the timeless—are both necessary, complementary rather than mutually exclusive. They need to be worked together in an embracing vision which is the final end of the entire sequence.

III

Side by side with the 'way up', the 'Affirmative Way', and to be explored at the same time, is the 'way down', with its acceptance of renunciation as a starting-point. This, indeed, is the alternative 'way' of the poem which, it is hoped, will lead finally to the same point as its fellow. We pass, accordingly, from the sense of *Erhebung*, from fleeting intuitions of an extra-temporal 'reality', to a consideration of life as dominated by the process of succession in time. This is 'time before and time after', in the dim 'twilight' of a world where there is no ordered direction, where no relationship is organic or, finally, real:

> Here is a place of disaffection
> Time before and time after
> In a dim light: neither daylight
> Investing form with lucid stillness
> Turning shadow into transient beauty
> With slow rotation suggesting permanence
> Nor darkness to purify the soul
> Emptying the sensual with deprivation
> Cleansing affection from the temporal.
> Neither plenitude nor vacancy.

This is, then, the 'place of disaffection', poised *between* the remote, barely human intuition of the 'still point', with its implication of distant, scarcely apprehensible meaning, and concrete but apparently meaningless flux. On the one hand, the 'lucid stillness', the 'transient' but real beauty of 'daylight', suggesting—but only suggesting—'permanence'; on the other a 'darkness' which, consciously accepted, *might be* a means to achieve meaning, a purification of the soul (in terms of traditional spiritual teaching), emptying the merely sensual through 'deprivation', cleansing the affection from its limitation to the temporal.

These are states which bear a potentiality of spiritual meaning: a meaning which is only to be achieved by consciously refusing subjection to temporal succession seen as an ultimate reality. Short of this deliberate choice, with its implication that there are valid motives for choosing, there is only a state of desolation which the poem now goes on to evoke. *Here*, in a world dominated by the temporal process (the world of 'time before and time after'), there

is only a 'place of disaffection', mirrored in the journey of the com-
muters on the London underground, described in terms which
recall the flow of the 'damned' across London Bridge in *The Waste
Land*:[30]

> Only a flicker
> Over the strained time-ridden faces
> Distracted from distraction by distraction
> Filled with fancies and empty of meaning
> Tumid apathy with no concentration
> Men and bits of paper, whirled by the cold wind
> That blows before and after time.

Here, in a world which considers the temporal process the *only*
reality—that is, not as *a* reality, significant in relation to something
barely apprehensible, but real, outside itself—even 'distraction'
becomes an 'unreal' shadow. Instead of 'light' or 'darkness' there
is only a 'flicker' replacing both: life is emptied of any possible
'meaning', dominated by 'apathy', incapable of the 'concentration'
which is a sign of the spiritual. The 'bits of paper' and the 'men',
like them, meaningless, carried on the 'cold', artificial subway wind
which is evocative of eternal damnation—it 'blows before and after
time'—are suggestive of a state of spiritual hopelessness. The
'souls'—and they *are* souls, in spite of all appearance to the con-
trary—are vomited out of the underground entrances into the
'faded air' of what Eliot, following Dante, had once called the
'Unreal City': vomited into a 'twittering', twilight world which is
neither that of light ('lucid stillness'), reflecting real if 'transient
beauty', nor of the true 'darkness' that may constitute, through the
conscious acceptance of limitation, an approach to the meaningful.

In this situation, the only remedy that offers itself is—it seems—
to 'descend lower', accepting 'perpetual solitude' in terms of the
creative 'way down', indicated by Heraclitus and mapped out in
detail by St. John of the Cross.[31] It should be remembered, as
relevant to an understanding of Eliot's conception, that the Saint
in *The Ascent of Mount Carmel*, and elsewhere in his commentaries,
distinguishes between two 'Dark Nights' through which the soul
must pass on its progress towards divine illumination and, even-
tually, union. These are, respectively, the *active* and *passive* 'nights'.
The first—the result of a *conscious* and *deliberate* evacuation by the
spirit of all the lower instincts and appetites which keep it back

from advancement in the ways of perfection—is entered upon following the soul's own initiative. The second, which corresponds to an advanced stage in the same ascent, is of its essential nature submissive, the result of a *divine* action upon the soul, calling it through a deliberate and accepted process of purgation to the recognition of its full range of possibilities.[32]

It should be emphasized that Eliot is, at this point, using these traditional teachings for ends of his own. He is not, immediately at least (though as much may turn out to be implied later), following a path which will lead directly, as St. John of the Cross had intended, to the illumination of the spirit. His concern is still with *concepts*, tools which may enable him to deal with ordinary, day-to-day realities; the hope is that by organization within a structure of this kind these realities may come to be seen as constituting a valid and purposeful unity. This is one way—no doubt there are others —of 'redeeming' what otherwise seems unmanageable, incoherent, and desolate. The 'way down' is potentially creative precisely in the degree to which it is consciously and willingly accepted, deliberately *chosen*. To choose this path, the second of the two proposed as alternatives in the epigraph of the *Quartets*, is to accept the reality of a world which has become, in its time-dominated state, empty of significance. The alternative answer to futility is now seen as a deliberate acceptance of 'deprivation' and 'internal darkness', which is distinguished from the preceding state of 'disaffection' by being based, not on mere tired acquiescence, but on deliberate and conscious *choice*.

The soul, accordingly, *chooses* this path as a *way* to something beyond itself:

> Descend lower, descend only
> Into the world of perpetual solitude,
> World not world, but that which is not world,
> Internal darkness, deprivation
> And destitution of all property,
> Desiccation of the world of sense,
> Evacuation of the world of fancy,
> Inoperancy of the world of spirit;
> This is the one way, and the other
> Is the same, not in movement
> But abstention from movement; while the world moves

In appetency, on its metalled ways
Of time past and time future.

The answer to the futility which is seen to be implied in all merely passive subjection to the temporal process lies, it seems, in a deliberately chosen, accepted forsaking of the *ego* which operates on all the levels of our time-conditioned and time-limited experience. Here again the poet is following the traditional writers who have explored the Dark Night of the soul. 'Sense', 'fancy', even 'spirit', under its temporal aspect, need to be put aside: and this both 'actively' and 'passively', in 'movement' and in 'abstention from movement'. They need to be put aside—we should repeat—not in the search for some esoteric illumination given to chosen spirits, but in the interests of daily living: for the temporal process is built into the fabric of each human existence, and only by seeing in it a ground for our conscious, deliberate choices—which may be of acceptance or renunciation, as each particular situation may demand —can we be delivered from the futility which it otherwise imposes. To live is to make choices, and to refrain from choosing is to die. This—it is suggested—may be the only path, in time, leading to liberation from the 'metalled', pre-determined ways of subjection to 'appetency' within the limits of mere succession, of 'time past and time future'. It is noteworthy that this 'movement' ends by a return to the phrase which introduced the problem of time, and its meaning in terms of experience, at the opening of the poem.

IV

After so much abstract, concept-creating verse, it is appropriate that the fourth section of *Burnt Norton* should take the form of a brief, more directly 'poetic' interlude. Like the similar section in each of the following quartets, it serves to remind us that we are dealing with poetry, not with 'philosophy' or abstract writing, and that the final test of the value of what is written lies, not in abstraction, but in the vital impact of language and rhythm. From this standpoint the passage emerges as a beautiful piece of evocative writing:

Time and the bell have buried the day,
The black cloud carries the sun away.
Will the sunflower turn to us, will the clematis

Stray down, bend to us; tendril and spray
Clutch and cling?
Chill
Fingers of yew be curled
Down on us? After the kingfisher's wing
Has answered light to light, and is silent,
The light is still
At the still point of the turning world.

Few passages in the *Quartets* demand more insistently to be *read aloud*, with an immediate, unconceptual response to the rhythms that underlie and mould meaning in relation to an emerging whole. The entire interlude is, deliberately and carefully, structured round the single, isolated word 'Chill'; what precedes—the two opening lines, with their incantatory, fairy-tale quality accentuated by the rhyme, the three verbs in the third and fourth lines joined by the repetition of 'to us' and leading up, through the deliberate break in mid-line, to the evocation of the 'tendril and spray' which, in a new and shortening line, 'clutch and cling' in nostalgic effect—leads up to this precise, disturbing moment; what follows expands from it to the final glimpse of reflected light in the passing flash of the bird's wing.

This is not poetry which makes its effect by complex imagery or by the use of calculated ambiguities dear to certain types of critical explication. It is the work of a poet, rather, who is aware of these things, but who here—and generally in the most successful passages of these poems—has chosen not to use them, may be said to have moved in a sense beyond them. This is, put simply, the poetry of the right word in the right place, where rhythm underlines and reinforces meaning in the simplest and most direct way possible: poetry which, far from being 'simple' in any limiting sense, represents the final distillation of an experience which is no longer dependent upon complexity. Not all, by any means, of the *Quartets* can be said to maintain this level, nor indeed—given the kind of poetry to which they belong—is it possible that they should; but where they do—and there are many passages of which this can properly be said—they can be seen as the final and logical outcome of everything for which Eliot had striven in the course of a lifetime devoted above all to perfecting his instrument of expression.

Beyond these general considerations, the effect of the interlude

—its place in the complete poem to which it belongs—is clear enough. Tender evocations of evanescent life and beauty—the experiences that time at once brings into being and destroys—are set against intuitions, equally time-conditioned and emotionally laden, of darkness and death. The tender, delicately clinging rhythms, where each dominant word is exactly placed in a succession of lingering, carried-over rhythmic units, make their appeal like the flowers, the 'tendril and spray' which 'bend' in solicitude towards us. They recall us by their natural sensuous appeal from the choice of hard renunciation which, however, the nature of our time-conditioned experience continues to impose upon us. The whole succession of verbs—'bury', 'clutch', 'cling'—together with the nouns and adjectives which accompany them—the 'black cloud', the 'curled fingers'—and the deliberately stressed and isolated 'Chill', all suggest death, cold extinction at the same time as they are associated with interventions of nature: the 'sunflower', the 'clematis', the 'yew' with its double association—always so evocative in Eliot's poetry—of death and immortality. At the close the counter-movement proceeding from 'Chill' affirms itself and points, with unobtrusive delicacy, to the larger themes developed elsewhere in the poem.

The experience conveyed has something of the quality which makes itself felt in the prose passages, already quoted, by Proust and in others, which could have been given, by such contemporaries of Eliot as E. M. Forster and Virginia Woolf,[33] but it gains something, perhaps, in relation to those passages, beautiful and moving as they are, by refraining f.om any suggestion of an explicit or didactic tone. The lines make their own effect in the process of development; there is no need for an explicit pointing of the symbolic significance. At the close the poignant evocation of fleeting natural beauty in the flash of the kingfisher's wing rests, for part of its appeal, on its passing quality, its end in 'silence'; but, at the same time, the beauty so summoned into being is held, 'still' recalled in the memory of the experience, related to the '*still* point', the ultimate creative source, with which the second section was more philosophically, abstractly concerned. The final lines on 'the turning world' can be seen, perhaps, as having some connection with the opening of the fifth poem in the *Ash Wednesday* sequence,[34] but what seemed there excessively convoluted, verbose, even confused in its effect, is now worked out in terms of an achieved and distilled clarity. The bird's wing flashes in relation to the sun, the source of natural light and, symbolically speaking, of illumination for the spirit: the last line of the interlude indicates the 'still point' already posited as the centre and meaning of the dance of experience.

V

In this way, the lyric interlude, whilst taking up on its own terms the 'philosophical' themes already developed, serves to introduce the final resolution of this first stage in the sequence. The resolution is, of course, provisional, as is inevitable at this point in the complete design, but it will itself serve as a foundation for further development. Here the central problem of the poem—that of the possible meaning and validity of our intuitions of an extra-temporal order—is taken up once more, this time in relation to the poet's specific task of artistic creation. Words, in poetry, and sound in music both involve movement, progression in time; but if they only existed in sequence it would seem to follow that their end and limitation is implied in their necessary death:

> Words move, music moves
> Only in time; but that which is only living
> Can only die.

The 'movement', however, is limited to the temporal aspect of these things, is made apparent 'only in time'. There may be an analogy here with life which, in so far as it is 'only living', considered only in terms of time, can only end in death. A further insight may be gained, it is suggested, when we cease to ask life for what it cannot, by itself, give us:[35] when, in other words, we take death into account as an inescapable and necessary aspect of the reality we call 'life'; and by so doing we are led to a conception of 'life' itself which is more than, or at least other than, merely temporal. In a similar way the 'words' and the 'music' which, when they are thought of as moving solely in time, must be seen as subject to their own kind of 'death' can also, once this impermanence is recognized, be found to achieve a significance which is timeless, statically permanent.

In other words, the struggle to attain a measure of significant expression through words or sounds and that to achieve 'meaning' through and beyond time are seen as closely related. Both, considered in relation to their temporal basis, reach only into extinction, the 'silence': 'Words, after speech, reach/Into the silence.' The 'silence', however, may itself provide the entry into a realm of permanence. If words have a 'meaning' which can be conceived of as surviving their temporal extinction, it must be through their achievement of 'the form, the pattern', by which their movement —passing outside the order of time which originally seemed to give them their 'life'—is given a 'perpetual' quality which transforms, gives a new dimension to the attainment of 'stillness'. In this way, it may be, the artist is concerned not with 'death', the stillness that follows the cessation of activity in time, but with a reflection— precarious, indeed, but not on that account less truly significant or spiritually evocative—of the 'still point' which traditional philosophy has seen as the source of the creative pattern. What began as a concept in the realm of abstraction is now restated in terms of the living necessities of artistic creativity.

The 'stillness', in other words, reached through the creative use of words in poetry or of sound in music, is, above all, a matter of dynamic relationships. Each part is seen as involved with every other part in an indivisible unity: a unity, moreover, which is a *new* creation, not to be adequately defined as the sum of its parts alone:

> Only by the form, the pattern,
> Can words or music reach
> The stillness, as a Chinese jar still
> Moves perpetually in its stillness.
> Not the stillness of the violin, while the note lasts,
> Not that only, but the co-existence,
> Or say that the end precedes the beginning,
> And the end and the beginning were always there
> Before the beginning and after the end.
> And all is always now.

The image of the 'Chinese jar' may serve to illuminate this harmony under the aspect of 'stillness'. That of the violin, 'while the note lasts', precisely because it seeks to balance the passing against the permanent, at once helps and confuses. It reflects in some degree the emotional apprehension of the timeless which certain artistic experiences seem to offer, but fails to express adequately the intellectual aspect, the sense of a 'co-existence' which may be apprehended as such, deeper than any emotional conviction could be. In this respect the 'Chinese jar', on account of its relative permanence, may serve—always within its limitation—as a less inadequate image. In so far as its material solidity conveys an impression of 'stillness' achieved through and beyond movement, so that it 'still moves'—'perpetually', but in its continuing, formal 'stillness'—it gives us, perhaps, as exact an image of our intuition of the 'still point' as we can hope, within our temporal limitation, to achieve.

The poet's awareness of these things is, inevitably, given the nature of his material, more precarious:

> Words strain,
> Crack and sometimes break, under the burden,
> Under the tension, slip, slide, perish,
> Decay with imprecision, will not stay in place,
> Will not stay still.

The struggle to attain expression through words and that to arrive at significant experience in time are seen as closely related. Words reflect life in so far as they 'strain', 'crack', 'break' in the effort to express, or to reflect (the preceding image of the light on the kingfisher's wing is to the point) the elusive extra-temporal core of our deepest intuitions. The 'stillness' of achieved form at which the artist aims is threatened at each moment by discordant, irrelevant 'voices' which seem to return it insistently to chaos. The words used fail to 'stay in place', will not cling with any degree of permanence to their final function, which is 'to stay still' in reflection of a form, an order achieved. Here, as ever, art—poetic or other—is seen as the reflection of a deeper reality: the word which is the poet's instrument becomes an image of 'the Word', the *Logos*,[36] shadowed in the desert by 'voices of temptation', surrenders to self-pity ('The crying *shadow* in the funeral dance'), and the delusion implied in 'The loud lament of the disconsolate chimera'.

The poem ends, initiating a pattern which will be followed in each subsequent part of the sequence, with a passage of shorter lines which sums up and gathers together the present state of its findings. If the 'detail' of the pattern of life, like the corresponding formal discoveries of art, is based on 'movement', changing and shifting emotion in time, the equivalent in terms of the spiritual life can be seen in the traditional concept, based on St. John of the Cross and other Christian writers, of the 'ten stairs': the stairs which the soul is continually ascending and descending—the way Up and the Way Down—'in ecstasy and humiliation'.[37] Moving up and down the stairs, in accordance with the alternative 'ways', the soul perfects itself in the doctrine of love:

> Desire itself is movement
> Not in itself desirable;
> Love is itself unmoving,
> Only the cause and end of movement,
> Timeless, and undesiring
> Except in the aspect of time
> Caught in the form of limitation
> Between un-being and being.

Love, seen under the aspect of time or movement, is 'desire', which can only reach fulfilment in relation to its true, 'unmoving' end: the same end, however, which is itself 'the cause and end of movement'. The argument, it need hardly be said, tends *not* to the rejection of 'desire' as such, but to a recognition of its necessary incompleteness. 'Love', in itself 'timeless' and 'undesiring', is compatible with and shadowed by 'desire' only under the aspect of temporal limitation: the aspect which found expression through the tenuous, transitory, but intense moment of illuminating experience recaptured in the rose-garden.

To that experience, accordingly, we return in the lines which end the quartet. There, in the garden, the reality of love was glimpsed, 'caught', as alone it can be caught within man's necessary and salutary subjection to the temporal order, 'in the form of limitation': 'limitation', however, which the preceding meditation on the original experience has suggested may be something more than illusion. Out of the stirring of the 'dust' on the bowl of rose-leaves[38] there rises—briefly and passingly indeed, but not for that less poignantly or truly—the intuition of possible life contained in 'the *hidden* laughter/Of children in the foliage':[39] laughter caught in its fleeting affirmation in the 'here' and 'now', but suggestive, in a way that only discursive thought can interpret, of the 'always', the permanent and unchanging reality. To see first the timeless through the temporal and then to obtain through the ordering of the elements given by temporal experience a glimpse of the pattern which is a reflection, limited indeed but true, of eternity, is at once the task of the artist and the key to the relationship that exists between his efforts and the obligations imposed upon him by his intermediate state—'Between un-being and being'—as a man. In relation to this intuited glimpse of the timeless pattern that gives its meaning to human experience mere temporal succession, in so far as it is unredeemed by relation to the reality which underlies it, is seen to be an unreal mockery: 'the waste sad time', stretching in empty and mechanical succession 'before and after'.

[3]
East Coker

The second poem in the series of *Quartets—East Coker—*takes up the argument at the point where its predecessor had left it. It is, as a poem, notably more concrete and personal, less concerned with the development of abstract concepts, than *Burnt Norton*. The title itself, which refers to the West Country village from which the Eliot family set out in the seventeenth century for the New World, has a personal and family meaning, is indicative of the poet as engaged in a search for his origins. The theme is temporal succession, the individual conscious both of his own place in time and of his necessary relationship to society and the need to affirm this even in a period of crisis and discouragement. It is no accident that the writing of the poem coincided with the outbreak of war in 1939 and its publication with the disastrous European events of 1940.[40] The implications of the doctrine of detachment, stated abstractly and universally in *Burnt Norton*, can be seen developed here in more personal terms, terms related to a definite time and place: England at war, engaged in a re-examination of her traditional assumptions.

I

The poem begins with a phrase evoking the circular movement of things in relation to the famous motto of Mary Stuart—*En ma fin est mon commencement*—which is, however, reversed to read deathward: 'In my beginning is my end'. The phrase, which takes up a theme already touched upon in the final 'movement' of *Burnt Norton* has, of course, a variety of philosophical implications. In terms of the philosophy of Heraclitus every moment of our experience is simultaneously an *end*—in as much as it is the result of a previous line of development—and the *beginning* of something new, projected into the future. Seen through the eyes of Aristotle, the position alters somewhat. According to this line of thought, every *beginning* points, of its very nature, to an *end*. The *final cause* may be said, in logical terms, to precede the *efficient cause*, in much the same way as—for the poet—the completion of a poem, in as much as it may be said to condition the beginning, precedes that beginning.

From this, given Eliot's general purpose, which is to use philosophical concepts to illustrate the processes of artistic creation, it is no more than a step to advance towards a Bergsonian conception of duration (*durée*), according to which the end may be said actually to *contain* within itself the beginning from which it has sprung. The argument posits that, since the past is seen to endure through the operation of memory into the present, all direct human perception is modified by the survival of earlier impressions. *Durée*, as Bergson puts it, 'is the continual progress of the past which grows into the future and which swells as it advances'.[41]

This range of ideas is important for an understanding of the complete pattern of the *Quartets*; but, for the moment, the aim is more limited, more closely related to our immediate experience as creatures involved in, and needing to react to, the temporal process by imposing upon it some conception of meaning. It is worth noting, in relation to the structure of this initial 'movement', that in its last line the reference to the 'end' is omitted, and that the concluding words indicate not an arrival, but a point of departure: 'In my beginning'. In this way we are led forward to the main theme of life as a journey in time towards an end progressively and meaningfully pursued: the theme, in fact, with the development and exploration of which the whole series is principally concerned.

For the moment, the emphasis is on 'succession', on what the concluding lines of the previous quartet saw as a prospect of time 'stretching before and after' in what threatened to be an unending vista of futility and waste.[42] Here, as befits the tone of the new poem, the prospect is more concretely and tangibly realized. Our concern is now to be with organic process, the rhythm of 'rising' and 'falling', life first asserting itself and then being assimilated to the death through which the preceding generations have passed. Death is now associated with *earth*, the key element in this quartet, as 'air' had been in the first; and the earth, besides being the repository of dead, finished organisms, is simultaneously engaged in the nourishment of renewed life.[43] 'In my beginning is my end.' Yes, certainly, but equally, and at the same time (for the Way Up and the Way Down are not so much alternatives as different aspects of a single process), 'In my end is my beginning'.

Once again, as in *Burnt Norton*, and as in the subsequent poems of the sequence, *time* is to be a principal concern of the new quartet: not so much, however, 'time' as a universal concept, but the actual, *lived* time of each individual being and of the race to which he belongs, the time in conformity to which each and every life finds its measure of personal fulfilment. There is a *time* for living and a *time* to die: a *time* for 'building' and for generation, for the creation of new possibilities of life, as well as a *time* for the natural dissolution of these things into their constituent elements. We are beginning, in fact, to glimpse a new context in which the alternative 'ways' can be considered. The Way Up, the way of affirmation, passes through the acceptance of life as creative and self-perpetuating. The Way Down, the way of negation, accepts death as an inseparable part of life, an element built into it from the moment of birth, shadowing it as darkness shadows light, destroying it under its temporal aspect, but providing, by contrast, the necessary basis for its affirmation. Birth and death—or death and birth—begin to be seen as manifestations of a single process,[44] neither comprehensible except in relation to its apparent opposite, both contributing, through acceptance and negation, to a reality the final term of which is life enhanced and freed from the limits of succession. This these poems seek to convey, not in terms of abstraction, but of realized experience.

Between these terms of life, or birth, and death lies the succession of events in time, conveyed in the movement of the sequent lines:

> a time for building
> *And* a time for living and for generation
> *And* a time for the wind to break the loosened pane
> *And* to shake the wainscot where the field-mouse trots
> *And* to shake the tattered arras woven with a silent
> motto.

And . . . and . . . and . . . and: considered in abstraction from individual lives, as a process impersonally recorded by the moving hands of a clock, the temporal process is a meaningless sequence leading to no significant conclusion, unfolding itself from no definable beginning to no conceivable end. This is the view of time to which the poets of the Renaissance, who were preoccupied with it to the point of obsession, sometimes gave the name of 'mutability': the view against which some of their finest poetry—Spenser's *Cantos* and Shakespeare's *Sonnets*—stands in tragic reaction. It is a view against which a twentieth-century poet needs to set such resources as he possesses,[45] for, even less than his sixteenth-century predecessors, can he assume the validity of the notion of time as a divine creation, proceeding from God's infinity and eventually returning to it.

This reaction, or counter-assertion, begins to take shape in the new quartet. The insertion into the temporal process of lives, individual and social, points, however tentatively or uncertainly, to a new element of indeterminacy. There is *a particular time* for each individual life, and for the life of the race or species to which each individual life belongs; and wisdom consists, for each creature possessed of consciousness, in understanding and accepting *his* or *her* time, moulding his or her existence in conformity to it and accepting as natural and finally life-giving the particular rhythm which it imposes. In this rhythm the reality of death plays an unavoidable and, it may be, an indispensable part. To live in accordance with it, to incorporate individual life into the appropriate pattern of succession, making the action of time naturally one's own individual rhythm, even when this implies (as it inevitably does) the acceptance of mortality, 'the time for dying' as well as the 'time for living'—this may prove to be the beginning of wisdom.

The rest of the first 'movement' of *East Coker* derives from this initial theme. Repeating the opening motto, we pass on—in a manner which can be paralleled in the opening section of each poem—to its particular manifestation in a definite moment of time, caught and, as it were, held in the quiescent village. '*Now* the light falls.' The writing is beautifully and precisely evocative, in a manner scarcely attempted in *Burnt Norton* (the rose-garden experience, though equally intense, is essentially different in kind, belongs to a world of dream reality rather than to an objectively realized scene), but now, and only now, fully appropriate to the developing theme:

> Now the light falls
> Across the open field, leaving the deep lane
> Shuttered with branches, dark in the afternoon,
> Where you lean against a bank while a van passes,
> And the deep lane insists on the direction
> Into the village, in the electric heat

> Hypnotized. In a warm haze the sultry light
> Is absorbed, not refracted, by grey stone.
> The dahlias sleep in the empty silence.
> Wait for the early owl.

To compare this with the recreation of the rose-garden experience in the previous poem is to be aware of a significant development in the direction of the real and the tangible. The 'rose-garden' intuition may or may not have actually happened—we are left deliberately uncertain—may have been either a real, if fleeting revelation, or the evocation of something that *might*—perhaps should—have happened, but which never really occurred. The house and the formal garden itself are left deliberately vague, only tenuously located in place. By comparison, the village of *East Coker* is splendidly realized, both visually and in terms of prevailing atmosphere. The emphasis, beautifully conveyed by rhythms which rest unerringly on the significant word, the truly evocative image (Eliot is a master of the word exactly and rhythmically placed so as to intensify what is basically a prose or conversational foundation), is focused on the 'fall' of light, on the 'deep lane/Shuttered with branches', closed to the living world outside, 'dark in the afternoon'. There is a 'hypnotic' tension in the 'electric heat' which recalls, but in a more tense, even sombre way, the 'autumn heat' in the rose-garden of the previous poem. Here, however, the emphasis lies not on the evanescent, fleeting presence of life, but on the 'empty silence', the foreboding expectation of 'the early owl'. Light here is 'absorbed', assimilated by grey stone, not—as in *Burnt Norton*—reflected in a momentary vision of the 'heart' of reality.

The different approach, however, may lead equally to a vision, though—appropriately, given the change of theme and tone in the new quartet—of a more material, less ethereal kind. In the dark evocation of 'a summer midnight', the dances of the primitive rites of a pre-Christian world live again in the imaginative summoning of the tenuous music of 'the weak pipe and the little drum'. These are associated, through the quoted words of the poet's sixteenth-century ancestor, Sir Thomas Eliot, author of *The Governour*,[46] with the life-continuing conjunction of matrimony:

> The association of man and woman
> In daunsinge, signifying matrimonie—
> A dignified and commodious sacrament.

Two and two, necessarye coniunction,
Holding eche other by the hand or the arm
Whiche betokeneth concorde.[47]

The archaic spelling, far from being a pedantic display of academic
precision, is needed to connect the moral, doctrinal content with
the older, immemorial rites on which it rests and which it is con-
ceived as fulfilling. The Christian sacrament at this point takes up
the rhythm of 'generation' expressed in the pagan dances of the
summer solstice: the life of individuals, coming together in the
fulfilment of a social imperative which is also an individual dedica-
tion, is integrated into the temporal pattern of the revolving sea-
sons, which imply life as well as death, the creation of new
existence on an accepted foundation of mortality. The life of man,
in other words, is now seen as inseparably united to the larger
rhythms of the world of nature, involved through recognition of
the temporal pattern in harmony and 'concorde'.

Beneath the whole 'movement', as we now begin to see, we are
made aware of a contrast between two possible attitudes to the
circular procession of life leading, for each successive generation,
to its inevitable death in time. The first of these is finally pessi-
mistic in what it seems to imply for each individual life; the second
points to an acceptance of the temporal design which prevails in
each individual generation and each single life as belonging to a
significant and living rhythm:

> Keeping time,
> Keeping the rhythm in their dancing
> As in their living in the living seasons,
> The time of the seasons and the constellations
> The time of milking and the time of harvest
> The time of the coupling of man and woman
> And that of beasts. Feet rising and falling.
> Eating and drinking. Dung and death.

At this point we are being invited to take up, under a new aspect,
more local and human, the conception of the 'pattern' expressed,
in Heraclitean terms, in the lyrical introduction to the second
'movement' of *Burnt Norton*. What was there seen as 'reconciled
among the stars' is now approached in terms of specific human
continuity, as an aspect of man's relationship to his distinctive

'time'. To live positively, it is suggested, is to accept the context given to each man by his sense of *his* appropriate time, without seeking to twist or force it in the direction of his own egoistic or, at best, partially understood desires. Men and women can accept, in a spirit finally creative, the '*living*' rhythm of the '*living* seasons' —the double emphasis on 'living' underlines the direction of the poet's intent when set against the entire 'movement's' persistent concern with death—and this indeed is what is implied in the pagan dances and their continuation in the married sacrament. Nevertheless, in case we should be tempted to an affirmation which would, at this stage, be premature, it is still, when seen from the point of view of its 'end' rather than that of its 'beginning', a rhythm of inexorable succession which leads finally in the order of time to 'Dung and death'. The meaning, the 'still point' at the centre of the 'dance', has still to be discovered; but this may be a starting-point[48] at any given time or place—'here/Or there, or else-where' (there is a kind of echo here, definite if not to be overly insisted upon, of the 'Quick now, here, now, always' at the end of *Burnt Norton*)—and the last word of this first section rests, signi-ficantly, on a 'beginning'. The 'beginning' here, it remains to be said, implies an acceptance by the individual—or by the society which represents, at his given time and place, his integration into the larger design of human endeavour—of the time-cycle as an inescapable condition, personal and historical alike, of human experience. To accept this reality as the 'end', or death, of all our efforts and affirmations corresponds, perhaps, to the Way Down of the Heraclitean epigraph. To see it, still acceptingly, as a 'beginning', the gateway to a new cycle of living experience, would then answer to the affirmative sense, the Way Up implying active and purposeful concurrence, of the same statement.

II

The second 'movement' of *East Coker* follows the pattern of the preceding quartet by opening with a 'poetic' passage in short and irregularly rhymed lines. These differ by offering no suggestion of any reconciliation of contraries 'among the stars', no glimpse of any creative pattern in either time or space. The emphasis is upon images of disorder covering nature and the universe. The normal sequence of the seasons is inverted and the death of nature prevails. 'Late roses' are filled with 'early snow', and the processes of declining life are paralleled by strife in the heavens, 'constellated wars'. The result is, at the last, the vision of a world consumed by 'destructive fire'[49] as prelude to the utter cold of extinction.

Poetry of this kind, however, 'not very satisfactory', as the poet himself puts it, cannot take us much further in the understanding of our problem. The true meaning, if it exists, has still to be defined in terms of discursive argument, of the kind already used in the corresponding section of *Burnt Norton*; and this involves the introduction of a theme not there treated, but destined to become increasingly important in the design of the following quartets, the poet's ever more anguished problem, 'the intolerable wrestle/With words and meanings'. The poetry itself is not the matter in question. 'It was not (to start again) what one had expected.' Poetry, in fact, resembles life in many respects, and not least in the need to meet the challenging obligation 'to start again', with all that this implies in the renunciation of apparent certainties. What is truly disturbing is the sense, universal to life and continually posing itself as a problem, of disillusionment, of having arrived, in this case on the threshold of old age, at something very different from the 'autumnal serenity' which the 'wisdom of age' was supposed to bring with it. The problem, which presents itself to all times and conditions of men, imposes itself with particular menace to a poet conscious of a world in collapse around him, a society which its own connivances and unwillingness to assert belief in its own professed values have brought to the verge of destruction.

Under these circumstances, from which the poet, like the rest of us, has no reason to feel himself exempt, the advice offered by 'the quiet-voiced elders' is seen only to have brought a sense of deception, the product perhaps of self-deception in those who expressed it. The 'long hoped for calm, the autumnal serenity' has turned out to be, for the poet who has looked forward to this inheritance, a delusion, the result of seeking to draw from the experience of the past lessons which, just because they derive from what is done and finished, can claim no relevance for a totally unforeseen — and unforeseeable — future.

This, indeed, seems to be, as the poet meditates upon it, a universal law of existence. Knowledge based on the experience of the past implies an interpretation which, when applied to the eternally new and unforeseen future, is necessarily and inevitably false. As Heraclitus again put it, no man steps twice into the same stream; for both stream and man, in as much as they are truly living entities, are endlessly subject to change. The quotation, like most so-called 'philosophic' statements, can easily strike us as an empty, or slightly pretentious abstraction; what the poet needs to do—and here does—is to make it live in relation to his individual, *lived* experience. The 'serenity' extolled as the end of the development of a life-time, advanced as its fruit and justification, leads only to 'hebetude', to a state of lethargy and disillusionment from which all real life is excluded. The 'wisdom' which the elders exalted, and which was exalted in them by others, as the fruit of their efforts of a life-time, the essence of what they desired to pass on to the following generations, becomes only 'a receipt for deceit' (once again we have the internal rhyme, a sure sign in Eliot of emotional involvement), 'the knowledge of *dead* secrets/*Useless* in the darkness into which they peered': or, perhaps more often and less impressively, the disillusioning reality from which 'they turned their eyes' in fearful self-deception. The situation is one which, besides answering to a disturbing, an almost intolerable personal realization, is seen to reflect a kind of law, to correspond to a necessary condition of human existence:

> There is, it seems to us,
> At best, only a limited value
> In the knowledge derived from experience.
> The knowledge imposes a pattern, and falsifies,
> For the pattern is new in every moment
> And every moment is a new and shocking
> Valuation of all we have been.

It would be wrong to think of this simply in terms of the progressive inflexibility of old age, relevant though that is. What we are being offered, as a reality and a warning, is something of a more universal application: something on which we may eventually build a positive, a life-directed reaction. Knowledge of the kind which can be derived from a contemplation of past experience—and there is a sense in which all experience is *necessarily*, in so far as it can be reflected on, past—is 'at best' of 'limited value' as a trustworthy guide to the present. Leading, in accordance with a universal human instinct, to the creation of a 'pattern', a picture of supposed meanings and relationships, it 'imposes' this upon the new and vital material which each living moment offers and, in the process of so doing, inevitably 'falsifies': for it is a condition of continuing to live that the pattern offered to us—or that which we create—must continually renew itself (it is *new* in every moment') and that every moment really lived offers us, not a comforting illusion of assimilation into the dead past, but something disturbingly and vitally different: 'a *new* and *shocking*/Valuation of all we have been.' To be 'shocked' is certainly to be appalled, to meet with something like terror the challenge presented to us; but it is also to be shaken forcibly out of the complacent range of our established prejudices, and so to be obliged, however uncomfortably, to *live*.

The statement is clearly not without relation to the more 'abstract' formulations at the opening of *Burnt Norton*. It repeats, in a more personal key, what was there said about all time being, of its very nature, unique and 'unredeemable'. It reminds us, again in a way more directly related to individual living, that 'what might have been' and 'what has been' can only be of real concern to us in as much as their effects are still alive and operative in the 'present'.

The meditation, in any event, disturbing as it may be (and to be 'disturbed' is, perhaps, a condition, uneasy but necessary, of being in any real sense alive), does not end simply in disillusionment. The 'valuation' offered by the renewal of human experience in time is not only 'shocking', disruptive of our comforting, and insulating assumptions, but 'new', and—as such—indicative of fresh possibilities of life. It constitutes, finally, a salutary warning against the tendency to impose upon our experience a premature and therefore falsifying pattern. It also brings with it a realization of the truth that the issues of the past are, in so far as they are finished and dead, incapable of offering any valid protection against the threat of possible 'harm' in the present.

The truth, seen in this way, becomes a delicate balance of positive and negative elements. The 'pattern' we must certainly believe exists, if only because our creative instinct impels us so insistently to form it. It is offered to us, however, as 'new in every moment', and can—accordingly—never be complete *in time*: can, therefore, never be accepted as final. Insecurity is, in this sense, a necessary condition of the act of faith by which we continue to live, and the 'wisdom' which the aging tend to extol as final and all-inclusive is in fact an illusion based in no small part on *fear*: fear of life, fear of the gift of self in which life consists, fear of recognizing the reality of any relationship to others or, ultimately, to what we call 'God'.

This is the 'disconsolate chimera' already summoned up in *Burnt Norton* and now recreated in a complex image which brings together the dark wood which opens the *Divine Comedy*,[50] the Grimpen Mere and the phosphorus-painted monster of *The Hound of the Baskervilles*:[51]

> We are only undeceived
> Of that which, deceiving, could no longer harm.
> In the middle, not only in the middle of the way
> But all the way, in a dark wood, in a bramble,
> On the edge of a grimpen, where is no secure
>   foothold,
> And menaced by monsters, fancy lights,
> Risking enchantment.

Such is the human situation, seen at a time of personal and universal stress, and imposing — as a condition of continuing to live in any real sense — the renunciation of all the easy consolations which offered themselves, in anticipation, as desirable goals and which have now turned out to be irrelevant in the face of an unknowable and menacing future.

The main line of the argument is now seen to carry on the process initiated in the corresponding 'movement' of *Burnt Norton*. Wisdom, it appears, cannot be in any ordinary or superficial sense cumulative, either for the individual or for the society to which he belongs. *In that sense* at least, the law of 'progress' is an illusion,[52] an evasion of the continually renewed obligation to exercise personal choice in relation to the living present:

> Do not let me hear
> Of the wisdom of old men, but rather of their folly,
> Their fear of fear and frenzy, their fear of possession,
> Of belonging to another, or to others, or to God.
> The only wisdom we can hope to acquire
> Is the wisdom of humility: humility is endless.

In *Burnt Norton*, we remember, the poet had spoken of the 'completion' of a 'partial ecstasy', the 'resolution' of a 'partial horror'.[53]

The meaning behind these phrases is now being incorporated into the substance of the developing sequence. *True* wisdom, as distinct from its appearance, which is a form of egoistic affirmation, is seen to involve what the poet calls *humility*: subject to the fresh experience of each moment as given, and the drawing out of its full implications before any attempt is made to impose upon it a 'pattern' which, if premature, is necessarily false, based on the no longer actual 'lessons' derived from the dead or superseded past. The 'pattern' is necessarily incomplete, can only be *living* in so far as it waits upon the present, recognizing its lack of finality. Meanwhile, it may be, the instinctive attitude already glimpsed in the dancers is, in this necessary state of half-knowledge, of imperfect awareness, more potentially valuable. They, in their long-vanished day, accepted life in the instinctive perception of the 'dance', with its implication of an underlying design; but—it has to be added— they are also *dead*, consumed in their mortality:

> The houses are all gone under the sea.

> The dancers are all gone under the hill.

The law of the time-cycle is, inevitably and necessarily, change. Earth and sea, the natural elements, absorb the works of man and subject them to mortality. The whole quartet can be seen as a meditation upon the implications of this reality.

III

The last lines of the preceding section imply a return to the *darkness* and as such serve to introduce what now follows. The new 'movement' opens with the words 'O dark dark dark'. Life is now seen in terms of the extinction which seems to be the end of all experience confined to the order of temporal sequence, and which now appears to be presaged in the imminent death of our own civilization. In this reality all the so-called 'leaders' of our society are involved:

> They all go into the dark,
> The vacant interstellar spaces, the vacant into the
> vacant—

for their lives have been lived in a void which reflects total absence of meaning, the lack of any vivifying or natural contact with the

outside universe and its permanent rhythms. The end of this state
of affairs can only be a 'silent funeral' which is itself without
meaning; for death itself, seen from this standpoint, has no signifi-
cance, leaves the 'sense' cold and 'lost the motive of action'. The
funeral is, indeed, 'nobody's', for the simple reason that there is,
in any proper sense, 'nobody', no being possessed of real, affirma-
tive personality or effective capacity for *real* choice, to be
'buried'.

In this situation the individual who is conscious of what faces
him can only rely on his own resources. The only course open to
the 'soul' is to be 'still', content to wait in a spirit of acceptance
upon the 'darkness' by which its life is conditioned:

> I said to my soul, be still, and let the dark come
>   upon you
> Which shall be the darkness of God.[54]

The last part of the phrase introduces a new element, and one
which is not at this stage capable of any strictly rational justifica-
tion. The mood, which can be seen as a development from that of
the corresponding section of *Burnt Norton*, is one of acquiescence
in a state now seen to be necessarily one of imperfect understand-
ing. Something more than despair, however, is now involved. The
'darkness' to which the 'soul' deliberately submits itself may turn
out to be something more than the 'vacancy' it contemplates
around itself: may be, in fact, nothing less than what the poet now
calls 'the darkness of God'.[55] To make this possible, in the mean-
time, it is necessary to 'wait': to attend upon events without the
premature effort or useless tension which the preceding section
has already presented as futile, in expectation of the moment of
illumination which may indeed come, but the arrival of which
cannot be forced or willed into being.

The fact that Eliot chooses, in the rest of this section and else-
where in the sequence, to rely upon explicitly religious formula-
tions in developing his theme should not hide from us the fact that
he is touching upon concerns which other English poets have
expressed and which can be seen as central to the very nature of
the creative process. Among those poets was John Keats who, from
an early stage in his short life, not only affirmed the need for
detachment in a poet's attitude to his art, but can be seen in his
letters transforming it into a corner-stone of his poetic philosophy.

The passages I have in mind constitute, perhaps, the best commentary on what Eliot was at this point trying to say. The essence of Keats' philosophy is Creative Detachment or, as he himself called it in a famous phrase, 'Negative Capability'.[56] As a young poet, still in the stage of assimilating the varied ideas and emotions which life so richly offers, Keats insisted that the artist must not exclude any experience until he has tested its possibilities to the full. His motto might, in effect, have been 'First accept, then judge', and it answers to the truth, observable in other matters of life, that those who believe they know all the answers to human problems before they have considered them in their unpredictable reality are rarely the wisest men or the best writers. The fact is that the poet's living material comes to him from beyond himself, must therefore be accepted totally and without prejudice before he can even begin to see whether it is capable of assimilation to the constantly maturing body of his total experience. It was this kind of detachment that Keats came to find in Shakespeare: the ability to lose his own character for his artistic ends (no loss of real personality is implied) in that of the beings and situations he is contemplating.[57] Never force issues, never impose abstract solutions upon life: this was the first creative principle that Keats came to see embodied in Shakespeare, and it was this that made Shakespeare the great master of his tragically short life.

These speculations—to take the matter a little further, in ways not finally extraneous to an understanding of Eliot—help us to interpret several passages in Keats' letters which have often been misunderstood. When he wrote, for example, 'O for a life of sensations rather than of thoughts',[58] he was not—as has often been believed—exalting mere irrationalism or promoting the exclusion of reason from the processes of living. He was rather considering 'thought' from the distinctive viewpoint of the creative artist and insisting that the poet's *initial* business is to *experience* fully and completely, to allow unity of outlook to come by a process of trial and error, through the operation of an intense concentration (Eliot might have called it contemplation) which must finally dissolve all inferior and discordant elements. 'The excellence of every art', Keats wrote, 'is in its intensity, capable of making all disagreeables evaporate, from their being in close relationship with Beauty and Truth.'[59] The 'disagreeable' here is that which refuses to be assimilated, which stands out as a discordant element in the pattern of finally shaped, mastered experience which is the poet's aim.

In view of this position what Keats rejected in 'thought' is its arbitrariness, the writing from pre-established positions: the absence, in other words, of what Eliot would call 'humility'. This is what Keats found incompatible in Wordsworth, whose greatness he recognized but whose poetic manner he described shrewdly in another letter as 'the egotistical sublime'.[60] Whilst responding to the 'sublimity' of such a poem as *The Ode on Intimations of Immortality* (a fine example of Wordsworth's expressive rhetorical manner), he none the less found this way of writing, and by implication of thinking, arbitrary and finally narrow; because a preconceived set of ideas had led the poet to exclude whole tracts of relevant human experience in the interest of a series of grandiose statements imposed upon, rather than springing from, the original life of the poem.[61] Keats, as a young poet, proposed to himself to begin at the other end. In so doing, he did not deny that poets must come, in one sense or another, to philosophize in the process of evolving the values on which their work must rest. He merely said that these values needed to *grow out* of experience, out of life, at least as much as they are imposed upon it. Or, to put it in another way, he affirmed that the answer to our problems lies finally, inescapably in ourselves: not in the text-books, however respected and respectable, which purport to sum up the 'wisdom' of previous ages. Hence, again, the remark on poetry which we find in a letter of 1818 to John Taylor: 'If poetry comes not as naturally as the leaves to a tree it had better not come at all.'[62]

Once more the insistence is on the idea of poetry as *growing out of life* by a natural, spontaneous process which needs, indeed, to be shaped, consciously guided into form, but which must first exist in its own right as a manifestation of life; for poetry, after all, *is* life, growing, developing, understanding, and this is perhaps the only real reason for paying attention to it. Ideas and systems will — must, indeed — come to the poet, as to all men; but they should not be forced anticipations which can only — in as much as they cut off later developments — impede free growth into maturity. In the meantime, and indeed at any stage, the state of the poet should be one of 'Negative Capability': that is, as he wrote in December 1817, 'when a man is capable of being in uncertainties, mysteries, doubts, without any irritable searching after fact and reason'.[63]

All this does not mean, of course, that ideas and their truth do not make their presence felt as the writer advances. To Keats himself this happened increasingly in 1818. 'There is but one road for me,' he writes, 'the road lies through application, study, and thought.'[64] This is right and natural, in as much as 'thought —the desire for truth—is a part, perhaps even the most important part, of that human experience which the poet aims at tasting in its totality; but the point is that it should come to the poet—to Keats as to Eliot—in the fullness of time not as something which he has neither the detachment to understand nor the power to express, but when the firm literary and imaginative basis for its assimilation has been laid. 'When the mind is in its infancy a Bias is in reality a Bias, but when we have acquired more strength a Bias becomes no Bias.'[65] And again: 'I will write independently. I have written independently without judgement. I may write independently with judgement hereafter. The Genius of poetry must work out its own salvation in a man; it cannot be matured by law and precept, but by sensation and watchfulness. *That which is creative must create itself.*'[66] That is possibly the most profound observation that has been made about the kind of poetry we often call romantic. Other kinds may be based on accepted principles which pervade and condition the writing; but the romantic poet is *by himself*, essentially on his own, and has to work out his salvation by 'sensation'— that is, by full exposure to experience—and by 'watchfulness', or the exercise of constant self-criticism. In this sense at least Eliot— whatever his immediate critical formulations may have been— shows himself in the *Quartets* as a poet who started from what was, whether he willed it or not, a 'romantic' situation.

The parallel with Keats may serve, always provided it is not pressed too far or made too literal, to illuminate the points which Eliot's poem makes in a different language. Various images—that of scene-changing in a darkened theatre, that of tense expectation in the underground train at an unexpected stop between stations— are introduced at this stage to suggest the recalling of the soul to an awareness of its real state. This is seen to involve, at this stage, a conscious, deliberate facing of the prospect of 'vacancy' which, whether we will it or no, is a necessary reality of our present lives. The 'bold imposing façade' of theatrical scenery is an illusion, soon to be 'rolled away'; the darkness in the tunnel, and the suspension of automatic motion, leaves the commuters alone with 'mental emptiness' and 'terror', forces them to see their lives outside the context of the daily, comfortable routine to which they instinctively cling in their life-long efforts to evade reality.

Reality, however, though evaded, continues to be there. It asserts itself in the form, precisely, of a horror of the prospect of 'vacancy'. The 'growing terror' which imposes itself on conversation in the unmoving train as talk, after 'rising' in a sub-conscious first reflection of anxiety, drops away, 'slowly fades into silence', is a reflection of the deepest of all man's fears, that of being confronted with the meaningless implications of his situation, the rooted fear of having 'nothing' to think about.[67] The fear itself—the poem goes on to indicate—is inescapable, but may be faced in a spirit which leads beyond it. A humble recognition of its reality is now seen to imply nothing less than the abandonment of all our most cherished illusions: abandonment even of those that seem most desirable, of 'hope' and 'love', in so far as these are conceived of as final and significant emotions within their temporal limitation. These are, in the present state of incomplete awareness, necessarily imperfect, even illusory:

> I said to my soul, be still, and wait without hope
> For hope would be hope for the wrong thing; wait
>   without love
> For love would be love for the wrong thing.

There is indeed beyond these illusions and half-glimpses the reality of 'faith', and without it the mood would be one of mere negation or despair. At this stage, however, 'faith', like 'the hope and the love' which it alone can illuminate, are seen to be 'all in the waiting'. The Dark Night familiar to so many of the spiritual writers must, in other words, precede the illumination which can only become a full and explicit reality after this partial negation has been accepted. The new 'commandment', accordingly, requires us to 'wait without thought', not because thought is wrong in itself (that would be far from the poet's intention, in Eliot as in Keats) but because it has to be recognized as an objective truth that we are 'not ready for thought'[68] and that thought, in so far as it involves us in the pursuit of premature and therefore misleading conclusions, can only lead us into paths of impoverishment and illusion. Similarly we are required to renounce 'hope', and even 'love', not because these are worthless or in themselves to be rejected—they

are, on the contrary, the essence of any life conceivably worth living
—but because they are, in time, necessarily incomplete and to build
on their supposed completeness is finally to close the doors to the
greater fulfilment which lies beyond them. If, recognizing this
reality, we are ready to accept the call to 'humility'—and this the
poet sees as simply a realistic view of our situation—then we may
be led to a true sense of the 'pattern' in which we are obscurely but
vitally involved. In this event, 'the darkness shall be the light' and
the 'stillness' (to return to the central image of *Burnt Norton*) 'shall
be the dancing'.

In the light of these considerations the poem returns, in a kind
of fugitive flash-back, to recall certain moments of personal intui-
tion of the kind foreshadowed in the rose-garden of *Burnt Norton*:

> Whisper of running streams, and winter lightning.
> The wild thyme unseen and the wild strawberry,
> The laughter in the garden, echoed ecstasy
> Not lost, but requiring, pointing to the agony
> Of death and birth.

The moments of illumination, again like the rose-garden revela-
tion, are seen as an 'echo', an echo not 'lost' or vain, but 'requiring',
demanding a positive effort of acceptance in humility. The sugges-
tion is that these moments of 'ecstasy' are only real in so far as we
are ready to recognize their impermanence. Their 'meaning' can
only become apparent to us in so far as we are ready to renounce
them, to accept them not as intuitions to be dwelt upon, recalling
the past in nostalgia, but as pointing to a reality beyond them-
selves. The 'ecstasy' calls for, 'requires' the 'agony' as part of its
significance: and the 'agony' is one of 'birth' through the accep-
tance of the reality of 'death'. 'Birth', be it noted, *follows* 'death' (as
the 'beginning' may be said to follow the 'end', reversing the initial
reversal of Mary Stuart's motto), rather than preceding it or affirm-
ing death as the end of the process that began with the emergence
of new life.

The positive, life-giving direction of the entire sequence is here
indicated, in effect, at what is perhaps its moment of stressed soli-
tude and isolation. In the light of what has just been said the
'movement' ends appropriately, with a summing-up—it is prac-
tically a translation—of the doctrine of the Negative Way (the
'Way Down', to return once more to Heraclitus) of St. John of the

Cross.[69] This states, in more explicitly theological terms, what the rest of the poem has been putting forward as a reality of specifically human experience. Since God is directly unapproachable, unknowable by those whose perception is humanly limited by its foundation in time, knowledge of his nature is only accessible to us through the way of recognized ignorance and negation. The only thing we can certainly know is 'what we do not know', because the nature of the real infinitely exceeds the limits which life has imposed upon us. The only thing we can truly be said to 'own' is what we are ready to give up, surrendering the illusion of possessions which we must, in time, lose for those, beyond temporal limitation, which are present though beyond our understanding. In time, where you really, logically, *are* turns out to be 'where you are not'.

IV

The interlude which, in the usual manner of these poems, constitutes the fourth 'movement', is an evocation of the Passion of Christ which, transformed into modern language, reminds us of some aspects of seventeenth-century verse, the characteristically 'metaphysical' *wit* of such a religious writer as Herbert. The attempt to transpose this very special kind of verse into a contemporary key, ingenious as it is, does not perhaps make for one of the most successful parts of the sequence. Too much, maybe, of what the verse seeks to convey remains on a rather frigid conceptual level without attaining to what would have been, in a 'metaphysical' writer, a true fusion of thought and feeling. It is possible to feel, too, that little in the previous development of the sequence has really prepared us for the introduction of an almost 'devotional' content against which, as we saw, Eliot in another mood issued a critical warning. He would have argued, we may suppose, that his purpose in writing these lines was not in any sense 'devotional', that the Christian concepts are used simply because they are accessible to his readers and because they are useful to convey what the poem has at this stage to say; but for one reader at least the lines fail to come to real life, are at best conceptually rather than poetically valid.

Be this as it may, the prevailing concept of the interlude sees the world in terms of a 'hospital', and each individual interned in it as a 'patient'. The 'wounded surgeon', whom we may hold to represent

the crucified Christ of Good Friday, exercises his healing func-
tion by probing with 'steel' the sick, 'distempered' part of our
common human nature. He is himself, under his aspect of man,
involved in the suffering which he has come to cure (his hands are
'bleeding'), but his severity, 'sharp' as it is, involves the divine
quality of 'compassion', aims at healing, 'resolving' what is, in the
absence of his action, the mystery, the 'enigma' of our fever-ridden
existence.

The 'dying nurse' of the second stanza is a figure of the Church,
herself involved as a human society in the limitations of mortality,
but offering—by virtue of her divine foundation—the prospect of
'health' to those who are ready to recognize the existence in them-
selves of sickness:

> Our only health is the disease
> If we obey the dying nurse
> Whose constant care is not to please
> But to remind of our, and Adam's curse,
> And that, to be restored, our sickness must grow
>   worse.

In conceiving of the Church in terms of a 'nurse', the poet seems
to be courting the danger of turning his concept of loving care into
something less attractive. The severity which is appropriate in rela-
tion to the divinely-ordered spiritual society seems to become less
so when translated into terms of a human being who exercises her
healing function towards the sick by being consistently careful 'not
to please'. In any event, attractive or not, the comparison is in-
tended to reflect the constant function of the Church as the severe,
unflinching one of reminding the human beings entrusted to her
care of the share of each one of them in man's fallen condition
('Adam's curse') and of the hard fact that, in order to be 'restored',
we must first accept the full consequences, in terms of subjection
to mortality, of our stricken condition.

The whole world, in short, to render the metaphor more explicit,
is a 'hospital' to house the sick, endowed by the 'ruined millionaire'
(a curious figure, this, perhaps more ingenious than explicit or
satisfying) who may be either Adam, as progenitor of the entire
fallen race, or Christ, the 'second Adam', in whose person the con-
sequences of the original Fall were happily restored. Adam,
originally endowed as a 'millionaire' in God's generous initial

economy, was 'ruined' by his rejection of the divine purpose for him. His ruin was the Fall, and the inheritance which he bequeathed as a result to all mankind was Original Sin. But—as the result again of an essential vital paradox—his very transmission of 'sickness' to his posterity opened the way to the free gift of Christ's redemption. As 'patients' in the hospital, it is required that we accept the reality of our condition; but it is essential also for us to recognize that it answers to a providential purpose—'the absolute paternal care'—which everywhere 'prevents', or forestalls, our utmost efforts to recover by anticipating and coming to meet them. To accept this in a proper spirit—'if we do well', referring both to the possible improvement in the patient's condition and to the positive nature of his own actions—is to receive through accepted death the final gift of life.

Meanwhile, death—'the chill'—dominates over our bodies and, in the form of fever, imposes itself upon our mental activity:

> The chill ascends from feet to knees,
> The fever sings in mental wires.
> If to be warmed, then I must freeze
> And quake in frigid purgatorial fires
> Of which the flame is roses and the smoke is briars.

By a living paradox, to receive the 'warmth' of life it is necessary to 'freeze' in 'frigid' fires of purification[70] thereby cleansing the imperfection of our temporal desires: once again, the purgatorial doctrine of Dante's Arnaud Daniel, so close at all times to Eliot's thought, makes its entry into this poem. Accepted in this spirit, the 'flame' of these purgative fires issues in the 'roses' which symbolize eternal life, and their 'smoke' is 'briars': that is, at once wounding and, beneath the necessary pain, bearing the flower of possible redemption.

The aim of the 'metaphysical' conceit is to blend life with the acceptance of the reality of death in a purgatorial, penitent spirit. The final verse—

> The dripping blood our only drink,
> The bloody flesh our only food—

refers directly to the Christian mystery of the Eucharist. This, indeed, together with what has gone before it in this interlude, is the first overtly orthodox reference in a poem which refuses at each stage to anticipate its religious implications. We 'like' to see this symbol of offered, and transformed, suffering as a sign of restored health, of the hope that our condition is one of 'substantial flesh and blood'; and, by a final paradox, we are enabled to see as 'good' the Friday which consummated the apparently final death and defeat of Christ—and, through our association with the atoning action, of ourselves—by the forces of evil and death. The paradox, indeed, with its intimation of life as springing from death, presents itself as a central turning-point for the entire sequence.

V

After the interlude in rhyming verse, the final 'movement' of *East Coker* returns, in a further development of the line of thought initiated in the corresponding section of *Burnt Norton*, to a consideration of the poet's personal situation, both as artist and as human being. We have already seen, in the second section,[71] that the approach of old age has brought him impressions, not of peace and 'autumnal' serenity, but of delusion and profound unease. Now, more directly, personally, as he looks back on the years lived between two world wars —'the years of *l'entre deux guerres*'—he finds, even more insistently, that what they have brought with them is a sense of loss and disorientation. Life is seen, as in the earlier passage, as a matter, not of resting upon one's laurels, but of seeing each moment as a fresh 'beginning': 'every attempt/Is a wholly new start, and a different kind of failure.' The 'failure', however, when more closely considered, implies a new start. This is most obviously related to the poet's struggle (a condition of his art) with his unending problem: the struggle, which may always seem to end in 'failure', to arrive at an adequate expression of thoughts and feelings which, as soon as they have been expressed, become 'the thing one no longer has to say'.

In this, as in so much else, the writing of poetry seems to reflect life. The impulse to use words accurately reflects another, still more universal, to find *form*, significance and coherence in the material given by experience. We are looking from a new point of view—that of the creative process as involved in time—at the problem represented by the symbols of artistic achievement in *Burnt Norton*: the 'Chinese jar' which 'Moves perpetually in its stillness', and the 'stillness of the violin, while the note lasts'.[72]

What had been seen in the first quartet from the standpoint of achieved form is now considered from that of *process* in relation to reality. Each poem, in so far as it is not a reflection of the past, and therefore *dead*, is *new*; but the language through which the experience finds expression is, on that very account, necessarily less than adequate:

> one has only learnt to get the better of words
> For the thing one no longer has to say, or the way in
> which
> One is no longer disposed to say it.

In our time, moreover, or so the poet feels, there is the additional problem of the universal deterioration of language into the 'general mess of imprecision of feeling', against which the writer aware of his distinctive vocation must also struggle.

Under these conditions, the example of the great poets of the past becomes, at least on a superficial view, discouraging. Has everything, perhaps, already been said, expressed beyond possible variation or improvement? The question is one, it seems, which imposes itself most insistently for the old, or for those who are conscious of the approach of old age, and who are particularly called upon to consider it. The answer is beginning to emerge as a particular application of the doctrine of 'detachment' already implied in the second and third sections of *Burnt Norton*. What was there stated in terms of relative abstraction is now taken up in closer relation to a personal, almost a 'professional' problem: a problem, however, which is seen at the same time to carry universal implications for human life. The idea of 'competition' against other writers engaged in the same quest needs to be renounced as involving direct personal assertion, if only because it is clear that the creative effort can never be completed in time. For the poet, as for the rest of men, in their various spheres of action, life reduces itself to the fight 'to recover what has been lost/And found and lost again and again': to recover what is, by an unvarying law of human existence, seen to be continually lost and found. 'Gain' and 'loss', seen in a proper spirit, are found to be irrelevant and only the 'trying', the endlessly renewed effort to achieve adequate expression, ultimately counts.

Not only therefore—to put the same point in another way, indicated at the outset of the quartet—is our 'beginning' our 'end', but our 'end' is seen as the occasion for a new 'beginning'. 'Home', the point of expected arrival, is 'where one starts from'. In the process of life's journey each individual experience becomes more complex, is seen to be involved in a 'pattern' which is not only personal but of 'dead and living':

> As we grow older
> The world becomes stranger, the pattern more
>   complicated
> Of dead and living. Not the intense moment
> Isolated, with no before and after,
> But a lifetime burning in every moment
> And not the lifetime of one man only
> But of old stones that cannot be deciphered.

The intense moment of experience—such as that recorded, for instance, in the first section of *Burnt Norton*—is now seen under a new light, not in timeless isolation, but as gathering into itself the accumulated intensity of 'a lifetime burning in every moment'. This lifetime involves not only the personal present but the immemorial past. It includes the intuition indicated through the reference to the anonymous dancers round the bonfire in the opening 'movement' of the quartet. There is a time to recall the dance in the 'evening under starlight', as well as a time to dwell on more intimate memories of a family nature, under 'lamplight' with 'the photograph album'. There is 'a time' for such things, a 'time' which these actions can in some measure 'redeem': always provided, however, that these evocations of the past are *not* taken as pretexts for evading the present, are not seen as final.

We are now ready for a new, still provisional conclusion derived from the present state of the incomplete but developing argument. The state of simplicity, originally caught through memories of moments of real or imagined personal illumination—of the kind so intensely and so fleetingly revealed in *Burnt Norton*—and there continually lost through the inability of man to bear 'much reality', may turn out to be the end of the long journey of life which thus becomes, in a special sense, a return to the intuitive foundations of our being. Between setting out and return, however, as we can now see, the vision precariously attained necessarily and continuously changes. New experiences at each moment make the previous picture incomplete. They enrich it if they are accepted in a spirit which the poet has called that of 'humility'; but they lead only to the death of the spirit if the personality submits to the comforting temptation to regard its personal condition of the moment as a satisfactory point of arrival, and seeks to affirm itself exclusively in the present, turning in upon itself in the process and becoming static in the contemplation of past (and therefore, in as much as it is exclusively past, *dead*) achievement.

This latter, the distinctive temptation of old age, is the extreme example of another and more universal one, which sees love (which is properly understood as liberation from 'desire') exclusively under the aspect of the satisfaction, 'here and now', of the passing, deathward-directed moment. True love, we can now begin to see, is quite another thing: 'Love is most nearly itself/When here and now cease to matter.' The aging, above all, should be chary of resting on the temptation which implies the surrender of the continued willingness to live, the refusal to accept the price which that willingness must imply. For the young the temptation may be nothing more than a distraction of the moment, from which recovery is always possible: for the old who fail to resist it, it can be nothing less than death. 'Old men ought to be explorers.' Renunciation of this imperative implies in the case of those approaching their old age an illusory resting upon the experiences of a past which is, quite simply, no longer there. It is for this reason that old men, above all, 'ought to be explorers', to whom—just because they are no longer young—'Here and now cease to matter.'

The meditation culminates in a brief phrase charged with meaning: 'We must be *still* and *still moving*'. *Still*: in other words, content to wait upon experience in the shadow of a knowledge which is necessarily partial, refraining from that premature imposition of a 'philosophy' which may seem to be a satisfactory—and comforting—affirmation of the self, but which is really, when more closely considered, its chief limitation. That is one side of the picture, but to it there corresponds another. We are also (and this applies not to the aging alone, though it must have a special meaning for them) to be 'still moving': always, that is, prepared to accept the challenge of the living present—in relation to which alone time is 'redeemable', or 'redeemed'—instead of taking refuge in an acceptance as supposedly final of the vision imposed and limited by the experience of the past.

In this way, the traditional doctrine of the Negative Way (the

Way Down of the epigraph), first advanced as a *concept* in *Burnt Norton*, begins to acquire a fresh, a fully personal and contemporary meaning. The human obligation at any given moment is to *advance* towards 'a further union', along a path likely to involve the reverse of facile comfort (the spiritual landscape is that implied in the reference to 'the *dark cold* and the *empty desolation*', the comfortless infinite water of the open sea which will play an important part in the next quartet), but which is now seen as a condition of continuing and expanding life. So the poem ends on a significant rectification of the equally significant inversion, at the opening, of the dead Queen's motto: 'In my end is my beginning'.

[4]
The Dry Salvages

There has been a tendency among critics of the *Four Quartets* to find *The Dry Salvages* the least successful poem in the series.[73] Some have found that there is too much *prose* in this part of the sequence, too much repetition of what they find to be tired and dispirited motives. Others—more deeply dissatisfied—have considered that the underlying thought is lacking in precision or fails to contribute in any valid way to what should be, they rightly feel, a developing and expanding argument. Others again, recognizing the difficulty which these findings present, have argued that the descent, as they feel it to be, from poetry to prose is a structural necessity, a stage of false, or at least premature resolution, through which the poetry has to pass before it can recover, assert its real strength in the final, inclusive resolution of *Little Gidding*.[74]

That there may be some measure of truth in these various views we need not deny. Some parts of *The Dry Salvages* do seem to read less poetically, even less conclusively, than what has gone before; and it may be that the poet, here more than in the rest of the sequence, is struggling with something like a partial failure or drying-up of the creative impulse. But that cannot be *all* the picture, for further consideration will discover in this third quartet an extension of theme that is surely deliberate and answers to a planned and coherent conception. If the motive which provided the starting-point for *East Coker* was primarily personal, the poet engaged, as it were, in taking stock of his situation at a given moment of particular stress and menace, that of *The Dry Salvages* looks beyond England to America; it takes in his earliest conscious memories and reaches out, beyond these, to the links—largely preconscious, essentially non-intellectual, unconceptual in kind—that bind his experience as an individual to that of the race to which he belongs. Whether he has succeeded in this new stage of his endeavour only the quality of the poetry can tell; but the attempt certainly answers to the logic of his design and not to have made it would have been to omit a link essential to the whole.

I

The opening 'movement' of the new quartet is, whatever we may think of what follows, one of Eliot's most sustained and evocative pieces of writing. It answers to the themes we have just indicated and sets the tone for the poem as a whole. The subject is now man's journey in time, which is simultaneously that of the individual engaged in recovering the instinctive, half-conscious memories of the human past. The sustained image which dominates the section, and which corresponds by its position to the rose-garden in *Burnt Norton* and to the ritual dances of midsummer in *East Coker*, is that of a great river running to the sea. More precisely, the river is the Mississippi of Eliot's earliest childhood memories in St. Louis;[75] but, in the process of being recalled by the poet it becomes something more, is associated with the efforts of the successive generations of men who have at various times fought, used, and been overcome by it. The river runs into the sea, and the part it plays in the poem implies at once a journey back into personal origins and, beyond this, a symbol of the history of the human race which each individual accumulation of experience in time in some measure recreates. The sense of the whole, uniquely eloquent passage emerges in the line which connects the two sections into which it is divided: 'The river is within us, the sea is all about us'. The river is life as movement in time, continual restlessness, the sea is the greater reality which surrounds us, the 'eternity' which we only penetrate at the moment—and at the cost—of dying.

The river, more precisely, is a symbol of the racial experience which runs as a determining factor, present even when undetected, in the life-blood of each individual man: much as in *Burnt Norton*, we remember, the poet spoke of 'the trilling wire in the blood' which 'sings below inveterate scars'. It is also the immemorial object of a kind of religious awe, 'a strong brown god'. It is possible to see in all this some reflection of the journey of the narrator into 'the heart of darkness' in Conrad's story of the Congo river.[76] That, too, was a journey profoundly ambivalent in its effects, at once deeply disturbing, destructive of supposed certainties and shallow assumptions, and obscurely indicative of new, hitherto unconsidered possibilities of life. On a more immediately conscious level the Mississippi river is seen as a witness to the history of man's continually expanding domination over his environment: initially a 'frontier' between himself and the still unconquered hinterland, then the route along which trade relationships pass, and, as such, at once 'useful' and 'untrustworthy', finally no more than a 'problem' confronting the development of civilized means of communication.

Man's civilizing achievement, in fact, finds one of its most powerful traditional images in the concept of the *pontifex*, 'the builder of bridges'. This is a real conquest, the product of his natural, distinctively human urge to control and master his environment; and, real as it is—indeed, precisely because it is so impressively real, because it has succeeded in covering over, disguising other orders of reality—it carries with it a corresponding peril. The danger, as the passage also makes clear, is that the 'god', who remains 'sullen, untamed and intractable' beneath all the efforts made to tame him by incorporation into the civilizing, domesticating process, will come to be taken for granted, in effect forgotten. Present though he still is in the subconscious depths of the human mind, both individual and collective, the 'strong brown god' can easily—too easily—be set aside, neglected as a presence in the advance of material progress:

> The problem once solved, the brown god is almost
>   forgotten
> By the dwellers in cities—ever, however, implacable,
> Keeping his seasons and rages, destroyer, reminder
> Of what men choose to forget.

As always when Eliot is writing well, the rhythmic placing of words is unerringly accurate and evocative. To read the lines appropriately is to respond to the cumulative echo of 'ever' and 'however' leading up to the menace of 'implacable'. It is also to take the sense of the river's 'seasons and rages' as pointing to the description of it as potential 'destroyer', the assertion of its inexorable presence as a reminder of all those realities—and not least those concealed, submerged within his own nature—which man has chosen in his self-created world of limited, finally self-deluding achievement, to place behind him, 'to forget'.

In responding to all this as we read, it is important to avoid the one-sided or simplified response. Man's civilizing achievement is a real one, a necessary expression of his humanity, one which finds its most complete affirmation in the process which has made of the original primitive being a *citizen*, a 'dweller in cities'.[77] In the same way, the poetry which he writes as a 'citizen' benefits from the cumulative achievement of tradition which enables him to incorporate into his own work, in the process of extending the 'frontiers' by his personal contribution, the findings of those who have gone before him.

What has been achieved in this way, however, has been at the cost of what has been, in the process, submerged, 'forgotten'. At the back of all man's 'advances', his necessary and impressive efforts to impose himself upon the world which surrounds him and which he has been largely successful in reducing to a convenience, the river remains present both as a powerful external reality and in the submerged memory of each individual member of the human race. Although normally 'unhonoured', 'unpropitiated' by those who have chosen to 'worship' the machine which is the instrument of their power, it is none the less still there, still a factor in shaping, if not the partly illusory present, the still undetermined future. 'Watching and waiting' it will finally assert itself, both in the rhythm of each individual life and as a link with the undying collective memory of the human race.

Eventually, indeed—and this is the next stage in the argument— the two realities, the conscious and the submerged, will come together. At any given moment in the life of a society, and in each individual life which in some measure recapitulates the accumulated experience of that society, it is true that, if 'the river is within us', the sea is 'all about us'. Like land and sea, life and death, the two conditions are inextricably interlocked: 'The sea is the land's edge also, the granite/Into which it reaches.' The sea throws back to the land, to the 'beaches'—again the echoing internal rhyme with 'reaches' intensifies the sense of interwoven relationship—the memories of a past, personal and racial alike, which we have so often seemed to 'forget', but which in fact contrives to live in these obstinate testimonies to an unrecognized reality, 'hints of earlier and other creation'. It 'tosses up' our 'losses' (once again the internal rhyme underlines and intensifies the sense) and brings back the remnants of our disasters. The objects it restores are dead, mere relics of what was once living and humanly meaningful; but they serve to remind us, by their very nature, of the final insignificance of what has been achieved—not in itself, for the achievement has been real, a distinctively human conquest—but in relation to the larger and more enduring rhythms of existence. For the 'voices' of the sea are innumerable, and the 'gods' which it represents beyond all human limitation.

The sustained passage into which this opening leads would be sufficient in itself to refute those who are inclined to see in *The Dry Salvages* little more than a failure in poetic power. It is a splendidly evocative piece of writing which, beyond its obvious quality as poetry, serves to concentrate the entire sense of the 'movement':

> The sea howl
> And the sea yelp, are different voices
> Often together heard: the whine in the rigging,
> The menace and caress of wave that breaks on water,
> The distant rote in the granite teeth,
> And the wailing warning from the approaching
>   headland   .
> Are all sea voices, and the heaving groaner
> Rounded homewards, and the seagull:
> And under the oppression of the silent fog
> The tolling bell
> Measures time not our time, rung by the unhurried
> Ground swell, a time
> Older than the time of chronometers, older
> Than time counted by anxious worried women
> Lying awake, calculating the future,
> Trying to unweave, unwind, unravel
> And piece together the past and the future,
> Between midnight and dawn, when the past is all
>   deception,
> And the future futureless, before the morning watch
> When time stops and time is never ending;
> And the ground swell, that is and was from the
>   beginning,
> Clangs
> The bell.

Few passages in Eliot use rhythm so sustainedly and with such success to draw together a variety of threads into a common and embracing whole. As it opens, the different 'voices' of the sea—the 'sea howl' and the 'sea yelp', both menacing in their connotation— are at once separated by being placed in different lines and beautifully held together in a common development, 'often together heard': the inversion of the normal order of verb and adverb serves to strengthen the sense of unity in distinction, as well as to provide the break in the line, after 'heard', which introduces a further set of cumulative impressions. From the 'whine' in the rigging we are led to the 'menace and caress' of the wave that breaks, with deceptive placidity, on 'water' (the combination of sound and contrasted meaning—'menace' set against 'caress'—is exceptionally evocative): but the mention of 'water' is followed by the more open threat of 'granite teeth', and this leads in turn to further echoes, 'sea voices' heard 'under the oppression of the silent fog' and leading, as the focal point of the whole passage, to 'the tolling bell'.

From this moment to the end of the first 'movement' the verse moves in a single, cumulative build-up that might properly be called rhetorical in its effect, to its natural conclusion. The effect is produced, essentially, by the interweaving of two themes, corresponding to surface current and under-tow, as they move to a common end. The surface current, we might say, is given by the time-theme, the sense of *human*, measured time bearing life along to its inexorable conclusion; but beneath this, moving—so to speak —as counter-current, not so much *against* the first as *under* it, modifying and qualifying it by its intuited presence, is another sense of time, not to be reduced to mathematical measurement or abstract division into 'past' and 'future', 'before' and 'after': the totality of 'time' as apprehended in the living moment we call 'the present' and as destined, in the continual process of becoming 'the past', to die. The two rhythms, simultaneously present on their different levels—which we might call, in psychological terms, the conscious and the sub-conscious, the personal and the racial, the civilized abstraction and its primitive foundation—converge together, meet in the central, unifying image of the 'bell'.

The bell, indeed, is destined to play a central part in the development of this quartet. At this point it is the 'tolling bell', indicative of the death in which all human effort ends and with which it is required to come to terms. At a later stage, it will merge into the Angelus-bell, indicative of the Annunciation and of the birth, the new life, which may emerge from accepted death.[78] Moved by the 'ground swell'—the under-current, as we have called it—it serves at this point to remind us of a dimension of life beyond any which we may seek to impose upon it: a dimension beyond the time which can be measured out, or 'counted', by men (or women) in their 'anxious, worried' subjection to the 'chronometer', to the mere impersonal succession of past and future.

The aim of the passage is now seen to bear reference to the problems originally posed for exploration at the opening of *Burnt Norton*. Its effect is to set the two temporal rhythms which were there posited — the mathematical impersonality of 'unredeemable' clock-time and the constantly shifting motions of each individual, *personal* apprehension of the temporal — into a living relationship. To every man there will come, in so far as he is sensitive, alive, a moment of true apprehension, which is not necessarily reassuring. The experience in the rose-garden, which provided a starting-point for the entire sequence, was such a moment, and it ended in retreat, in the reassertion of what passes for 'reality'. Now, with the intervening development and reflection behind us, we can hope to take the problem a little further. The intuitive 'moment' is seen as that in which the individual becomes aware, as he succeeds in abstracting himself from his normal subjection to the limits of temporal succession, of the sound of the 'tolling bell' as reminder of 'what men choose to forget'. The result of this insight is not — we must repeat — necessarily or immediately encouraging. It comes in an intermediate, uncertain moment, 'between midnight and dawn', when the past is seen as 'all deception' and the future as 'futureless'; and what it recalls is the universal reality of death, which is certainly the end of 'time' for each man and woman and which may prove — on further reflection — to be the occasion for entry into eternal life. The beautiful rhythm which runs through the passage serves to unite the two currents — the temporal and the timeless — through the images of 'river' and 'sea' which respectively convey them, until they are brought together in the concluding clangour of the bell.

II

If the opening 'movement' of *The Dry Salvages* is one of Eliot's most sustained and evocative passages, the rhyming section which provides the first part of the second is apt is leave readers uneasy. The rhyming scheme, which is a free adaptation of the *sestina* form used by Sidney in a poem from the *Arcadia*,[79] is, of course, an exceptionally difficult one to handle. The poet no doubt chose it in part out of attraction for the very challenge it represented. He is also likely to have felt that the long final rhymes, and the effect of a stanza endlessly turning upon itself, answered to a sense of desolation which we can see as carried on from the preceding section: the sense, in other words, of the sheer, unending repetition which limitation to mere temporal succession — 'time before and time after' — seems to involve. The recurrent rhymes emphasize the circular, essentially closed nature of the experience they contemplate; and they end in a 'calamitous' assertion — which the poet calls an 'annunciation': the word is used three times in the *sestina*, with developing significance — of what he seems to see as a process of universal drift and death.

Acceptance of this intention, however, and of its logical place in the development of the sequence cannot prevent us from asking certain questions which a reading of the *sestina* raises. In the first place, it is possible to feel that the rhymes are sometimes insufficiently tied to meaning. This is especially the case with the long endings in '-less' — 'devotionless', 'oceanless', and 'erosionless' — which are apt to leave us wondering whether the monotonous, falling syllables are an adequate reflection of, or a substitute for sense. The test here would seem to be one which can be applied to all poetry. Do the rhymes serve effectively to point a meaning necessary to the poem; or do they not rather seem to indicate a certain weakness in the thought, a tendency — it might almost be said — to evade clear definition of the problem in hand? This is an impression that a good deal of Eliot's later prose writing is apt to give us, but which seems, so far, to have been kept very successfully out of his poetry. Could it be, we find ourselves asking, that on this occasion at least some of the weaknesses of the prose are communicating themselves to the verse?

Questions of this kind lead in turn to considerations perhaps even more important, which may have implications of a limiting kind for a good deal of Eliot's later work. These lines *do* appear to read as depressed, even tired verse; and it is perhaps not unfair to say that tiredness, a peculiar surrender to depression which may involve the struggle with a certain failure in creativity, is one of Eliot's principal problems as a poet. There may be too much exhaustion here, too marked a predisposition to find life arid and unrewarding: and, as is always the case at the moments when this sense prevails, too much prosiness, too many limp and exhausted rhymes.

This is not to say that it would be fair to leave the matter there. Beneath the sense of depression which seems to permeate these lines, Eliot is aiming, with whatever difficulty, at conveying a sense of development. This he does, essentially, by the placing of the three references in the *sestina* to 'annunciation': for each of these is seen, on reflection, to carry a step further the sense established in its predecessor. The first mention of the '*calamitous* annunciation' would seem to correspond—as we have said—to a sense of life as unendingly subjected to a repetitive and apparently meaningless process in time. The second, or 'last annunciation', appears to take us a step further. It answers to the death which may seem to be a final confirmation of desolation, but can conceivably be thought of as representing a challenge to that sense of the meaningless, if accepted in the spirit for which the entire sequence is arguing. To speak of *death* in terms of an 'annunciation' is, after all, in itself to alter the common concept we have of it, to join it, however obscurely or tentatively, with the notion of a possible *birth*.

The theme, clearly, has connections with preceding parts of the argument. To 'redeem' the time is—we are beginning to see—to accept the reality of the death which is inextricably interwoven with it, which its very nature implies; and to live significantly is not to evade this issue—in which the entire problem of the human meaning of time is, as it were, concentrated—but to resolve it in relation to what we may call, not necessarily with theological implications, an *act* of faith. It is this act, finally, which underlies the concluding reference in the *sestina* to the 'one', the unique and irrepeatable 'Annunciation'. Here, of course, Eliot *is* making use of his own, personal beliefs. This, unlike the other two, which can be seen as merely foreshadowing it, is the definitely *Christian* Annunciation (it is significant that here, and here alone, the word is given a capital letter), prelude to the 'historical' Incarnation which brings with it, for a believer, the only conceivably valid redemption of the temporal process. Eliot is still not writing a devotional poem, or assuming readers who share with him common beliefs; but he *is* asking those readers to accept, as a symbol conveying his meaning, the Christian assertion of a unique *event* by which, at a given historical moment, the significant, the meaningful reality which we call 'the spiritual' (the term is sadly worn, but more or less irreplaceable) projected itself with redemptive consequence into the temporal process. The *event* is one which calls for, because it itself symbolizes it, an answering *act* of faith: an *act* of acceptance, made in a spirit which excludes all thought of return or withheld commitment and which is inspired by the conviction that accepted 'death' will lead to a 'birth' into new life, that indeed only by recognizing the reality of death as an aspect of life is the 'birth' of new life conceivable.[80]

Round these successive points of focus, with the sense of developing *meaning* which they imply, the *sestina* weaves its desolate pattern of unending repetition. According to the statement with which it opens this is the inescapable reality which governs all life in time. There is no conceivable 'end', but simply' addition', one meaningless and isolated fact following its predecessor: this and, beyond it, the continual destruction of the supposed certainties of the past — 'what was believed in as the most reliable' — without their replacement by any corresponding significance in the present. Here, evidently, we are being invited to take up once again the theme, developed in the second 'movement' of *East Coker*, of the necessarily falsifying nature of 'the knowledge derived from experience'.[81] In *The Dry Salvages* this becomes a panorama of desolation affecting all human generations to the end of time:

> There is no end, but addition: the trailing
> Consequence of further days and hours,
> While emotion takes to itself the emotionless
> Years of living among the breakage
> Of what was believed in as the most reliable —
> And therefore the fittest for renunciation.

Added to this, as if it were not enough, is the 'final addition' provided by the bitter personal experience of advancing years: the 'Pride or resentment at failing powers',[82] the experience of 'unattached devotion' separated from any satisfying or adequate object of faith, the sense of life as 'drift' and the premonition of approaching and unavoidable 'shipwreck'. Taken together these things point to the 'undeniable' death implied in the sound of the bell which rounded off the first section and which is now felt to herald the 'last', the final 'annunciation'.

All this, read in isolation from the *sestina* as a whole, might seem to amount to little more than a repetition, perhaps intensified and rendered more desolate, of the attitude to the 'wisdom' of the old men already expressed in *East Coker*. This, in a poem which depends on the sense conveyed in it of a developing exploration of experience, would be a serious flaw. Such a development, however, proves on closer reflection to be present. It is true, and perhaps true in a limiting sense, that under the circumstances which these lines describe, life adrift on the sea of experience is seen as an unending, or continually repeated struggle in the face of a future that is liable 'Like the past, to have no destination'. The attitude of the 'fishermen' to their situation does, however, introduce something like a new element. 'Forever bailing', asserting their will to survive under conditions which seem to be endlessly unfavourable, they are moved (and it is at this point that the mood begins to shift) by an obscure faith that unites their efforts to the struggle of the anonymous generations which have preceded them in an enterprise that may appear to defy rational definition but which also corresponds to a tenacious affirmation of the human instinct to live. It is this that underlies their efforts in the face of 'lowering' North East winds, as they sail 'Over shallow banks unchanging and erosionless', making their endless and apparently unfruitful — 'unpayable' — trips 'For a haul that will not bear examination'.

That the 'haul', the result of all this effort, may not seem to justify itself in the light of a reasonable evaluation of what the fishermen — or any man living in, and limited by, 'time before and time after' — may expect to find is evidently true. The fact remains that the effort continues to be made, unendingly repeated; because it seems to be inspired by an obscure, but tenacious, instinct for life which drives the human race (and the individuals which compose it) beyond the evidence of helplessness.[83] As such, it answers to an initial affirmation of faith: not faith indeed directed to an object, or validly supported by reason, but a basic instinct which asks to be recognized, and one on which — just conceivably — something may be built. Certainly there is no easy consolation here, gained by ignoring the inconveniently real:

> There is no end of it, the voiceless wailing,
> No end to the withering of withered flowers,
> To the movement of pain that is painless and
>   motionless,
> To the drift of the sea and the drifting wreckage,

The bone's prayer to Death its God. Only the hardly,
  barely prayable
Prayer of the one Annunciation.

Such life as the fishermen can show is still subject to the action of
the temporal process. The answer to the question posed at the open-
ing of the *sestina* — 'Where is there an end of it?' — seems to be that,
within the process itself, 'There is no end of it'. The flow is unend-
ing, meaningless, and finally destructive of life. The flowers that
have 'withered' remain so, the experience is one of 'pain' indeed,
and of a pain that seems to be senseless, in a way without reality:
'painless' and, at the same time, inexorably fixed, 'motionless',
leading to nothing beyond itself. Life seen as subjected to mere
succession is 'drift', and the endless drift of broken 'wreckage' at
that. The 'bone', being itself dead, can only pray to 'Death its
God', and this seems to be the final confirmation of desolation.

It should be noted, however, that both 'Death' and 'God' are
now given capital letters. The possibility is emerging that an
acceptance of death as an inexorable reality in time may lead to the
possibility of birth, to the affirmation of an 'Annunciation' that is
'one', unique and not, of its very nature, subject to temporal
repetition. The final affirmation is that the only conceivable *end* of
the tragedy of lives conceived as limited by their subjection to the
process of succession in time is that of religious acceptance and the
dangerous, inexorable assertion of *choice* which it implies. It is an
end, however, still almost inhuman in its remoteness, though it
carries with it in the poem's most explicit reference yet to Christian
doctrine a hope for the final redemption of the temporal process by
which all human life is conditioned.

The act of acceptance which is thus implied must, however, be
something more than an abstract gesture. The poem does not seek
to argue, but to convey an experience. It does not even demand
acceptance as *true* of the Christian belief it uses, but only a willing-
ness to find it appropriate as a symbol conveying lived meaning.
What has been stated needs at this stage to be related to the
developing exploration with which the whole series is concerned.
We return, accordingly, in a passage which again may strike us as
somewhat prosaic, almost deliberately unpoetical, to a considera-
tion of the complex pattern of temporal experience. The second
part — the 'counter-statement', as we have called it[84] — of the
'movement' which opened with the *sestina* takes up once more —

but now in an expanded, less immediately personal sense—the theme already indicated in the concluding section of *East Coker*:

> It seems, as one becomes older,
> That the past has another pattern, and ceases to be a
>   mere sequence—
> Or even development.

The notions of 'sequence' and 'development', which might at an earlier stage have seemed adequate to convey a sense of life as purposeful are now seen to be unduly limited, in as much as they presuppose, and are restricted by, the notion of mere succession. The years, in other words, bring with them the sense of a pattern in the past: not only, at this point, the past of the individual, but also that of the race to which each individual person belongs. This is positive, in so far as it answers to a broadening of vision which has been prepared for in the early stages of this quartet, and especially in the river passage of the first section; but, unless clarified, it is not enough. The 'pattern'—we are now told—is not to be thought of as a mere 'evolution', for this would be misleading, a 'partial fallacy', in so far as it leads the individual to separate himself from, to 'disown' a past which he thinks has been simply superseded by the onward movement of events. The truth, rather, is that we *are* our past, in so far—and in so far only—as *our* past, that past which is personal and individual to each one of us, continues to live in our present circumstance, lending it a fruitful depth of perspective which it would otherwise lack. The poet's meaning here is notably more important, more truly expressive of his design, than his expression which, with its somewhat pedantic reproof of 'the popular mind', may serve, by reading rather aridly and pettily, to distract attention from the point that is being made.

As an alternative to the merely 'sequential' view of our experience in time, the poem now concentrates on those moments of unique if transitory clarification with which we have been concerned since the original glimpse of elusive insight in the rose-garden. Their effect is one of 'sudden illumination', more fundamental—we are told—than any sense of immediate well-being ('Fruition, fulfilment, security, or affection', or even, a little flatly perhaps, 'a very good dinner') can be. The time has now come to find a place for them in the view of time which has been emerging from the sequence as a whole. Appropriately, therefore, the moment of intuition recorded in *Burnt Norton* seems to be recalled, but as seen now under a new light:

> We had the experience but missed the meaning,
> And approach to the meaning restores the experience
> In *a different form*, beyond any meaning
> We can assign to happiness.

As a result of the tentative 'approach' to meaning recorded in the various stages of the sequence the original moment of intuitive experience has acquired a sense which is necessarily more discursive, even prosaic, but also more capable of being related to what we choose to call the 'real'. The new meaning is not to be confused with 'happiness' as we generally understand it. It may even have implications of 'agony', of barely tolerable tragedy, but it points to a conceivable redemption of the temporal process. We are beginning—however abstractly, even unpoetically—to see a way to satisfy the need, posited at the beginning of *Burnt Norton*, to 'redeem the time', to make the temporal sequence which dominates our existence something more than an arid, death-directed panorama of repetitive futility. The original experience, which seemed to have been lost, is now 'restored', but under a different aspect which serves to distinguish the truly living from the dead: 'restored', in other words, in a *new* form, beyond any superficial notion of 'fruition' or 'happiness'.

At this point, furthermore, we return to take up what has been from the beginning a principal theme of this quartet. The past experience thus revived, 'restored' in relation to an emergent sense of 'meaning', is seen to involve more than a single life-time. The redemption of the past implies, among other things, the uniting of the individual life to that of the generations and races that have contributed in the course of time—through the easily misunderstood process we may call, if we choose, 'evolution'—to the formation of the present reality. The effect is to lead back as far as the 'ineffable', the still subconsciously present experience of primitive terror:

> The backward look behind the assurance
> Of recorded history, the backward half-look
> Over the shoulder, towards the primitive terror.

The reference here is once more back to the 'dweller in cities' who

—we remember—has '*almost* forgotten' the river, 'the strong brown god', who remains none the less a presence, obscure but potentially threatening, beneath the life that has been constructed on his domination. Once again, a superficial reading of 'evolution' will consider these memories of the racial past as superseded, no longer actual: whereas a deeper understanding will show them to be presences, still capable of contributing to, and indeed enriching, the pattern of our present living.

What is needed is to see 'the past experience revived in the meaning', which 'Is not the experience of one life only/But of many generations'. In other words our reading of the past, personal, and historical, is valid just in so far as it has meaning for the present. The 'moment of agony' in our lives—even those occasioned by 'hope' or 'dread' for what turns out to be, following *East Coker*, 'the wrong thing'[85]—are also seen as 'permanent': not absolutely, indeed, for impermanence is inseparable from our lives, but 'with such permanence as time has'. Their 'permanence' results from our ability to see them as sharing in, and contributing to, the pattern, the 'meaning' which the sequence as a whole is seeking to develop and which can never, in time, be complete or final.

This 'permanent' aspect of what presents itself to us under the guise of suffering, 'agony' is a reality—the poet finally reflects—which can be appreciated better through our loving participation in the 'agony' of those near to us than in our own. In our own lives, as we normally experience them, the 'agony' of the past is carried away, in the process of becoming 'past', by the onward moving 'currents of action' which bear us irresistibly onwards; we are once more reminded of what was implied figuratively in the river meta-phor of the opening 'movement'. It is the nature of the river to move ceaselessly onward bearing the *débris* of the past—'hints of earlier and other creation'—along with it. Similarly, our own 'agonies' are buried or submerged in our subsequent experiences, whereas those of others, close to but distinct from ourselves, re-main 'unworn by subsequent attrition'. That, it may be, is an important function of friendship, of loving relationship, in the enriching of human life. For it is true, and indeed necessary, that 'People change, and smile': but true also that the 'agony'—in this like the river—'abides'.

At the end of this line of thought we can begin to see that 'time the destroyer' is also 'time the preserver', and be ready to return with renewed understanding to the image of the river. The river may be said to 'preserve' the elements of life even in the process of destroying them. Conserving its own life of unending flow, it carries along with it in its course a cargo of wreckage and, in theological terms, of the human reality implicit in the notion of an original, and redeemable, Fall from grace: 'The bitter apple and the bite in the apple'. The 'ragged rock' in the 'restless waters' recalls the moments of agony already referred to. These are normally concealed, covered over, by 'the currents of action', but they are still present; for—as we have just been told—'the agony abides', and may be seen, when the appropriate season comes—'the sombre season/Or the sudden fury'—to be 'what it always was'.

III

The third section of *The Dry Salvages* follows the normal pattern of the quartets in setting out to explore the consequences in *moral* terms, for personal decisions and behaviour, of the positions reached in the previous 'movements'. Like the rest of the quartet, it expands its theme notably beyond any merely individual experience. A point has been reached at which the poet needs to develop his thought by reference to an external, 'objective' statement: not the explicitly Christian references which he has already introduced, and which answer to an *experience*, a lived intuition, rather than to an analytic development of conceptual thinking, but something which he can hope to use with greater detachment.

He finds what he requires in the meditations of the Hindu god, Krishna, in the *Bhagavad-gita*,[86] on the implications and limitations of action. This bringing together of elements drawn from the religious traditions of East and West is not, of course, new in Eliot, who had already made use of something similar in *The Fire Sermon* section of *The Waste Land*. Nor does it mean that the poet—who studied Sanskrit and Eastern religious thought at Harvard, and who once confessed to having been left in a state of 'enlightened mystification' as a result[87]—is out to present himself as a competent expert in these matters. The ideas found in the Hindu scriptures interest him as material for poetry: more accurately, perhaps, as an example of what may be derived from the Way Down, the negative way of renunciation, whereas the emerging Christian component in his thought is seen rather as affirmative, as implying the redemption of the temporal process through the essentially active concept of 'Incarnation'. This does not mean, however, that the two approaches are to be seen as mutually exclusive, or that one is 'better', finally more positive than the other. Rather they are mutually completing, and the final result will be to show that they are—in Heraclitus' phrase—'the same'.

In the passage of the *Bhagavad-gita* to which Eliot refers, Arjuna has questioned the rightness of becoming involved in a battle which will cause him to fight against his own relatives. Consulted in this matter, the god Krishna replies with a consideration of the nature of 'action' itself. He says that action, 'rightly performed' or 'rightly renounced' (and the emphasis is on 'rightly', on the essential purity of motive), brings with it freedom. *Both* the action performed and the action renounced, he goes on to say, are better than the action merely 'shunned', the essential *choice* evaded. The connection with Eliot's own use of the alternative ways of Heraclitus —the Way Up and the Way Down—is obvious. Their equivalent in terms of the *Bhagavad-gita* is to be found in the alternative ways of 'knowledge', or contemplation, and 'action':

> The wise see knowledge and action as one; they see truly.
> Take either path and tread it to the end; the end is the same.
> There the followers of action meet the seekers after knowledge in equal freedom.

The relation of these considerations to the intuitions concerning the nature of time which the poem has been developing constitute the sense of the section.

From the point of vantage now proposed we begin, in the opening lines of this 'movement', to look back on findings already established. At the heart of the entire development of the series there has lain a growing conviction, which we have been approaching from diverse points of view and which received its original impulse from the fleeting intuition in the rose-garden, that the future and the past are meaningless, as concepts, unless caught under the aspect of the present. Up or down, backward or forward in time, the present moment is finally the only reality: everything else, in so far as it is accessible to us, is in fact *there*. We have indeed the illusion of being carried forward in time, but there is only one real or significant development, as distinct from the 'deceptions', the one-sided notions of 'evolution' and so forth, which were discussed in the second section and there dismissed as means of evading or 'disowning' the past;[88] the significant development lies not in time, but in the order of *consciousness* concentrated on the living and present moment. It is this order as rendered apparent, *incarnated*, through acts of *choice* issuing in *action* that the poet, using Krishna's injunction for ends of his own, is now incorporating into his developing theme.

The approach to Krishna's statement, which thus provides the point of meditation on which the entire 'movement' turns, is through a series of images that evoke, in deliberately enigmatic form, just this sense of past and future as intertwined, mysteriously centred on the present. The future may sometimes be seen in terms of the past, as 'a faded song, a Royal Rose or a lavender spray', charged with the nostalgia of 'wistful regret' for those who are, unlike those remembered in a past 'no longer there', by contrast 'not yet here to regret'. In either case the mood of nostalgia — 'Pressed between yellow leaves of a book that has never been opened' — is not to be dwelt upon to the exclusion of the living challenge offered by the present. The 'yellow leaves' are *dead*, as much so when they refer to our anticipated escape into an imagined future as they are when they seek to recall, and to live by, what is vanished and done with. The simple truth — simple though we are unable, in general, to recognize it as such, or to face it steadily — is that 'time is no healer: the patient is no longer here'.

After this introduction, which serves to link this new stage in the poem with what has gone before, the implications of viewing life in terms of a development in *consciousness* are explored by the consideration of human existence through the image of a traveller engaged on a long journey at the end of which he will not be the same individual as when he set out:

> Fare forward, travellers! not escaping from the past
> Into different lives, or into any future;
> You are not the same people who left that station
> Or who will arrive at any terminus,
> While the narrowing rails slide together behind you;
> And on the deck of the drumming liner
> Watching the furrow that widens behind you,
> You shall not think 'the past is finished'
> Or 'the future is before us'.

The continual development of identity through a process of necessary incompleteness is one aspect of the journey; the other, not less essential, is that in terms of time the traveller cannot hope 'to escape from the past' into 'different lives, or into any future'. In the last analysis the only possible, or *real* destination of those who 'fare forward' is the present. Awakening into true *consciousness* implies, in fact, liberation from any idea that the past is finished and done with or that the future lies simply 'before us'. The point of the voyage is to be seen, if at all, when we are able to hear the 'voice descanting (though not to the ear,/The murmuring shell of time, and not in any language)': the 'voice' which is made accessible to the traveller in a condition in which 'time is withdrawn' and in which past and future can be contemplated in a truly conscious state, 'with an equal mind'. The journey, in effect, is that which bears each individual human being to the end of *his* time in death, and our temporal actions acquire their true meaning when they can be seen and valued in the light of a death accepted as at once inevitable and redeeming.

Like so many other aspects of his sequence, Eliot's treatment of time can be illuminated by reference to that of previous poets. The case of Shakespeare offers interesting parallels. His poems and plays were written at a moment when the medieval and Christian conception of the temporal process as having a *beginning* and directed towards an *end*, a meaningful point of arrival in accordance with a posited divine purpose, was giving way to the sense of a continual, unending flow, without conceivable beginning or end. The resulting dichotomy is a main theme of many of the plays. Hotspur, slain by Prince Hal at the end of *Henry IV, Part I*, asserts with his dying breath that 'Time . . . must have a stop';[89] but the end of his life, dedicated to traditional and rhetorical conceptions of 'honour', is seen as becoming 'food for worms' (the conclusion is put into his mouth by his more dispassionate rival) and it is not clear that personal aspirations are in any way relevant to the onward march of an unending temporal sequence.

Much the same could be said of many of the *Sonnets*:

> Like as the waves make towards the pebbled shore,
> So do our minutes hasten to their end.[90]

True, but the 'end' itself is seen, in the conclusion to the same sonnet, as indifferent, if not hostile, to all personal aspirations. 'Time', the poet goes on to say,

doth transfix the flourish set on youth,
And delves the parallels in beauty's brow,
Feeds on the rarities of nature's truth,
And nothing stands but for his scythe to mow.

In the face of this inexorable reality the poet can only assert his aspiration towards love and value in terms of hope, arriving at a conclusion that is only rhetorically convincing:

And yet to times in *hope* my verse shall stand,
Praising thy worth, despite his cruel hand.[91]

Belief in the worth of the object or person celebrated is essential if poetry is to be convincingly written or life to be convincingly lived; but to affirm that this is *necessary* is not to establish it as *true*, and, as always at these moments, the Sonnet ends on a note of rhetorical assertion from which the sense of *real*, as distinct from *affirmed* conviction, is absent.

In his great tragedies Shakespeare treated the theme with greater subtlety and wider implications. *Macbeth*, perhaps in some sense the most 'metaphysical' of the plays, is possibly the best example. *Macbeth* is the tragedy of a man who is led, against the warnings of his conscience, to do violence to his own nature by seeking to lay hold of time and to force it in accordance with his desires. His first thought on hearing the ambiguous revelation of the Witches is to allow events to take their course in accordance with the natural pattern: 'If chance will have me king, why, chance may crown me,/ Without my stir.'[92] The reaction is, as far as it goes, natural and prudent. The point is that it does not go far enough, that choice is in fact imposed upon a man as a necessity of his nature. As it happens, some of Macbeth's deepest instincts are pressing against it, and the influence of those around him on his weak and indecisive moral will drives him in the opposite direction. Lady Macbeth stresses for her husband the need to deceive, to accept a split between the appearance he presents to the world and the inner reality. She conveys this split in terms of the temporal process: 'To beguile the time,/Look like the time:'[93] the 'time', the circumstance of a life lived in the normal flow of succession which the future murderer is enjoined to seize, to subject to his own ends.

Each man, the play would seem to say, lives in his own appropriate and natural time, and to accept this reality is a law of life;

whereas to attempt to *seize* time, doing violence to its natural course and seeking to force it in accordance with the obscure drives of a consuming ambition, is finally to *kill* it, to make life itself meaningless. And so, at the turning-point of his tragedy, Macbeth makes the discovery that, having chosen against his nature as a time-conditioned creature, he is no longer *free* to choose, that choice itself has become empty in his regard:

> I am in blood
> Stepped in so far, that, should I wade no more,
> Returning were as tedious as go o'er.[94]

'Tedious' is the key word here. Macbeth's determination to wrest the temporal process, to force time to his own unnatural ends, has made his obligation to choose meaningless. At the last, this conviction of emptiness makes itself felt through his sense of a subjection to the temporal process itself, seen now as empty and devoid of sense:

> To-morrow, and to-morrow, and to-morrow . . .
> a tale
> Told by an idiot, full of sound and fury,
> Signifying *nothing*:[95]

a procession of events in the face of which he is conscious only of a decline into senseless old age and irreparable loss.

These considerations give a measure of perspective to Eliot's own exploration of the time theme, which has now reached a stage of resolution. As always, his attitude to the temporal process is seen to rest on the attempt to balance the two terms of what seems to present itself as an inescapable dilemma. Time, it has been asserted at an earlier stage, is at once the foundation of our experience and, so it would seem, its enemy; it is at the same time 'destroyer'and 'preserver',[96] the solvent of our past experience and the element which—like the river with its burden of accumulated *débris*—preserves that experience, carries it along with itself into the present. Without time, life as we know it would be inconceivable; with it, our intuitions of a state of 'consciousness' not subject to destruction are constantly threatened by extinction. The key to the possible reconciliation of these contradictions would seem to lie in a recognition of the simultaneity implied by our experience when sufficiently explored. The true value of our actions only begins to emerge when we are able to abstract ourselves from the time in which they were realized; and the sum of our past experiences, always concentrated on the reality of the 'present', only assumes its complete meaning at the moment in which the pattern, which in time is being constantly renewed, is complete, the moment, in other words, of each individual, present death:

> Here between the hither and the farther shore
> While time is withdrawn, consider the future
> And the past with an equal mind.
> At the moment which is not of action or inaction
> You can receive this: 'on whatever sphere of being
> The mind of a man may be intent
> At the time of death'—that is the one action
> (And the time of death is every moment)
> Which shall fructify in the lives of others:
> And do not think of the fruit of action.
> Fare forward.

In this way, considered in the light of the thoughts expressed by Krishna and refashioned (not necessarily in the same way) by the poet, the traditional idea of 'the good death' acquires a new meaning. On the one hand, the pattern of human lives in time is always incomplete, always subject to the impact of new experiences in so far as we accept life's injunction to 'fare forward'. Under this aspect, it can only be called complete at the moment in which life ends and time ceases to be relevant. On the other hand, since time itself is now understood to be only a partial reality (for, as we tentatively proposed at the outset and as we have now found reason to believe, 'Time present and time past/Are both perhaps present in time future'), the moment of 'death' cannot be considered as an isolated terminal point, but covers in a very real sense the whole course of each individual existence: 'The time of death is every moment'.

Every moment, in other words, in our lives carries implicitly contained within itself the sense of an *end*, and is accordingly a kind of death; but every moment, we can now see, also represents a possible *beginning*. As the motto quoted in reversal at the opening of *East Coker* and re-ordered at the end of the first section there has it: 'In my end is my beginning'. Krishna's meditation on the significance of human action in time is now seen to have a bearing on this. It is the quality of our actions at each moment that determines the quality of our lives and, in so doing, shall be seen to bear fruit, 'to fructify in the lives of others'. This has little to do with tangible, observable results in the temporal sequence of things, since such consequences are bound up with and limited by time, like the 'fruit, periodicals, and business letters' which the traveller takes with him to provide distraction on his journey, to offer him a means of escape from the pressing awareness of empty temporal sequence: 'Not fare well,/But fare forward, voyagers.' To consider dispassionately the consequences of any choice we may have made —particularly in relation to a matter of more than personal importance—is to be aware that, when we made the choice, its ultimate results were largely beyond any possible foreseeing on our part. To choose is to insert one's own small decision into a field which infinitely surpasses our grasp or understanding of it.[97] We may anticipate, at best, the immediate result of the decision we have made; but the further we move from that result the more evidently we enter a reality which may well be contrary to our wishes and which is certainly beyond our control.[98] To say this is not to conclude that it is *unnecessary* to choose. Our choice has been made, and—by being made—has become incorporated into the order of reality to which it belongs. It has made its contribution, uniquely and irrepeatably, to a pattern which would not have been the same without it, and, in so far as our motives were good, it has contributed in a positive way to that pattern and is to that extent justified.

The point of contact between the injunction to 'Fare forward' and the advice offered to those facing old age in *East Coker*—'Old men ought to be explorers . . . We must be still and still moving'[99] —is sufficiently apparent. Now, however, in the light of the broadening theme of the sequence, we can see this less as a piece of personal counsel than as a universal law, or condition, of life. 'Fare forward', on this level, means something essentially distinct from a mere journey in time, though time was the starting-point and the reality of such a journey is implied by the very condition of human existence. It means increasingly detachment from any notion which regards the present self as a final reality, points to the exploration of what *East Coker* called 'another intensity',[100] another and more inclusive order of consciousness. This, if anything, *is* reality. These reflections lead the poet to understand something of

Krishna's meaning in relation to his own experience, and so to a mood of acceptance tempered with a certain optimism. The end of the journey of life has become the key to its beginning, and experience is seen at the last as an invitation to confidence. Once again: 'Not farewell,/But fare forward, voyagers'.

IV

The fourth section of *The Dry Salvages* once again takes the form of a short lyrical interlude. Less 'poetical' than the corresponding passage in *Burnt Norton* and less 'ingenious' than that of *East Coker* it answers to the spirit of the poem to which it belongs, and takes up in concentrated form several of the more significant themes there developed.

The poem is, in the first place, a prayer for all travellers, and as such it is appropriate in relation to what have been some of the main concerns of this quartet. It is addressed to the 'Lady' whose shrine is situated on the 'promontory': the same headland, we may think, from which was heard in the first section (and continued as an undertone in the *sestina* of the second section) the 'wailing warning' of destruction and mortality. The 'fishermen' of the *sestina*, engaged in the unending task of 'bailing', of maintaining the tenacious instinct to live under apparently hopeless conditions, reappear in the reference to those 'whose business has to do with fish', as do the 'worried anxious women' who, in the first section, lay awake between 'midnight and dawn', trying to 'piece together the past and the future', and who are now evoked as having seen 'their sons or husbands/Setting forth, and not returning,' helplessly subjected to the more dramatic and catastrophic vicissitudes of war.

For all these, and indeed for all travellers on the sea, the 'Lady' is asked to intercede:

> Also pray for those who were in ships, and
> Ended their voyage on the sand, in the sea's lips
> Or in the dark throat which will not reject them
> Or wherever cannot reach them the sound of the sea
>   bell's
> Perpetual angelus.

The beautiful internal rhythms of the passage—the echo of 'ships' before the open ending of the first line and 'lips' at the close of the second, the cunning inversion of the closing lines leading up to the 'Perpetual angelus', which itself takes up the final 'clang' of the bell at the end of the superbly constructed first 'movement' — are a sign that here at least the poet is fully in control, engaged in drawing his material triumphantly together. The 'Lady' is also, in Dante's phrase from St. Bernard's prayer in the last Canto of the *Paradiso*, 'Figlia del tuo figlio',[101] 'daughter of thy son'. As such, she is the recipient of the angelic salutation which conveyed 'the one, barely prayable Annunciation' of the *sestina*; and as such, she is asked to offer her prayer for those who have been unable to receive the message of the sea bell, in which the menace of death — so powerful at the end of the opening section — is transformed into an intimation, an 'Annunciation', of perpetual rebirth.

V

At this stage, it may be useful to undertake a brief summary to establish the point now reached in the exploration of experience, individual and human, with which the series of *Quartets* has been concerned. We began, in *Burnt Norton*, with a consideration of the possible implications of the fleeting moment of insight which seemed to be offered, 'really' or imaginatively, in the rose-garden. This was felt to have a positive 'meaning' which, however, faded away, because 'human kind', living in time and conditioned by this fact, 'cannot bear very much reality'. Reflection, however, developed through the sequence, has now brought the poet to the point in which he is able to posit the relevance of what he calls 'Incarnation', in which time and the timeless may be said to meet in true significance. Approach to this *reality* — as it is now in the process of becoming — involves an increase in *consciousness*, implies liberation from 'time before and time after', 'the waste sad time' considered as mere sequence. In *The Dry Salvages* this need has been considered in relation to the injunction of Krishna to Arjuna, in which the god affirms that true consciousness is achieved through liberation from temporal sequence. We need to *choose*, either to perform action or to abstain from it, but in either event to make our choice in full and explicit awareness of what we are doing.

In either case, whether we choose to act or to abstain — and these alternatives can be seen as corresponding to the Way Up and the

Way Down of the first quartet—we are not to shun the need to choose, which life itself imposes; but whatever choice we make needs to be made in freedom from the pressure of 'time before and time after'. *Action* and not *the fruit of action* is to be our proper concern; for right action will produce good fruits (though not necessarily, or even often, those we foresee) in its own right, not because of our immediate and often short-sighted concern with the results in time of what we have chosen to do. It is no doubt because he felt the need of a corrective for that excessive concern with results, the determination to impose the immediate interests of the self brutally and short-sightedly, which has been perhaps the besetting sin of our Western culture, that Eliot chose at a crucial point in his argument to call in a voice from the East to redress the balance.

The final section of this quartet aims, accordingly, at pulling together the various intuitions previously explored, from *Burnt Norton* onwards, into a more inclusive statement. This will not be a conclusion—there is still another poem to come—and it may even involve, as a necessary stage, a partial sacrifice of poetic intensity;[102] but it will represent an indispensable step in the advance towards such a conclusion. The step will be taken in the light of the central reality, as it is now to be affirmed, of Incarnation as a bringing together into unity of time and the extra-temporal, flesh and spirit, the moment of intense and living intuition and the concept that may serve to give it meaning. The latter concept, moreover, is now in the process of being expanded to include historical and 'racial' experience as well as that of the individual.

First, however, we are reminded, in a passage which may seem excessively didactic, of the false or misleading ways in which men, enmeshed in time, seek to find significance in the temporal process itself: in other words, to forestall, and by so doing, to 'control' the future. These attempts, which recall Madam Sosostris' manipulation of the cards in *The Waste Land*, are involved in 'time before and time after'. They are therefore without relation to the achievement of *consciousness* which, although initiated in time, involves a liberation from mere sequence.

This is what Krishna meant when he said that action, based on choice, was necessary, but that both choice and action should be undertaken in detachment, without thought of the immediate 'fruits of action'. Such attempts habitually involve an escape into the 'pre-conscious', whereas it is an *increase* in consciousness at which we now aim. The parallel already drawn with Macbeth's tragic career is especially significant in this connection. In the long run these are evasions, 'pastimes and drugs' undertaken to disguise from ourselves what has become the intolerable nature of a reality seen as mere meaningless sequence: 'Men's curiosity searches past and future/And clings to that dimension.' What we have now found is that it is precisely this clinging which is, in a fundamental sense, a denial of the real conditions of living.

This preoccupation is counterbalanced by the poet in a passage of splendid eloquence, which more than compensates for anything arid or merely prosaic in what has gone before. He asserts that the true human concern is a preoccupation with the temporal process which merges, by a natural development, into the kind of vision associated with the saint:

> to apprehend
> The point of intersection of the timeless
> With time, is an occupation for the saint—
> No occupation either, but something given
> And taken, in a lifetime's death in love,
> Ardour and selflessness and self-surrender.
> For most of us, there is only the unattended
> Moment, the moment in and out of time,
> The distraction fit, lost in a shaft of sunlight,
> The wild thyme unseen, or the winter lightning
> Or the waterfall, or music heard so deeply
> That it is not heard at all, but you are the music
> While the music lasts. These are only hints and guesses,
> Hints followed by guesses; and the rest
> Is prayer, observance, discipline, thought and action.
> The hint half guessed, the gift half understood, is
> Incarnation.

The vision, if it is to be attained at all, is connected with an act of acceptance: an act which involves risk, adventure—and here we may recall the surrender which Mr. Prufrock failed to make in Eliot's first important poem—an affirmation of faith in life, a *giving* in *love*, through which alone time can be said to be conquered.

It is the 'saint', indeed, who is distinguished by his ability to *maintain* this level of awareness, making it the consistent centre of his life. Because he has *given* more, he has received a correspond-ingly greater measure of insight into being, into what it means to be really, fully *alive*. The saint, however, is an extreme case at the positive end of the human scale. For the rest of men—for 'most of us', as the poem now has it—there is only the fugitive glimpse of a revelation, 'the moment in and out of time', exemplified in the experience in the rose-garden and still more tenuously glimpsed in the evocation of such things as the 'wild thyme' and the 'winter lightning' of the waterfall: glimpses we remember, already intro-duced in *East Coker*[103] and seen there not as 'lost', simply carried away by time, but as 'requiring', pointing to the experience of reality through the 'agony' of 'death' and 'birth'.

These are now seen, more clearly, as 'hints and guesses', or 'hints' followed by the process of reflection—'guesses'—with which the whole sequence has been concerned. The meaning of these moments of intuition lies, for 'most of us', in the relation of these experiences to daily living. The exploration of them in the process of artistic creation represents for the majority of human beings immersed in and conditioned by the temporal process, the limit of spiritual possibility. The rest is 'prayer, observance, discipline', leading to a glimpse of the reality which is here called, explicitly, Incarnation—'the hint half guessed, the gift half understood'—the point of union in which time and eternity coincide.

The poem ends, in the usual passage of shorter lines, with a statement of reconciliation in the light of this central concept of Incarnation, 'The point of intersection of the timeless/With time.' The 'union' that has seemed to be 'impossible' is there achieved, past and future 'conquered', in terms of individual living finally 'reconciled'. 'Action', just because it is not seen under the aspect of mere sequence in time, becomes meaningful, is found to emanate from a 'source'. 'Right action is freedom/From past and future also': the 'dance'—to return yet again to *Burnt Norton*, in a con-cept now enriched in relation to the experience developed through the sequence—is given meaning, form, in connection with the 'still point'.

In the final passage, the end of human life is seen as the achieve-ment of 'freedom' from the enslavement of 'past and future'. 'Most of us', though we have had experiences which dimly indicate this, are unable to realize this freedom 'here', caught up as we are in the deception of a process wrongly regarded as final. Under this aspect,

our normal lives of day to day become a continual new beginning —
a 'trying' — following upon an equally continual 'defeat'; at this
point, we are reminded of the unending efforts of the fishermen in
the *sestina*.[104] In the light of what we are now in the process of dis-
covering we can be 'content' with this present condition, accepting
our death — our 'temporal reversion' — as a part of the process which
we can now see (remembering also the dancers of *East Coker*) in
relation to the 'yew-tree', the graveyard symbol of immortality,
itself connected with the creative rhythms of nature, 'the life of
significant soil'.

[5]
Little Gidding

After what may have seemed a partial failure of imaginative power in *The Dry Salvages*, the final quartet — *Little Gidding* — finds the poet restored to the fullness of his creative energy. The poem, indeed, can be read as the fitting summing-up of the efforts of a life-time, Eliot's last important achievement as a poet. Logically enough, it is the most explicit in theological terms of the entire series. Though still in no sense what Eliot would have called a 'devotional' poem, the time has evidently come for the concepts worked out in the earlier quartets to serve as focal points for the significant organization of experience, to show what they can do in the way of generating poetic life, illuminating both one man's experience and its relationship to that of the humanity of which he forms a part. The poet is still not concerned to ask his readers to share his own beliefs, or even to argue in any explicit sense that they are 'true'. The question of 'truth', indeed, is not raised, may even — from the standpoint assumed in these quartets — be irrelevant or incomprehensible. All that is required of the reader is that he should be willing to 'suspend' such disbelief as he may feel for the purposes of responding to the poem as poetry.[105] The traditional ideas which it uses are to be justified in so far — and only in so far — as they are felt to 'work' in terms of the poetry, in as much as they allow the unprejudiced reader to feel that the initially random emotional material offered by life is being meaningfully pulled together into a pattern; and that the result — always in relation to the actual poetic experience — is a clarification of what may have seemed initially confusing, frustrating, or incoherent. In other words, the poetry of the *Quartets* requires to be read as what it is: as poetry, not as a substitute for 'philosophy' or theology. It offers what poetry has distinctively to offer, and both its achievement and its limitation are those inherent in the process of poetic creation.

Once again the starting point of the poem is an evocation of place by which the emotion is focused, tied down — as the nature of poetry would seem to require — to one man's localized experience. What we are now given, however, is something different from the memories, in the previous poems, of significant moments in the poet's own past, real or imagined: different from the country house and the deserted rose-garden of *Burnt Norton*, the silent village of *East Coker*, or even the great river of *The Dry Salvages*, in their successively expanding logical order. The place has become an object of pilgrimage, a symbol of the spiritual reality which may serve to relate the poet's own convictions, as we have seen them taking shape through the series, to the particular spot and the definite tradition in which he feels that they may most appropriately flourish. The spot is Little Gidding, the site of an Anglican religious community founded by Nicholas Farrar in 1625, broken up in 1647 as a result of Cromwell's victory in the English Civil War, ruined by fire and—as far as the chapel was concerned—rebuilt in the nineteenth century. These successive vicissitudes are creative as well as destructive; they indicate both the tenacious life of the spirit and the strength of the forces which periodically act to undo its manifestations in time. By virtue of these vicissitudes the remote, forgotten village serves in its unmemorable, unspectacular present as a focal point, an 'incarnation' (as we have now learnt to call it) in time and place of the kind towards which the entire series has been pointing and which it is now, in its final stage, ready to affirm. We must add, however, that the affirmation is made, not in a spirit of challenge to values or ideas more commonly accepted, but simply as a presence, a point of concentration, in relation to which the vital forces developed through the sequence may fall naturally and unobtrusively into place, be found to justify themselves in terms of the emotional life they are able to generate.

I

Fire emerges from the beginning as the master element of the new poem, as air had been in *Burnt Norton*, earth in *East Coker*, and water in *The Dry Salvages*. The assertion of the idea of Incarnation as a unifying concept at the end of the previous quartet leads logically to an anticipation of 'the baptism of the Holy Ghost with fire'[106] which is Whitsun or Pentecost. The symbol assumes various forms, distinct but interwoven, in the course of the poem, and their interrelationship constitutes indeed a large part of its substance. We are made aware in succession of fire as leading to the destruction of the old life, with both its comforts and its illusions; of fire as purifying, as illuminating, and—finally and inclusive of all these other aspects—as symbol of the Divine Love in relation to which human attachments become freed from the limitations of 'desire', to be seen at last in their true and timeless context.

The symbol which assumes these successive forms is, of course, more explicitly Christian, overtly theological, than any so far used by the poet, and this is logical in as much as he has come to see that the resolution of his problem requires an incorporation into the tradition which represents his own human situation in time. Except in such a context, as he now understands, a man cannot exist in any complete sense as a fully realized human being. To advance the symbol in this way and at this stage is not, of course, to posit its uniquely exclusive validity. Whatever Eliot the Christian believer may have been disposed to hold in this connection, Eliot the poet is careful to avoid any such finality of assertion. There are other 'incarnations', no doubt equally valid for those who experience them, and it is no part of a poet's function to denigrate them or to assert the superiority of his own; but this is the one which has best corresponded to his position in place and time, and upon which he can most fruitfully build. Once again we must stress that what we are about to read is not in any sense a work of Christian 'devotion', even in the meaning in which a poem by, say, George Herbert might be so called (and the spirit of Herbert is indeed present in the poem), but an effort to relate a fully contemporary experience to certain concepts of a theological nature, to see if, and if so in what sense and to what degree, they can finally be said to 'fit'. If it now seems possible, as a result of the preceding development, that the concepts can give 'meaning' to the experience, it remains true that only the experience can give life to the concepts, can save them from remaining mere empty abstractions.

To give body to his new intuition of love expanding beyond the limitations of desire, the poet evokes in his opening lines a 'season': a season, however, 'not in time's covenant', outside what he calls 'the scheme of generation'. The passage in which this is conveyed is one of Eliot's most successful and sustained pieces of writing:

> Midwinter spring is its own season
> Sempiternal though sodden towards sundown,
> Suspended in time, between pole and tropic.
> When the short day is brightest, with frost and fire,

The brief sun flames the ice, on pond and ditches,
In windless cold that is the heart's heat,
Reflecting in a watery mirror
A glare that is blindness in the early afternoon.
And glow more intense than blaze of branch, or brazier,
Stirs the dumb spirit: no wind, but pentecostal fire
In the dark time of the year. Between melting and
    freezing
The soul's sap quivers. There is no earth smell
Or smell of living thing. This is the spring time
But not in time's covenant. Now the hedgerow
Is blended for an hour with transitory blossom
Of snow, a bloom more sudden
Than that of summer, neither budding nor fading,
Nor in the scheme of generation.
Where is the summer, the unimaginable
Zero summer?

The poet's aim is to create, through image and rhythm, the sense of a 'season' outside the normal order of succession, uniting apparent opposites in a reflection of what has now become, beyond the scheme of nature, the embodiment of a new condition of the spirit. This is the unity of 'midwinter spring', creating light without heat, reconciling opposite sensations in a natural reflection of the spiritual order which looks forward to the still remote, 'unimaginable zero summer' of fulfilled, timeless consummation.

It is an order at once 'sempiternal' and involved in the life of nature. 'Suspended in time', to which its constituent elements belong, it yet partakes of the timeless; steeped in the darkness of winter, from which it is in the process of emerging, it none the less radiates the 'brightness' and 'light' of a season of rebirth which is finally—though *only* finally, at the end of a process which, in time, can only be dimly intuited—outside the natural order from which its elements derive. 'Frost' and 'fire', 'cold' and 'heat', a 'glare' and 'blindness'—all, in themselves, natural, even if contrasted manifestations—are brought together into a new, a 'supernatural' relationship, and the result is a 'fire' more intense than any natural 'blaze' of 'branch, or brazier': the reference here is, surely, to the relighting of fires outside the churches in the early morning which follows the darkness of Good Friday in the traditional Holy Week ceremonies.[107] The fire kindled in this way is one which introduces a new order of life, which 'stirs the dumb spirit', 'pentecostal' in 'the dark time of the year'.

In accordance with the sense of this unique, subjective 'season', the 'soul's sap quivers', poised between 'melting' and 'freezing' in a life that is now issuing into the order of the spirit, untouched by 'earth smell/Or smell of living thing.' It is not, of course, that 'earth smell' — 'smell' of the kind associated with the activities of the dancers in *East Coker*[108] — is to be repudiated as disgusting or repugnant; it is simply that we are now concerned with another order of reality, neither altogether separate from nor entirely limited by it. This is life, but life in the order of the spirit, 'not in time's covenant': a sensation of 'spring time' and rebirth, indeed, such as we experience commonly in our own lives, but no longer subject to 'time before and time after', or to the normal sequence of the seasons. The memory of that sequence remains, is evoked once more through the bloom of the hedgerow, a reminder of the passing beauty of the natural order as revealed in 'transitory blossom': *real*, even obsessively recreated in the beauty of the image, but seen now in a relationship, at once paradoxical and revealing, to 'winter snow', transferred into a reality outside 'the scheme of generation'. The opposites are blended in the anticipation of a perfect harmony which — concerned as it still is with spring and winter, the temporal succession of the seasons — is no more than a premonition of what the state of full consciousness will be, in perfect union, at the zenith, the 'zero summer': a condition still 'unimaginable', but now dimly conceivable as a possible aspiration, by those who continue to feel themselves enmeshed in 'before and after'.

But, concerned though we now are with an experience 'suspended in time', pointing beyond the natural order, we are still in a definite place, taking a definite path which we have chosen with a definite end in view. We are, in fact, in England and on the road to Little Gidding, which we are approaching in the natural, 'voluptuary sweetness' of 'may time'. This is where the spirit has manifested itself, become 'incarnate' in time and place, for an English-speaking Christian. Indeed, the association with George Herbert is of particular significance for a poet who feels himself engaged, as he approaches the end of his career, in the effort to understand and define his relationship to the literary tradition to which he belongs. The point of arrival is the same for all those who, with varying

degrees of understanding, have at one time or another embarked
upon this journey of the spirit: for the defeated Charles I—the
'broken King'—who after his decisive reversal at Naseby in 1647 is
said to have prayed at the chapel, as for the modern tourist who is
not aware of the true object of his pilgrimage. In either event Little
Gidding, seen as a tangible place approached

> when you leave the rough road
> And turn behind the pig-sty to the dull façade
> And the tombstone,

presents itself as only a 'shell', the 'husk' of a 'meaning' which once
presented itself as vital and operative in a way no longer imme-
diately apparent. The true purpose of the journey only breaks out
from beneath the 'shell' when the purpose originally 'figured' by
the pilgrim in his coming has been transformed in relation to his
sense of an end which leaves it 'altered in fulfilment'. The relation
of this to the concept, developed in *The Dry Salvages*, of life as a
journey constantly changing and developing in time,[109] is by now
becoming clarified. Only through an act of faith, a personal com-
mitment to what is conceived, beneath its desolate appearance, as a
continuing source of life outside and beyond the order of time, can
the 'place' be seen in its true, timeless significance.

This, in fact, responds to what has been emerging through the
whole series of poems as a necessary condition, inexorable but
potentially vivifying, of existence: a law foreshadowed in the re-
flections on the deceptive nature of 'autumnal serenity' in *East
Coker*,[110] and confirmed in *The Dry Salvages* where the poet told
us that 'approach to the meaning restores the experience/In a dif-
ferent form.'[111] At this particular moment the path to the 'mean-
ing' takes the pilgrim behind and past a 'tombstone', the importance
of which in relation to the complete pattern is unobtrusively
emphasized by a break in the rhythm. The 'place', in other words,
needs to be seen, beyond its immediate temporal situation, as in a
real sense 'the world's end'. There may perhaps be other possible
ways, not less valid, one perhaps for each individual being who
bears with him on his life's journey his own particular cargo of
unique experience; but, for the purpose of the poet engaged in the
writing of his poem, this is the *end* of the purely temporal, just as
death was the end for so many in the war years during which the
poem was written:

There are other places
Which also are the world's end, some at the sea jaws,
Or over a dark lake, in a desert or a city.

For each and every man there is a 'place', which he can anticipate
but not avoid, where he is called upon to contemplate the fact of
death in relation to life as he has lived it. All such 'places' are con-
ceivably valid, none can properly be called insignificant; but this
particular spot, in England and in relation to the experience of a
twentieth-century poet concerned with his relationship to his own
past, personal and ancestral, is the 'nearest', the most immediate
place in which an intuition of the spiritual, the extra-temporal
order, can be rendered 'incarnate' in place and time.

The 'way' which has been pursued, under a variety of possible
approaches, throughout the sequence, and which has insistently
proved to point 'beyond the end you figured', to be 'altered' in the
process of 'fulfilment', now approaches a point of arrival. The con-
dition of reaching it is that already established in the preceding
poems. It demands detachment from 'sense and notion', con-
sidered as self-sufficient ends, and from any manifestation of cur-
rent curiosity, mere historical research, or journalism. The essence
of the experience is submission leading to 'prayer' in a place where
prayer has in the past seemed to prove valid. Prayer, in turn, is
conceived as leading to contemplation, an experience beyond words
or 'the sound of the voice praying'; an experience which represents
the taking up, in a more fully *conscious* spirit, of the kind of fugitive
intimation tenuously glimpsed in the initial experience in the rose-
garden. 'Prayer', in fact, is the reality which the moment of illu-
mination in the garden is seen to posit when it is advanced beyond
the stage of intuition to that of fully 'conscious' reality.

To achieve contemplation, however, is not to weaken, but rather
to intensify, to render more *real*, the bond by which we are united
to our fellow-men, past and present. Above all, perhaps, it means
at this point communion with the dead, who still live in us and
with whom we can share experience of the contemplative reality—
the reality outside time, by relation to which our experience in time
is rendered valid—which formerly inspired the community of
Little Gidding.

The relationship which thus links us to the dead turns out to be,
paradoxically, a living one of unity in the Pentecostal 'fire', for 'the

communication/Of the dead is tongued with fire beyond the language of the living.' The 'intersection' of the 'timeless moment' with time (which is, as we saw in the previous poem, 'Incarnation', the assumption by the timeless reality of physical and temporal form) is revealed at a determined and tangible point: the point, for this poet and at this time, is Little Gidding. It is here, 'in England' and, at the same time, 'nowhere', outside the temporal process. The purpose of recreating the place is seen to lie outside time, to be realized in *prayer* by which we may aspire to touch upon a true *consciousness* of what we are. Prayer, conceived in this way, unites us in a living relationship with the *tradition* which has formed our thoughts and feelings; it makes us one with the dead who live again in what is seen to be the Incarnation, the point—and we remember 'the still point' of *Burnt Norton*—at which the 'timeless moment', 'intersecting' with time in a relationship to which it brings meaning becomes the logical crown of the process of human and spiritual living.

II

The 'lyrical' passage which once again, following the usual pattern of the quartets, opens the second 'movement' is beautifully precise in its adaptation of rhythm to the requirements of meaning. Its background, like that of the entire section, is that of the apparent collapse of a civilization, the destruction and desolation of war. There is also, of course, a more immediate reference to the ruin of the chapel in Little Gidding, and to the destruction and abandonment of the values and beliefs for which it once stood. That was the result of civil war and there is a sense, Eliot would seem to suggest, in which our own greater catastrophes amount to the pursuit of self-destruction. In its development the passage picks up in succession the elements—air, water, earth, and fire—which have been present throughout the sequence, and weaves them into a pattern of doom:

> Ash on an old man's sleeve
> Is all the ash the burnt roses leave.
> Dust in the air suspended
> Marks the place where a story ended,
> Dust inbreathed was a house—

The wall, the wainscot and the mouse.
The death of hope and despair,
This is the death of air.

It is worth remarking that the principal images used in these lines
reflect others which have already appeared in earlier parts of the
sequence. The roses of *Burnt Norton*, which were there associated
with the dust disturbed on a bowl,[112] have now become 'ashes on
an old man's sleeve': 'houses' which were, in *East Coker*,[113] incor-
porated into the unchanging rhythm of birth and death, crumble
into dust, and the 'mouse' behind the 'wainscot' and the 'wall'
recalls the one that shook 'the tattered arras' in the earlier poem.

In the second stanza, similarly, 'water' and 'land' are alike 'dead',
and the 'soil' (again of *East Coker*) has become 'parched', 'evis-
cerate', drained of life. We seem to be once again in the Waste
Land. The final effect is one of ruin, in which the desolation pro-
duced by man's unending wars answers to his abandonment of the
'foundations' upon which the previous achievements of his civiliza-
tion have rested:

Water and fire succeed
The town, the pasture and the weed.
Water and fire deride
The sacrifice that we denied.
Water and fire shall rot
The marred foundations we forgot,
Of sanctuary and choir.
This is the death of water and fire.

The links which unite nature and man have fallen apart, and their
death 'derides' our forgetfulness of the past—the 'marred founda-
tions' of our way of living—as formerly commemorated in the
chapel and now ruined. This is the true death, brought by the
action of 'water and fire' upon a society which has turned its back
upon its basic traditions—or found, perhaps, that these traditions
have betrayed it, can no longer represent for it a source of life; and
which, after witnessing 'the death of earth', the collapse of its fer-
tility under the action of 'flood and drouth', is now in the process
of being finally consumed by fire.

The main body of the 'movement' which follows this introduc-
tion is also one of the most important passages of the sequence.

Eliot has told us that it involved an elaborate effort to recreate, in terms of the special requirements of the English language, Dante's *terza rima*.[114] He has also told us that he found it one of the most difficult passages to write in all his experience as a poet. Once again, as is so often the case with Eliot, the successful overcoming of a technical challenge becomes the point of departure for an important personal expression. The reference to Dante is not an accident, for the poet is engaged in an effort to revive and evaluate his own experience, in terms of concepts in which the example of the Italian poet plays a decisive part. The setting of this ghostly episode is London, at dawn and at the end of an air-raid. The city is seen under the likeness of hell (the two worlds, the poet asserts at one point in a phrase that might have come from *The Waste Land*, have become 'much like each other'): the point in hell, more precisely, at which Dante was astonished to meet his former tutor, Brunetto Latini.[115] What Eliot's *persona* meets, however, in his guise as an air-raid warden engaged on his dawn round, is no single or identifiable figure, but 'a familiar compound ghost', made up in the first instance of the dead poets who have contributed in various ways to his own work: Dante, Shakespeare, Mallarmé, Yeats, and—no doubt—others less easily identifiable. It is essential to understand, however, if we are to respond to the full scope of the poet's intention, that we are here dealing with an intimate self-confrontation. What the poet meets in his great predecessors is, in a very real sense, nothing other than *himself*: 'I was still the same,/Knowing myself, yet being someone other.' The great writers who are remembered in the course of the passage are there in so far as they have been incorporated into his own work, and become accordingly a part of himself. What we are witnessing here is the recreation of an effort at self-assessment, an attempt both to look back upon and to evaluate the results of a life-time dedicated to the writing of poetry, and to define his present situation as an individual and as a member of the human race.

The time, then, is dawn at the end of a London air-raid, the 'uncertain hour before the morning' after the nightly ending of 'interminable night'. The 'dark dove' is the enemy raider, a kind of parody—also bringing its own kind of fire—of the symbol of the Holy Spirit, and the 'dead leaves' are the shrapnel of the guns which rattle 'like tin' on the asphalted pavements of the deserted city streets as the poet turned air-raid warden makes his rounds and as the smoke of the fires of destruction rises 'between three districts'. It is at this point, poised between night and morning, destruction and relief, that he meets the 'familiar compound ghost' who recalls the 'brown baked features' of the Brunetto Latini met by Dante in the course of his journey through Hell. The 'ghost', as we have already said, is at the same time one, and many. It is in fact composed of all the dead poets whose work has contributed to Eliot's own, figures felt to be 'intimate' presences in his own thought and expression, and yet—because they have been translated, re-created in terms of his own sensibility—finally 'unidentifiable'.

Confronted in this way the poet 'assumes a double part'—that of the dreamer immersed in his dream of the past and that of the waking poet considered in the light of his present situation—and hears the ghostly echo of Dante's greeting to Brunetto: 'What! are *you* here?'[116] The meeting is described, of course, as taking place in what the poet presents as a twentieth-century equivalent of Hell, but the description is modified by the essential awareness of a state of dream; for, even whilst speaking, 'we were not. I was still the same,/Knowing myself, yet being someone other.'[117] The effect is one which deliberately combines intimacy and distance; for, while the poet recognizes himself in the 'ghost'—since the dead poets have become part of himself—they are at the same time separate, capable of being seen with a certain detachment: 'Too strange to each other for misunderstanding'—misunderstanding of the kind which an impossible assertion of identity would imply. The intimacy of the 'meeting' can produce 'concord', can be illuminating, just in so far as it seems to have been situated outside the order of time, to have 'no before and after' and to take place 'nowhere'. Poet and ghost, thus stripped of all accidental qualities (as is appropriate in hell), walk together, as Dante and Brunetto had done —a condemned soul and a man of living flesh—'in a dead patrol'.

The confrontation is made explicit in the imagined dialogue which follows. Eliot is here, in a very important sense, addressing himself to his own most intimate awareness of 'what he has become'. The 'ghost' will not therefore speak to the poet of 'thoughts and theory', because the ideas of the past are no longer—in as much as they are past—to the present point:

> And he: 'I am not eager to rehearse
> My thoughts and theory which you have forgotten.

> These things have served their purpose: let them be.
> So with your own, and pray they be forgiven
> By others, as I pray you to forgive
> Both bad and good. Last season's fruit is eaten
> And the fullfed beast shall kick the empty pail.

The connection with the attitude towards 'past' events developed through the whole course of the sequence—a deliberate renunciation of them in so far as they are 'past', done with, finished—is sufficiently apparent. These things have, at best, 'served their purpose', and need now to be seen, from the standpoint of the life of the present and its continually renewed challenge, as having done so. Now, like all dead, 'past' things—'past', in fact, just in as much as they are dead—they can serve only, in personal terms, as material for forgiveness. Even their nature as either 'bad' or 'good', important as it was at the time when they mattered (because they were then the result of *real*, living acts of choice), have become irrelevant, 'last season's fruit', eaten, vanished beyond recall. Historically speaking, this conclusion can be applied to the issues so passionately fought over during the English Civil War, with which the creative years of Little Gidding and its then living community were so closely concerned; and this is a theme which will be taken up before the end of the poem.

For the moment, however, the primary concern is elsewhere: in fact with the language to the use and perfection of which the poet has dedicated his life. 'Last year's words' express only last year's needs. Those of the present, which point towards the future, 'await another voice', which can only come into being after the past, conceived of as final or as in any way binding upon the present, has been renounced:

> For last year's words belong to last year's language
> And next year's words await another voice.

Whether, and if so to what extent, that voice can be the poet's own, or whether it must wait on the revelation of the future, is very much an open question. If it *is* to be his, it can only be as the result of a ceaseless effort of renovation, the painful but necessary renunciation of the old and acceptance, perhaps equally painful but necessary, of the perpetually new challenge which the living present involves. Perhaps, however, the question is not even valid, in as much as the very posing of it may represent an aspect of that desire to affirm the self and its importance which, as we now know, it is a condition of life to renounce. The advice given by Krishna to Arjuna, as recalled in *The Dry Salvages* — to act without considering 'the fruit of action'[118] — may also be of application here. Meanwhile, since the 'two worlds' — 'heaven' and 'hell' respectively — have become 'very much like each other', the voice from Dante is very pertinent to the living poet's situation.

In all this, the poet is taking up, and inserting into his new, developing context, ideas advanced in earlier parts of the sequence. The past, we have learnt by now, *is* past and, as such, cannot be restored to life. 'Last season's fruit' is indeed eaten, and our past actions and decisions, good and bad alike, cannot be altered. All we can do in respect of them is to ask and extend forgiveness, where that is appropriate, in a spirit of mutual compassion. Beyond that, to live is to accept the challenge of the present — even, and not least, the comfortless and desolate present — whilst looking towards the future; there is a clear connection here with the thoughts on the supposed 'wisdom' of old age already developed in *East Coker*[119] and with Krishna's final injunction in *The Dry Salvages*: 'Not fare well, but fare forward, voyagers'.[120]

In the light of this it is appropriate that the 'compound ghost' should now refer more explicitly to the poet's central concern with speech, his 'civilizing' and social vocation to 'purify the dialect' — and with it the thoughts and feelings which the 'dialect' expresses and to which, in great measure, it gives form — of the 'tribe'. It is here that the dead poets make their presence felt with particular intensity as a living influence on the present. 'To purify the dialect of the tribe' is the translation of a line from the French poet Mallarmé,[121] and in speaking of the poet's vocation to 'urge the mind to aftersight and foresight', we are brought close to the spirit of words spoken to Virgil in Dante's presence by Ulysses in Canto XXVI of the *Inferno*.[122]

This line of thought, indeed, occupied a prominent place in Eliot's conception of the poet's function throughout his life. For him, a large part of the poet's task — his distinctive 'vocation', if we will — lay in the perfection and purification of the resources of expression at the disposal of his society; this 'vocation' the poet exercised through his incorporation into the 'tradition' which he received and which his own work, by the very fact of its existence, modified and enriched. The recognition of the vocation stated in these terms involves, in turn, a detached estimate of the poet's own position, now on the threshold of his own old age. This is the prospect in time with which he, like all men, must come to terms, and it is conveyed with a force and poignancy almost unique in its kind in the *Quartets*:

> Let me disclose the gifts reserved for age
>> To set a crown upon your lifetime's effort.
>> First, the cold friction of expiring sense
> Without enchantment, offering no promise
>> But bitter tastelessness of shadow fruit
>> As body and soul begin to fall asunder.
> Second, the conscious impotence of rage
>> At human folly, and the laceration
>> Of laughter at what ceases to amuse.
> And last, the rending pain of re-enactment
>> Of all that you have done, and been; the shame
>> Of motives late revealed, and the awareness
> Of things ill done and done to others' harm
>> Which once you took for exercise of virtue.
>> Then fools' approval stings, and honour stains.
> From wrong to wrong the exasperated spirit
>> Proceeds, unless restored by that refining fire
>> Where you must move in measure, like a dancer.

These words are given to the imaginary interlocutor, the 'compound ghost' who fulfils in the episode the function of Brunetto Latini; but nowhere in the poem are we more conscious that this is in fact an intimate, even an agonizing self-assessment. The tone is, in the first instance, bleakly tragic, further than ever from the 'autumnal serenity' advocated by the deceiving voices of the earlier passages. This, indeed, is one of the most moving evocations in poetry of the *reality* of old age and what it brings with it. The soul sees itself caught, in 'exasperation' and 'frustration', in a progress 'from wrong to wrong', a chain from which the only issue lies in a spirit finally purgatorial, the spirit in which the Provençal poet Arnaud Daniel in Canto XXVI of the *Purgatorio* accepted the *fire* of Purgatory and was thereby incorporated into the dance, the measure, of love.

It is not to be believed, in any event, that acceptance of this kind

offers an immediate or easy gateway to what we generally call
'happiness'. It is, however, for Eliot the only possible path leading
to personal salvation. The only possible answer to a universal and
inescapable challenge lies in moving into the dimension of purga-
torial fire and accepting the reality of torment, which will not be
the less immediately tormenting for this acquiescence; not only
this, but to do so in the creative spirit of acceptance which Dante's
concluding line in this Canto implies: *Poi s'ascose nel foco che li
affina*: 'And then he hid himself in the fire which purifies him'.[123]
It implies an assumption of *consciousness*, the alternative to which,
in time, is subjection to the process of decay, to bitterness and the
ceaseless torture of memory operating on a world of opportunities
missed and decisions mistakenly taken; whereas to accept purga-
tion through 'fire', recognizing the deficiencies of the past in the
act of moving beyond them, is to assume, in suffering, a position in
the dance of significant reality which is controlled from the 'still
point' posited in *Burnt Norton*. As the section ends, and in contrast
with this intimate revelation, another day breaks on the still 'dis-
figured', untransformed street, and the self-communion in dream
is broken, through the 'all clear' signal, with 'a kind of valediction'.

It is clear that the passage we have been considering represents,
in more senses than one, a decisive stage in the ordering of the
Quartets. The poet is, we have suggested, *confronting* himself, seek-
ing to arrive at some estimate of what his life-time of creative
endeavour has achieved, what it can mean to him and what its
significance can be in relation to the human undertaking—the
'tradition' in which he is incorporated with the writers of the past
—to which he has sought to make his contribution. It may, there-
fore, be an appropriate occasion for us, as readers, to ask ourselves
certain questions. What, we may fairly ask, does all that we have
read in following this series of poems add up to in terms of actual,
definitive achievement? In trying to answer this question we shall
perhaps begin by recognizing something that is evident in the
passage we have just considered: that Eliot's poetry, here as else-
where, operates within certain limitations. He was a poet to whom
inspiration—if that is the appropriate word—did not come easily,
whose moments of achieved vision needed to be supported by hard
and unremitting effort, the 'sheer plod'[124]—to use Hopkins' phrase
—of continuous composition. He was also acutely—perhaps even
prematurely—aware of the oncoming of old age and its constrictive

effects; not every poet would compare himself, at the age of forty, and as Eliot did in *Ash Wednesday*, to an 'aged eagle' which questions the usefulness of continuing to 'stretch its wings'.[125] The problem lies in a sense of the progressive closing and hardening of the channels of imaginative perception that have led the greatest writers to look out with a dispassionate, almost frightening honesty, upon the real, the infinitely enriching and disturbing world that lies beyond the limits of the self. In his essay on William Blake[126] Eliot pointed to the presence in his subject of this 'naked vision;' he also indicated, at least by implication, a certain uneasiness that this presence produced in him.

These are factors that operate—we may agree—in a certain limiting fashion upon Eliot's poetry, when we compare him, for example, with the greatest of his English-speaking contemporaries, W. B. Yeats. The *Quartets* prove abundantly that he recognized the importance of renewal as a condition of life for any poet who desires to remain such beyond a certain age. Indeed, the renewal of the creative imagination under the conditions imposed by advancing years and a difficult environment could be described as the guiding theme of the entire sequence; but it must be added that such renewal did not come easily to Eliot, that the *Quartets* were written with the struggle which this implies—and the very real possibility of failing in it—very much in mind.

Yet it would not, perhaps, be right to let the matter rest there. The problem is one which Eliot understood, and with which he constantly grappled in some of his best poetry; nor was it his alone. It is very movingly conveyed, for example, in Wordsworth's lines —which are among his most poignantly personal—from the Twelfth Book of *The Prelude*:

> The days gone by
> Return upon me almost from the dawn
> Of life: the hiding-places of man's power
> Open; I would approach them, but they close.
> I see by glimpses now; when age comes on,
> May scarcely see at all; and I would give,
> While yet we may, as far as words can give,
> Substance and life to what I feel, enshrining,
> Such is my hope, the spirit of the Past
> For future restoration.[127]

Wordsworth is not a poet who is commonly associated with Eliot, but there are—it seems to me—important points of coincidence here. 'The hiding-places of man's power' might be a not inadequate phrase to describe what the Eliot of *Burnt Norton* was seeking through the recreated experience in the rose-garden; and his initially dispiriting conclusion that human kind 'cannot bear very much reality' is not unlike Wordsworth's sense that these 'hiding-places', as he approaches them, become inaccessible, 'closed'. For both poets the problem seems to be that of making something, creating some equivalent for what can already be seen only 'by glimpses' and is likely soon to be lost; and for both the solution appears to be to create, always within the limits which the power of expression imposes, 'substance and life' conveyed in words to replace the direct experience which is and can be no longer available. Finally, both poets seem to see their effort as in some way involving an incorporation into what Wordsworth calls 'the spirit of the Past' and Eliot—less personally, more intellectually—'tradition'; and for both this effort of bringing back to life a still significant past becomes a step to 'future restoration'.

We might state the parallel in another way by saying that Eliot, like Wordsworth was acutely aware of the problem which the obligation for self-renewal represents for any creative artist, and more especially for one who, operating outside a received and accepted tradition, has passed beyond the stage of romantic adolescence.[128] The problem, indeed, is not one which affects literature alone, but which has a more general application. It is a disturbing thought—but, I think, very largely a true one—that there is normally a limit to what the imagination can produce, in terms of life continually renewed, out of its unaided resources. Perhaps only a small minority of the human race—how small it might be tactless to enquire—is at any time capable of receiving a new idea, of forming a genuinely *new* impression or making a genuinely new judgement, after the age of twenty-five;[129] and perhaps it is this small part that, in terms of creative achievement, ultimately counts.

If these considerations are in any way valid it may be that Eliot produced in the *Quartets* poetry which reflected not so much a failure in creative energy (though we have found occasional signs of this in the poetry) as a permanent aspect of the human condition. Eliot was not a Shakespeare, whose final comedies are as original, as essentially innovative as anything else he wrote: not a

Dante, who concluded his great design in the *Paradiso* with passages of unsurpassed speculative daring and linguistic mastery:[130] not a Cervantes, who wrote after an interval of fifteen years the second part of his *Don Quijote*, even fuller of pathos, humour, and insight than the first.[131] These are perfect examples of the eternal flowering of the creative spirit, and Eliot's work clearly belongs to a lesser order of achievement. But this is not to say that he has not his own valid contribution to offer. The merit of the *Quartets* — or of what is positively valuable in them, which is the greater part — lies in the intelligent, honest, and finally positive facing of the problem. Read as a whole, the sequence abundantly confirms Eliot's recognition of the need to see every human end as simultaneously a beginning, his awareness that the inescapable condition of imaginative life — that is, of life *tout court* — is unending renewal. Moreover, he does not simply *say* this — it has often been said before — but incorporates it into a living process of poetic creation. It is for this reason that he writes, as we have seen,[132] in *East Coker* that 'old men', and they above all, 'ought to be explorers', and goes on to say: 'We must be *still* and *still moving*'. *Still*, certainly, in the sense of being content to wait on experience as perpetually and inexhaustibly given; but also *still moving*, always, that is, open to the challenge of the living present, rejecting the temptation to rest comfortably upon tired repetitions of a 'wisdom' derived from the past.

To convert this conviction of necessary renewal into poetry, which is one way among many of making it operative in life, was not a thing that came easily to Eliot, as perhaps the corresponding effort does not come easily to most of us in the conduct of our personal concerns; but the *Quartets* do represent a continuing and disciplined effort to do just that, to turn to poetic account what needs to be seen, and honestly recognized, as a limitation and a problem. The success of this effort is to be judged, not in terms of philosophical argument or doctrinal assertion, but in the light of what poetry, as a distinctive human activity, has to offer: words placed in meaningful and cumulative conjunction, reaching out beyond themselves to produce in their relationship to one another a sense of shape and meaning, of creative and enriching pattern. To say this is to outline, as Eliot will do later in this final quartet,[133] an ideal for poetic speech which reflects, on consideration, nothing less than an ideal for life. Seen in this way the end of poetry becomes something ultimately beyond itself, though only communicable on its own distinctive terms. It becomes the reflection, through the various stages of one man's necessarily limited experience, of the tradition which has made him what he is: the tradition upon which his own poetry rests, in so far as it is alive and therefore inescapably unique, and upon which it will in turn act, by the very fact of its existence, as a modifying and enriching reality.

III

Having carried through his act of self-confrontation with the 'familiar compound ghost' who both is, and is not, himself, the poet is ready to take up again his theme of detachment and its relation to love. The exploration of the central and creative reality of the love made manifest in the quartet's central image of fire is, indeed, the theme of this final poem and the justification of the whole sequence. There are, as we now know, two aspects of this love which, properly understood, complete one another. They correspond respectively to the Way Up and the Way Down, attachment and detachment. Each has its proper and positive place in the conduct of life; and between them there is the negative condition of 'indifference' which is, finally, a rejection of life itself.

The three 'states' to which these attitudes lead are precisely distinguished as the 'movement' opens:

> There are three conditions which often look alike
> Yet differ completely, flourish in the same hedgerow:
> Attachment to self and to things and to persons, detachment
> From self and from things and from persons; and, growing between them, indifference
> Which resembles the others as death resembles life,
> Being between two lives — unflowering, between
> The live and the dead nettle.

These alternative states present themselves to the mind as 'nettles' in so far as the grasping of any of them involves a real measure of pain, but the two positive ones 'flower', are productive and alive, whereas the state of indifference which lies between them is of its nature 'unflowering', dead. 'Memory', working upon these conditions, brings 'liberation', freedom from subjection to time; for by it we are able to see the actions of the past, personal, and historical, without being involved in the immediate and necessarily distorting passion of their enactment, expanding our experience of love beyond the limitations of 'desire', freeing ourselves from attachment to the premature hope of the future as well as from undue clinging to a past that is no longer with us. In this way the themes explored in the earlier parts of the sequence are drawn into a new and more inclusive context, 'redeemed' in relation to the living and creative reality of love which the poem is now, and only now, prepared to postulate as the crown of the complete design.

The immediate result of this new perspective is seen to be a recognition of personal freedom:

> not less of love but expanding
> Of love beyond desire, and so liberation
> From the future as well as the past.

This assertion of a liberating detachment, which is expressly and deliberately distinguished from negation, the rejection of life, is fundamental to the way of thinking developed in the course of these poems. To be human in any real sense is to advance the area of freedom, and the poet is now exploring the conditions under which, for him, such freedom is attainable. He goes on to illustrate his meaning by examples drawn from life, both personal and historical. In the spirit of the assertion about the nature of love just put forward, he says, we can aspire to look at our larger loyalties in a similar spirit of 'liberation'. These loyalties can be either restricted or fulfilling, according to the manner in which they are conceived and the quality of the love they generate. 'Love of a country', for example, which is apt to begin as an extension of self-love—'attachment to our own field of action'—and which is, as such, vainly or prematurely assertive, can be seen in its more positive truth when we are able to look beyond these aspects of it in the spirit—we might say—of Krishna's counsel to Arjuna in *The Dry Salvages*: once we have seen, in other words, that 'action' itself, which so often leads to results beyond our possible calculation of them, is in itself 'of little importance though never indifferent'.

All this leads to the conclusion that our actions matter, and matter just because they require of us the exercise of choice and a measure of personal commitment, because they involve an assertion of life.

Once the choices have been made and carried through, however, to the best of our committed ability, the result becomes unimportant, matter for renunciation, in so far as it is necessarily beyond our foreseeing, assimilated to a pattern larger than any we can anticipate and which only the passage of time can reveal in its completeness. (The pattern is, indeed, only seen as complete when it is *past*.) What is true of our present, personal choices applies equally to our understanding of those made by other men in the past, which seem to have contributed to our present situation. It affects, in other words, our reading of what we call history. If we seek to interpret it from the limiting viewpoint of self and to draw from it 'lessons' designed to conform to our own necessarily short-sighted purposes and judgements, it can only become 'servitude'. Only once the events and issues which composed it have been considered in detachment, through an exercise of the 'memory' which unites us, beyond our own limited perspective, to the collective experience of the race to which we belong, can our understanding of 'history' become a source of 'freedom'; in much the same way as, in a more personal order, the 'faces and places' which were immediately dear to us in the past, which the self within its limitations loved 'as it could', have vanished *in time* to become 'renewed, transfigured', once the necessity of this 'vanishing' has been accepted, in 'another' and more inclusive 'pattern'.

Given the associations of the place—Little Gidding—which has given this quartet its point of departure, it is natural that these reflections on history should give place to a meditation on the English Civil War and its contending parties. It was under the impending shadow of civil strife that Nicholas Farrar founded his community and as a result of the outcome of that strife that it was destroyed. Similarly, it was in the midst of what he saw as a vaster and more destructive civil conflict that Eliot conceived and wrote his poem. The ruins of the chapel, however, are not seen by him simply as a symbol of the destructive consequences of division. The meditation which comprises the second part of this 'movement' and which is separated from what has gone before by the use of shorter lines to which we have become accustomed, is introduced by a phrase taken from the fourteenth-century mystical writer Juliana of Norwich, who learnt in the course of one of her visions[134] that 'Sin is Behovely'—in other words, a necessary or inescapable aspect of human life—but that, beyond this necessity, it will eventually be seen to have its place in the greater design of the Divine Love; so that, in the final outcome and contrary to every immediate appearance, 'all shall be well', gathered into the final reconciliation to which the entire living process tends.

In a way which finally illustrates this statement, the contending parties in the Civil War can now be seen, in the detachment which distance in time makes possible and indeed imposes, as united beyond their immediate differences by a harmony of underlying intention. It is not, of course, that these differences were not real, or seriously held. They were, on the contrary, often followed to the point of death; but we, who have become their heirs in time, are now in a position to appreciate what we have inherited from both factions and to ignore, or at least to set in proper perspective, what must inevitably have seemed at the time irreparably divisive. The individuals who composed these factions, most of them (like the rest of us) 'not wholly commendable', though a few on either side —Milton and Marvell, perhaps, among them—were touched by a 'peculiar genius', can now be envisaged as 'United in the strife which divided them'. Charles I, his Archbishop Laud, and his minister Strafford, who died for their cause—'three men, and more, on the scaffold'—together with others who were 'forgotten' in exile, are seen as united with Milton, their adversary who also died, 'blind and quiet' after having experienced what must have seemed to him the death of his hopes and the ruin of his most deeply held convictions.

To see this reality, and to respond imaginatively to it, is not to fight again battles that are over and finished. *Both* parties are now seen to 'Accept the constitution of silence' and to be 'folded' in the 'single party' of those who have at any time been ready to fight, from their respective points of view, to maintain what they understood to be the values of the spirit and who have suffered the universal human experience of precarious victory followed by inevitable defeat. The struggle is in fact unending, like that of the individual as explored in the previous poems; and it reminds us of the poet's own preoccupation, in *East Coker*, with the equally endless effort to incorporate new meanings into forms of expression that are always on the point of becoming old, inadequate in relation to the reality that calls for definition in the present.[135] At each stage, we 'inherit' from the victorious and the defeated alike, much as—in the suggestion originally put forward at the opening of

Burnt Norton—'what might have been' and 'what has been' contribute, each after its own distinct fashion, to the reality, the 'end', 'which is always present'. From the 'fortunate' we have derived the fruits of their victory, from the 'defeated' something less tangible but not perhaps ultimately less valuable: a 'symbol' of love 'perfected in death'. Milton's party eventually suffered political defeat, but out of that defeat he made *Paradise Lost* and *Samson Agonistes*; Andrew Marvell, too, was numbered among the defeated, but he was able, in his *Horatian Ode*, to celebrate the courage on the scaffold of the King, his enemy, in an act of generous recognition, of 'common' humanity.[136]

The point is, of course, that the struggle is never-ending, however the forms under which it manifests itself may seem to change. The spirit of detachment exercised through memory—which is in this case the proper understanding of what we call 'history'—will show that societies, like individuals, are always victorious and, in the long run, endlessly defeated: victorious in the affirmation of the distinctive life which animates them, defeated in the death which, properly understood, is a necessary and inescapable aspect of life itself. As *East Coker* has already put it, 'For us, there is only the trying';[137] but to 'try' is to affirm the possibilities of the human condition, in a word to 'live'. To return, with the poet at the end of the 'movement', to the words of Juliana of Norwich, 'All manner of thing shall be well' in so far as our motives are grounded, beyond immediate partisan passion or useless self-assertion, in a spiritual conception of love as the foundation of our actions and 'the ground of our beseeching'.

IV

The fourth 'movement' of the quartet is devoted, once again following the pattern already established, to a short lyrical interlude. In this, the raiding 'dove' of the second section has become the symbol of the Holy Spirit, as it appeared, according to the New Testament account, on the first Whitsun:

> The dove descending breaks the air
> With flame of incandescent terror
> Of which the tongues declare
> The one discharge from sin and error.

> The only hope, or else despair,
>   Lies in the choice of pyre or pyre —
>   To be redeemed from fire by fire.

The transformed 'dove', like the enemy aeroplane, brings with it a 'flame' which, however, is now linked, beyond the original and still valid association, with the prospect of liberation from 'incandescent terror' through the 'tongues of fire' which, in the Acts of the Apostles, inspired the first Christians to speak in diverse languages — 'tongues' — testifying to the reality of their overwhelming experience 'as the spirit gave them utterance'.[138] The fires of material, man-made destruction, already present in the second 'movement' of the poem, are now revealed under a new light for which the intervening development has prepared us. They are seen not simply as destructive of the fabric material, and moral, of what we choose, not without presumption, to call our 'civilization', but as bringing a measure of release: 'discharge' from the 'sin and error' which have led to this prospect of ruin through the exercise of man's distinctive privilege — which is also his obligation — of 'choice'. In this case the 'choice' is between life and death, between the 'fire' which destroys and that which purifies, once projected into prayer in a proper consciousness of what we are at last prepared to see as 'sin'.

It should be noted that the stanza just quoted suggests that the conditions of 'hope' and 'despair', which we normally assume to be contraries, are rather different aspects of a single reality. Like the opposed states of 'life' and 'death', they are inescapably intertwined. From the experience of 'fire' as such, with all its unmitigated pain, there is indeed no escape. A true recognition of the human dilemma, and of its possible resolution, starts from this point. Neither is there any easy consolation. Each element in the choice which has to be made, because it is at every moment a condition of continuing to live, will bring with it not comfort immediately, but an increased sensation of torment. The final question, however, remains to be asked, and it is now answered:

> Who then devised the torment? Love.
> Love is the unfamiliar Name
> Behind the hands that wove
> The intolerable shirt of flame
> Which human power cannot remove.

We only live, only suspire
Consumed by either fire or fire.

The reality of 'torment', then, needs to be accepted: but, once the acceptance has been made, detachment from immediately personal preoccupations may lead to a recognition of the truth, which is that the pain is devised in the name of Love, that the fire of 'incandescent terror' is in fact, when properly understood, the redeeming action of God. This, perhaps, is the only valid way of 'redeeming the time'.

The affirmation of 'Love' as a creative factor in the processes of life—even in those which present themselves under the aspect of pain, or 'torment'—brings us to the affective heart of the conception which animates these poems. We may, indeed, be surprised that it has not come earlier. Apart from a few brief references[139] the word has been almost conspicuously absent from the earlier poems of the sequence. There has been a good deal about 'desire', generally in a limiting context, but little about what might have been expected to be, for a poet of avowedly Christian inspiration, the unique reality of 'love'. In its absence the prevailing tone of these poems may have seemed on occasions excessively severe, the repeated emphasis on the need for detachment lacking in a certain desirable human warmth.

We can now see, however, that a judgement of this kind would be at least premature. It is true to the design, the 'method', as we have called it, of the *Quartets* that the open statement of its harmonizing theme should have been deliberately held back whilst the ground was being prepared for its assertion, until it could be seen to fall naturally and unobtrusively into place. Where dogmatic assertion and sustained argument are both rejected as inappropriate to the nature of these poems, the relevance of a positive statement of this kind lies in its power to illuminate what has gone before and to give life to what follows. The earlier poems are to be read, in other words, not only for themselves, but as preparatory stages in a developing pattern, the complete sense of which is revealed, at the end of the process, in the light of an affirmation of 'love' as the ultimate reality by which human life is rendered tolerable and finally justified. 'Love' has become, as it were, the indispensable missing piece in the puzzle, implicitly present from the beginning but only now affirmed for what it is: the irreplaceable and crowning reality which confers life, 'meaning' upon the completed creative process.

We can now see more clearly the sense in which the *Quartets* can properly be called 'religious' poems. The recognition of 'love' as a source of life, a transforming and vivifying presence, has been from the beginning the aim of the entire sequence. This is the *end* of the 'exploration' on which we have been engaged, the goal of our human journey. In relation to it the various elements which have gone to the making of the earlier quartets—the stress laid on the need for detachment, the recognition of death as an inescapable aspect of life, and the awareness of human subjection to the limitations imposed by time—are now, but *only* now, seen for what they are: not as reflections of a limited, even a dispiriting condition, but as pointers towards a reality which confers upon them such significance as they have. For a religiously oriented view of life this reality *is* Love; and, we might add, to live is quite simply to be capable of loving. In terms of the central Christian affirmation, as it is stated most simply and inclusively by the author of St. John's Gospel, God *is* Love—and by 'God' we may mean what these poems call 'reality': the 'reality' described in *Burnt Norton* as being largely beyond our capacity to 'bear' in time.[140]

To advance this statement as an all-embracing abstraction is, however, one thing; to make it live in terms of poetry which derives from an honest twentieth-century experience is quite another. This is the heart of the problem which faced the author of these *Quartets*. If, writing as a poet of his own time, he has refrained from stating this conviction at an earlier stage in his 'exploration', this may in part be because he feels that the sense of the word 'love' has become unduly limited in the prevailing usage of the world around him. Its meaning has become largely confined to the relationship between the sexes: in other words, to one particular manifestation of what in the course of these poems has been called 'desire'. In making this point, it is important not to falsify the poet's intention. We are not being required to deny the value of this manifestation, which is indeed both natural and central to life. It is possible to find passages in Eliot's writing, both in poetry and prose, which might support such a reading, which are indicative of negative elements in his own experience against which, both as man and as poet, he may have needed to react. Something of this may even survive in the reference to the '*intolerable* shirt of flame' which cannot be removed, made acceptable, by any exercise of 'human passion'. Love in its habitual human forms is, in Eliot, often, and perhaps unduly, a difficult and uneasy compulsion; but the tendency of this sequence, as this passage asserts it, is surely—however we may respond to the stress which is undoubtedly present in it—away from these negations and in the direction of a more positive, a more life-affirming attitude.

This affirmative reaction has now to be understood in a specifically 'religious' sense. The argument which supports it has rested, traditionally, on a recognition of man's creaturely incompleteness. According to this view, what is valuable and positive in human experience can only maintain itself when it is seen as positing a reality greater than, necessarily outside and beyond, the self. To see love exclusively under the aspect of 'desire'—even natural, 'right' desire—is, so the argument runs, to commit the human error of mistaking the part for the whole: to see it, in other words, as inescapably limited by its final subjection to death. As we learnt at the end of *Burnt Norton*, 'Desire itself is movement/Not in itself desirable', whilst 'Love is itself unmoving,/Only the cause and end of movement,/Timeless, and undesiring/Except in the aspect of time'.[141] This is the reality that, in the lines we are considering, presents itself as 'torment', the bitter recognition of what love, seen under this aspect of limitation, at once insistently requires and is unable to attain. The 'solution', for these poems, lies in a recognition of the need to affirm the reality of love 'beyond', though not in opposition to, 'desire'. All human experience in time—and *all* human experience is, as we saw in *Burnt Norton*,[142] at least initially subject to the temporal process—points, necessarily and of its very nature, beyond itself; and the point at which it aims is most fully apprehended by men when, having accepted the commitment of faith which reason can recognize but not accompany, they assert the full measure of their capacity for love.

To see life in this way is, clearly, to extend our conception of 'love' beyond anything implied in our language of daily use; and to affirm this extension so that it lives in the light of the experience conveyed, made actual, in the poetry is, it might be said, the final aim of the sequence. Every manifestation of life is to be seen as the expression of a 'love' which is, of its very nature, creative; because to be alive, in any proper sense of the word, is quite simply to be 'in love'. Once again the use of this familiar, even trite phrase, needs to be extended to cover a greater truth; and once more, the effect is to throw light upon, to complete, certain intuitions fleetingly present in the earlier poems of the sequence. When we respond to a prospect of natural beauty or to a powerful aesthetic experience—of the kind associated with the achieved 'stillness' of the 'Chinese jar' or the note of the violin in *Burnt Norton*[143]—we can be said, for as long as the corresponding emotion lasts, to be 'in love' with the object of our contemplation. The sensation we experience is of its nature precarious, necessarily incomplete; but it is, within its limitation, real and indicative—in the argument which sustains these poems—of a reality greater, more permanent than itself. The statement of this perception can be applied, in turn, to other orders of human experience. The love which one human being feels towards another was celebrated in the classical tradition, from Plato and Cicero to the Renaissance, under the term of 'friendship'; this love which is given, in the form of physical or sexual attraction to which we sometimes tend to limit the use of the word, one particularly intense and elusive expression, is perhaps the most valuable and living manifestation open to human beings in time of this same creative reality.

The specifically 'religious' implications of these intuitions, as developed in the *Quartets*, are by now sufficiently clear. They amount to an attempt to restate, in relation to a contemporary experience, concepts rendered familiar by a long process of traditional development. According to these concepts the principle of life which, for want of a better word, we call 'God' is distinguished from that of man by its immeasurably greater, more inclusive capacity for loving. It expresses itself supremely in the act of *creation*, through the affirmation of a love which, in a timeless gesture of spontaneous *giving*, wills the object of its contemplation *to be* and, in so far as its nature permits, to be *free*: for 'God'—according to the line of thought which Eliot is now incorporating into his 'exploration' as the final, hitherto missing piece which completes his puzzle—is distinguished from men by his capacity to love the entire range of the creation which, in the limitless overflow of his creative generosity, he has willed to be free.

Man, on his side, can be said to 'live' just in so far as he is able to share, in the measure of his own corresponding capacity to give, in this design. This he does by expressing through the choices which govern his own life the degree of love of which he is capable:

a degree which, in relation to that of 'God', is necessarily limited, in time, to the contingent and the particular, but which remains within the extent of its capacity a genuine source of life.

Who then devised the torment? Love.

The affirmation that we live in the measure of our love, and in as much as we are capable of loving, is the conclusion—the *end* which the opening of *East Coker* already posited[144]—to which the whole design of the *Quartets* has pointed, and which they are now, and only now, ready to affirm. The affirmation is, we must stress, something more in the poet's intention than an assertion of comfortable, academic 'Platonism'. It is not made in abstraction from the difficulties to which it gives rise and which constitute an integral part of the poetry; for these—and ultimately nothing less than these—are implied in the reference to continuing 'torment'. The difficulties are indeed real, and they are not to be met by unsupported assertion or academic argument. There have been times, even in these poems, when it has been possible to feel that his conclusion was one which presented itself to the poet as difficult, even barely acceptable: times when the living, positive attitude to which it points seems to be obscured by a continuing struggle with intractably unloving, separating elements in his reading of human experience; but here, and in the lines which lead to the completion of the reconciling, harmonizing design, the reality of the 'love' which has been glimpsed in the course of the 'exploration' is affirmed, given its appropriate expression as the natural and necessary goal of man's journey in time.

In relation to this line of thought the human reality so far considered under the name of 'desire' at last falls naturally into place. The creative and the destructive aspects of fire, far from being mutually exclusive, are now seen as reconciled in the divine, 'unfamiliar' Name which conveys the ultimate reality of Love. Hercules, who was both a classical 'god' 'and a man of heroic stature', in whom the early Christian artists of the catacombs saw a prefiguration of the Christ, died—as a man—on his pyre, consumed by human passion, or 'desire', in the form of the poisoned shirt of Nessus. The divine Love too can present itself as an 'intolerable shirt of flame' which no 'human power' can of itself 'remove'. Our 'choice' lies, accordingly, through accepted pain, through the recognition of a need to 'live'—or 'suspire', like the souls in Dante's

Purgatory[145] — by a choice between the fire of destruction, which is one with that of passionate self-affirmation, and the burning away of the spiritual impediment of self-love on an accepted sacrificial pyre:

> We only live, only suspire
> Consumed by either fire or fire.

The choice itself is not to be evaded, for it is imposed by nothing less than the reality, as we have now come to understand it, of the human condition. Either way, it is the end of life to be *consumed*: the word carries with it the double implication of consummation and destruction ('hope' and 'despair', we remember); it conveys the essential meaning to which the fire symbol — common, in terms of Eliot's sequence, to Heraclitus and Dante — ultimately aspires.

V

The final 'movement' of *Little Gidding* is at once a conclusion to this quartet and a drawing together of the themes and symbols explored through the series as a whole. The starting-point is the idea, put forward in the form of a hypothesis at the beginning of *Burnt Norton*, of the continuity and 'co-existence' implicit in human experience as realized in time. What was there an abstract and tentative proposition, the statement of a mere possibility, can now be restated in terms of the experience accumulated through the sequence. For individuals and societies alike, death and birth are now seen as woven together, inseparable aspects of a single reality:

> What we call the beginning is often the end
> And to make an end is to make a beginning.
> The end is where we start from.

Here we are returning, of course, to the opening phrase of *East Coker*, which was itself a development in more human, historical terms, of the abstract hypothesis of the nature of time put forward in *Burnt Norton*. If the final achievement of *consciousness* lies, as the entire development of the series has tended to show, in the recognition of a final reality outside the process of temporal sequence, the *end* to which our lives are directed (if they are to be seen as meaningful at all) is in fact 'where we start from'.

The point is further illustrated by an analogy with the poet's craft, a theme which has occupied Eliot's thoughts from the beginning of the series and which is now ready to fall into place:

> every phrase
> And sentence that is right (where every word is at home,
> Taking its place to support the others,
> The word neither diffident nor ostentatious,
> An easy commerce of the old and the new,
> The common word exact without vulgarity,
> The formal word precise but not pedantic,
> The complete consort dancing together)
> Every phrase and every sentence is an end and a
>   beginning,
> Every poem an epitaph.

In a 'right' sentence, as in a 'right' life or a 'right' society, every word finds its 'place' in support of every other word, 'neither diffident' nor self-assertively 'ostentatious', bringing together tradition and novelty (the 'old' and the 'new') in easy, natural 'commerce'. The result is 'The complete consort dancing together', where 'Every phrase and every sentence is an end and a beginning': an echo, in other words, of the pattern, the 'dance' in which life itself, when properly understood, achieves its measure of 'meaning'. In writing, which is in this as in other respects a reflection of life, every phrase can be seen as the 'end' of one process of experience, and as the gateway opening out to its successor.

This leads, logically, to a consideration of the place of death in the complete process. Every poem, seen from one point of view, becomes the 'epitaph' of a completed experience, just as every moment in the life of an individual can be seen as a step towards extinction. 'The time of death is every moment', as *The Dry Salvages* put it in the course of a meditation on the words of Krishna.[146] Yes, but equally, in the timeless pattern of consciousness towards which human reality tends, physical death is not a final end. It is true that

> any action
> Is a step to the block, to the fire, down the sea's throat
> Or to an illegible stone,

where the 'block' recalls the death of Charles I and his supporters, the 'fire' both the ruins of the chapel at Little Gidding and the destruction caused in London by war-time bombing, the 'sea's throat' the pervasive image of *The Dry Salvages*, and the 'death by drowning' (which takes us back as far as *The Waste Land*) the end of many of those engaged in sailing with the war-time convoys in the Atlantic and the Arctic. It is true also, however, that *this* is where—necessarily and inevitably—we have to start in our own effort to grasp the complete process. 'We die with the dying', in so far as we are called upon, 'required', to share with them their sub-jection to time-conditioned mortality; but it is equally true that we are 'born with the dead' in as much as we can see ourselves united with the preceding generations in the 'common' possession of tradi-tion. Through this tradition the dead are re-affirmed through us, contribute to making us what we presently are. In that sense, which is not one of final pessimism, the reality of accepted death is the point 'where we start from'.

All this points, as we approach the conclusion of the poem and of the series as a whole, to a re-assertion of the relevance of history in the light of a deepened understanding, which the poems have given us, of the implications of our individual experience. To be 'with-out history' is in any event not to be 'released from time', as the more superficial among us may like to believe, but rather to be enslaved to one isolated and finally meaningless point in the com-plete process. (Here incidentally we perhaps see the real implica-tion of the reference, which seemed at the time a little patronizing, to 'the partial fallacy' of current notions of evolution in *The Dry Salvages*.[147]) Human history becomes, when properly understood, 'a pattern/Of timeless moments,' in which the past is neither dead nor oppressively dominant, but is given its place, its *meaning*, in relation to the timeless design. In that design, the realities of life and death—'The moment of the rose and the moment of the yew-tree'—both have their place, are finally 'of equal duration', because *both* are implicit in 'every moment' of our experience in time. History, in this sense and at the moment with which the poem is concerned, is 'incarnate' in Little Gidding, 'now' and in England.

The transition to the final summing-up, for which we are now prepared, takes the form of a quotation from a fourteenth-century English treatise on contemplative prayer known as *The Cloud of Unknowing*. It affirms the emotional moving force, as the poet is now ready to declare it, of the entire sequence: 'With the drawing of this Love and the voice of this Calling'.[148] In the light so provided the call of the bird and the reality of the 'love' glimpsed at the outset of *Burnt Norton*,[149] and there given tenuous, fugitive expression, are reaffirmed, reasserted in relation to the development between.

The conclusion, accordingly, takes up the main symbols and metaphors developed in the course of the sequence with the object of weaving them together into a final unity. *Final*, of course, it is necessary to stress, in relation to the sequence itself and no more: for this conclusion answers not to a complete experience (we have already had reason to see that no living pattern is, or of its nature can be, complete until death removes it from the order of time), but to the present state of the still uncompleted exploration. Life in time, as we have found in *East Coker* and *The Dry Salvages*, is to be regarded in terms of a voyage of discovery: a voyage, however, the end of which is to bring us back to the initial moment in which we stepped—in *Burnt Norton*—through the 'first' gate into the experience of the rose-garden, which we now see in the light of the intervening development as having a new, a more universal significance:

> We shall not cease from exploration
> And the end of all our exploring
> Will be to arrive where we started
> And know the place for the first time.

To the original and fugitive intuition of an order of timelessness there has now been brought the awareness that, in terms of the 'consciousness' which the entire sequence has been concerned to develop, the concepts of 'beginning' and 'end' are to be seen as differing aspects of a reality that is finally, in its true nature, not reducible to 'time before and after'. The end of the process of 'exploring' is to discover the 'beginning', to 'arrive where we started/And know the place for the first time;' the moments of intuition scattered through the poem return, 'half-heard', like the echo of the bell in *The Dry Salvages*[150]—which was at once the tolling bell indicative of death and the Angelus announcing the birth of a new order of life—as intimations of true consciousness.

To these intimations, and their expression in the earlier poems of the sequence, we now return for the last time in a final convergence of themes:

Through the unknown, remembered gate
When the last of earth left to discover
Is that which was the beginning;
At the source of the longest river
The voice of the hidden waterfall
And the children in the apple-tree
Not known, because not looked for
But heard, half-heard, in the stillness
Between two waves of the sea.

The 'gate', the voices of the children in the tree, 'heard, half-heard', all represent the glimpses, intuitions of a possible reality, from the previous poems. Added to them now is a fleeting reference to the myth of the Garden of Eden and to the river flowing from its source in the original Paradise: also, maybe, but in a sense now transformed, to 'the bitter apple and the bite in the apple' of *The Dry Salvages*.[151] These intuitions, in turn, are associated with the voice of the bird in *Burnt Norton* — 'Quick now, here, now, always'[152] — conveying an intense but passing sense of awareness at 'the point of intersection', where time and the timeless finally meet: the 'point' with which the first discursive passage in *Burnt Norton* began, and which we have now learnt to call, under its temporal aspect, which is the only one accessible to us in time and the flesh, 'Incarnation'.

The end of the completed process is now, at length, ready to be affirmed in terms of living. It lies in the attainment of nothing less than 'A condition of complete simplicity', the 'cost' of which, since it has to be commensurable with the value of what is to be attained, is the total surrender of self: 'not less than everything'. The point to which this renunciation leads is the conquest of strife, of sin and death, in the light of the vision once vouchsafed to Juliana of Norwich: 'all shall be well and/All manner of thing shall be well.' The whole poem, and with it the sequence in its totality, is rounded off by taking up once again the symbol of fire — this time indicative of Love as the ruling principle of all creation — in a Dantesque reconciliation of the symbols of 'the fire and the rose'. All opposites are brought together, finally transformed, in the lover's knot, the 'rose', woven from the element of purifying and transfiguring fire. As the flame becomes a flower, the rose-garden and the chapel, desire and love, nature and grace, are finally seen in their true relationship as vitally and creatively 'one'.

NOTES

NOTES

THE WASTE LAND
[1] Introduction

1 See *Ulysses, Order and Myth*, published in *The Dial*, November 1923.

2 *Purgatorio*, XXVI, 117.

3 Submitted at Harvard in 1916, and published in 1964 under the title of *Knowledge and Experience in the Philosophy of F. H. Bradley*.

4 The passage is taken from Bradley's *Appearance and Reality*.

5 From an essay on *Leibnitz' Monads and Bradley's Finite Centres*, published originally in *The Monist* (October, 1916) and reprinted in *Knowledge and Experience in the Philosophy of F. H. Bradley*, p. 204.

6 *ibid.* p. 204.

7 Essay on *Hamlet*, 1917, from *Selected Essays, 1917–1932* (London, 1932), p. 145.

8 *ibid.* p. 273.

9 *The Use of Poetry and the Use of Criticism* (London, 1933), p. 155.

10 *Selected Essays, 1917–1932*, p. 14.

11 The volume entitled *Adonis, Attis, Osiris*, which Eliot mainly used, was first published in 1906.

12 Published in 1920.

13 It is not, either from our point of view or the poet's, important to decide whether or not Miss Weston's theories can be considered to be scientifically valid. Their importance lies, for us, in their availability and their relevance to the intention of the poem.

14 It will be noted that, in the discussion of *The Waste Land* in this and the following chapter, we have not made reference to the questions raised by Ezra Pound's editing of the poem, a subject on which the recent publication of Eliot's manuscript has thrown a great deal of light. The omission is not accidental. We are dealing, in the first place, with the poem as it now stands in its definitive form, the form in which it asks to be judged. In the second place, if it is true that Pound's judgement contributed in an important way to the making of the poem (more especially in the many cases where his suggestions represent the suppression of inferior, sometimes embarrassing or imperfectly relevant matter), it is also true that Eliot had the intelligence and — we might add — the humility to recognize that his friend was right and to make his suggestions his own.

[2] The Poem

1 *The Canterbury Tales*, General Prologue, 1–18.

2 Compare, for example, the following from *Portrait of a Lady*, II:

> Now that lilacs are in bloom
> She has a bowl of lilacs in her room
> And twists one in her fingers while she talks.

The sense of tension, of nervous dissatisfaction, implied in the lady's gesture, is a typical Waste Land situation.

3 Note to line 218 of *The Waste Land*.

4 See *The Waste Land*, V, *What the Thunder Said*, 331–46, and p. 48 below.

5 See the poet's notes to lines 20 and 23.

6 Compare, for example, the effect of such lines as the following from *La Figlia che Piange*:

> I should find
> Some way incomparably light and deft,
> Some way we both should understand,
> Simple and faithless as a smile and shake of the hand.

What 'both' parties in the relationship 'should understand', what is implied in the deceptively simple gesture of trust—the 'smile' and the 'shake of the hand'—which should bring them together, is in fact the reality of betrayal.

7 The word 'nothing' has an important function in the development of *The Waste Land*. The poem will return to it at some of its central moments of significance, more especially in the second section, *A Game of Chess*. See p. 35 below.

8 On the possibility of forestalling, and thereby dominating the future, and on the illusion which this represents see the passage in *Four Quartets* (*The Dry Salvages*, V), considered on p. 177 below.

9 See the poet's note to line 46.

10 Compare these lines from early poems by Eliot:

> The brown waves of fog toss up to me
> Twisted faces from the bottom of the street.
>> (*Morning at the Window*)

> Among the smoke and fog of a December afternoon.
>> (*Portrait of a Lady*)

> The yellow fog that rubs its back upon the window-
> panes.
>> (*The Love Song of J. Alfred Prufrock*)

11 Compare Eliot's remark in his essay of 1930 on Baudelaire:

> damnation itself is an immediate form of salvation—of salvation from the ennui of modern life, because it at least gives some significance to living.
>> (*Selected Essays, 1917–1932*, p. 375)

12 *Inferno*, XV. We are reminded of the encounter with the 'familiar compound ghost' that will play so important a part in section II of *Little Gidding*.

13 Webster's text reads:

> But keep the wolf far thence, that's foe to men,
> For with his nails he'll dig them up again.
>
> (*The White Devil*, IV, iv)

14 Thomas Middleton's *Women Beware Women*, II, ii.
15 *Antony and Cleopatra*, II, ii.
16 *Cymbeline*, II, iv.
17 See, more especially, the description of Belinda's dressing table in *The Rape of the Lock*, I, 121 ff.
18 The sense of disillusion and loss has never, perhaps, been more movingly, and more ruthlessly, conveyed than in certain speeches uttered by Antony in his moments of defeat. We may think, in particular, of the following:

> . . . when we in our viciousness grow hard,—
> O misery on't!—the wise gods seal our eyes;
> In our own filth drop our clear judgements; make us
> Adore our errors; laugh at's, while we strut
> To our confusion.
>
> (*Antony and Cleopatra*, III, xiii)

> All come to this?—The hearts
> That spaniel'd me at heels, to whom I gave
> Their wishes, do discandy, melt their sweets
> On blossoming Caesar; and this pine is barkt,
> That overtopt them all. Betray'd I am:
> O this false soul of Egypt! this grave charm,—
> Whose eye beckt forth my wars, and call'd them home;
> Whose bosom was my crownet, my chief end,—
> Like a right gipsy hath, at fast and loose,
> Beguiled me to the very heart of loss.
>
> (*ibid.* IV, xii)

It is no disparagement to Eliot to recognize that, by comparison with these passages, *The Waste Land* is seen to belong to a lesser order of creation.

19
> Thou wast not born for death, immortal Bird!
> No hungry generations tread thee down;
> The voice I hear this passing night was heard
> In ancient days by emperor and clown.
>
> (Keats, *Ode to a Nightingale*)

20 See p. 51 below.
21 Marvell's famous lines read, of course, as follows:

> And at my back I always hear
> Time's winged chariot hurrying near;
> And yonder all before me see
> Deserts of vast eternity.

> The grave's a fine and private place,
> But none, I think, do there embrace.
> *(The Coy Mistress)*

22 See line 61 of *The Burial of the Dead.*

23 The contrast is of a kind which Eliot had already used to much the
same effect in his earlier poetry. Compare the following, from
Sweeney Among the Nightingales:

> The host with someone indistinct
> Converses at the door apart,
> The nightingales are singing near
> The Convent of the Sacred Heart,
>
> And sang within the bloody wood
> Where Agamemnon cried aloud,
> And let their liquid siftings fall
> To stain the stiff dishonoured shroud.

24 In this comment Eliot refers to the discovery of the internal com-
bustion engine, and speculates on the effect which this may have on
the poet's sense of rhythm as expressed in his work.

25 See *The Burial of the Dead*, line 67.

26 This is one of the passages of the poem which has gained most, in
proper reticence and discretion, from the poet's acceptance of
Pound's suggested excision of the inferior, and indeed repellent
verses, into which the passage was originally expanded. See the
passage titled *Dirge* printed in *The Waste Land: A Facsimile and
Transcript*, ed. Valerie Eliot (London, 1971).

27 Compare Mr. Prufrock's question and the negative answer:

> Do I dare
> Disturb the universe?
> In a moment there is time
> For decisions and revisions which a minute will reverse.
> *(The Love Song of J. Alfred Prufrock)*

28 See Eliot's note on line 411.

29 It is worth remembering that in his early essay on *Hamlet* (1917)
Eliot had already referred to *Coriolanus* as one of Shakespeare's
'assured artistic successes'.

30 See line 31 of *The Burial of the Dead.*

31 Compare *The Hollow Men*, V:

> Between the desire
> And the spasm
> Between the potency
> And the existence
> Between the essence
> And the descent
> Falls the Shadow.

32 The sense of a difference between the actual and the possible, between what actually occurred and what *might* have been is frequent in Eliot's poetry. We could compare with the passage under consideration the use of the conditional in the very early poem *La Figlia che Piange*, and remember also the episode (reflecting a real or possible event) of the rose-garden in *Burnt Norton*. See p. 98 below, and especially the lines

> *What might have been* and *what has been*
> Point to one end, which is always present.

This last statement, indeed, reads very much like Eliot's final resolution of a dichotomy fundamental to his experience.

33 The essay on *Thoughts after Lambeth* includes the following comment:

> When I wrote a poem called *The Waste Land* some of the more approving critics said that I had expressed 'the disillusionment of a generation', which is nonsense. I may have expressed for them their own illusion of being disillusioned, but that did not form part of my intention.
>
> *(Selected Essays, 1917–1932, p. 344)*

ASH WEDNESDAY

1 See *East Coker*, III and p. 142 below.
2 Grover Smith (*T. S. Eliot's Poetry and Plays*, Chicago, 1956, p. 141) points out that St. John of the Cross uses the story, which appears in the medieval bestiaries, of the eagle which in old age flies towards the sun and renews its youth as a parable of spiritual regeneration for 'the old man'. See *The Ascent of Mount Carmel*, II, xiii.
3 See *Ash Wednesday*, VI, and p. 83 below. The line of thought is taken up again, in a changed and expanded context, in *Little Gidding*, III: see p. 200 below.
4 'Hail, Mary, full of grace, the Lord is with thee. Blessed art thou among women and blessed is the fruit of thy womb Jesus. Holy Mary, Mother of God, pray for us sinners now and at the hour of our death.'
5 I *Kings*, xix.
6 *ibid.*
7   Nel mezzo del cammin di nostra vita
       Mi ritrovai per una selva oscura,
       Che la diritta via era smarrita.
                (Inferno, I, 1–3)

8 *Inferno*, I, 52–4.
9 *Ezekiel*, xxxvii, 3.
10 *The Waste Land*, V, 353–4: 'Not the cicada and dry grass singing'.
11 *Ecclesiastes*, xii, 5.
12 *Paradiso*, XXXIII, 1–39.

13 *Paradiso*, XXXIII, 142–5:

> All'alta fantasia qui mancò possa:
> ma già volgeva il mio disio e'l velle,
> si come rota ch'igualmente è mossa,
> l'amor che move il sole e l'altre stelle.

14 St. Ignatius Loyola, *Spiritual Exercises, Principle and Foundation.*
15 Compare the reference to Hercules and the shirt of Nessus in *Little Gidding*, IV:

> Love is the unfamiliar Name
> Behind the hands that wove
> The intolerable shirt of flame
> Which human power cannot remove.

See p. 204 below.
16 *Genesis*, iii, 8 ff.
17 *Purgatorio*, XXVIII to XXXIII.
18 *Ezekiel*, xxxvii, 5.
19 *Ezekiel*, xxxvii, 21–2.
20 For Virgil's exposition of the plan of the Mount, see *Purgatorio*, XVII, 91–139.
21 *Purgatorio*, IX, 94–102.
22 The phrase is taken from Eliot's Introduction to the Everyman edition of the *Pensées*.
23 *The Waste Land*, V, 339.
24 *Murder in the Cathedral*:

> Fluting in the meadows, viols in the hall,
> Laughter and apple-blossom floating on the water,
> Singing at nightfall, whispering in chambers,
> Fires devouring the winter season,
> Eating up the darkness, with wit and wine and wisdom!

25 *The Waste Land*, I, 36.
26 Compare, for a fuller statement of this theme, *East Coker*, III, and p. 142 below.
27 Compare *Burnt Norton*, II:

> To be conscious is not to be in time . . .
> Only through time time is conquered.

See p. 113 below.
28 From the preparation for the Communion in the Mass: 'Lord, I am not worthy. . . . but speak only the word, and my soul shall be healed'.
29 *Vita Nuova*, chapters iii, xiv, xviii, and elsewhere.
30 *Purgatorio*, XXVII, 35–6.
31 *Purgatorio*, XXX.
32 See especially *Vita Nuova*, xliii.

33 Compare the following passage on the 'Divine Pageant' of *Purgatorio*, XXIX, from Eliot's essay on Dante: 'It belongs to the world of what I call the *high dream* and the modern world seems capable only of the *low dream*.'

34 Compare the following comment from the Dante essay: 'I arrived at accepting it [the 'pageantry' of the *Purgatorio* and the *Paradiso*] only with some difficulty. There were at least two prejudices, one against Pre-Raphaelite imagery, which was natural to one of my generation, and perhaps affects generations younger than mine.' (*Selected Essays*, p. 248)

35 *Purgatorio*, XXIX.

36 The use of the 'yew' as a symbol of this double nature is recurrent in Eliot's poetry. Compare *The Dry Salvages*, V, and p. 180 below.

37 Eliot made a rather similar point, at about the same time, in his pamphlet *Thoughts After Lambeth* (1931: reprinted in *Selected Essays, 1917–1932*, p. 377): 'The World is trying the experiment of attempting to form a civilized but non-Christian mentality. The experiment will fail; but we must be very patient in awaiting its collapse, meanwhile redeeming the time: so that the Faith may be preserved alive through the dark ages before us; to renew and rebuild civilization, and save the World from suicide.'

38 'My people, what have I done to you; or in what have I grieved you?' The words are taken from the Latin liturgy for Good Friday.

39 See Eliot's essay *For Lancelot Andrewes*, reprinted in *Selected Essays, 1917–1932*, pp. 331–43.

40 Compare the reference in *The Dry Salvages*, II to 'The bitter apple and the bite in the apple'. See p. 167 below.

41 *The Waste Land*, IV, and p. 46 above.

42 See p. 71 above.

43 See p. 80 above.

44 Compare *The Dry Salvages*, III: 'The time of death is every moment.' See p. 173 below.

45 Compare *The Journey of the Magi*:

> This set down
> This: were we led all that way for
> Birth or Death? There was a Birth, certainly,
> We had evidence and no doubt. I had seen birth and
> death,
> But had thought they were different; this Birth was
> Hard and bitter agony for us, like Death, our death.

46 *Pericles*, V, iii.

47 *The Winter's Tale*, III, iii.

48 Compare Eliot's phrase in his essay on Dante when, speaking of the *Vita Nuova*, he writes: 'There is also a practical sense of realities behind it, which is antiromantic: not to expect more from *life* than it can give or from *human* beings than they can give: to look to *death* for what life cannot give.' (*Selected Essays, 1917–1932*, p. 261)

49 See *The Dry Salvages*, III, and the passage from *Little Gidding* quoted on p. 199 below.

50 *Paradiso*, III, 85: E in la sua voluntade è nostra pace.

51 Already at the end of *The Waste Land*, as we recall, the protagonist had sat on the shore with the desert behind him.

FOUR QUARTETS
[1] Introduction

1 From *The Music of Poetry*, reprinted in the collection *On Poetry and Poets* (London, 1957), p. 38.

2 *Shakespeare and the Stoicism of Seneca* (*Selected Essays, 1917–1932*, p. 137).

3 This was, in fact, a commonplace of scholastic philosophy. Compare the following passage from St. Thomas Aquinas:

> Now in treating of the divine essence the principal method to be followed is that of remotion. For the divine essence by its immensity surpasses every form to which our intellect reaches, and thus we cannot apprehend it by knowing what it is. But we have some knowledge thereof by knowing *what it is not*; and we shall approach all the nearer to the knowledge thereof according as we shall be enabled to remove by our intellect a greater number of things therefrom.
>
> (*Summa contra Gentiles*, quoted in *Thomas Aquinas: Selected Writings*, ed. M. C. D'Arcy, S. J. London, 1939, p. 97)

4 In his published address on *American Literature and Language* Eliot wrote as follows:

> The Mississippi of Mark Twain is not only the river known to those who voyage on it or live beside it, but the universal river of human life—more universal, indeed, than the Congo of Joseph Conrad. For Twain's readers anywhere, the Mississippi is *the* river.
>
> (*To Criticize the Critic*, London, 1965, p. 54)

5 In formulating what follows I have found my own ideas considerably clarified by Dame Helen Gardner's observations in Chapter II of her book *The Art of T. S. Eliot* (London, 1949).

[2] Burnt Norton

1 Essay on *George Herbert* (London, 1962), p. 24.

2 For a persuasive exposition of this view, see D. W. Harding's essay *A Newly Created Concept* from *Experience into Words* (London, 1963).

3 For a good example of this kind of argument, see George Orwell's essay on the poet, printed in *Poetry London* (Oct. 1942).

4 See, for example, the remark quoted on p. 88.

5 See St. Augustine, *Confessions*, XI, xxvii:

> Suppose, now, the voice of a body begins to sound, and does sound, and sounds on, and list, it ceases; it is silence now, and that voice is past, and is no more a voice. Before it sounded, it was to come, and could not be measured, because as yet it was not, and now it cannot, because it is no longer. Then therefore while it sounded, it might; because then there was what might be measured. But yet even then it was not at a stay; for it was passing on, and passing away. Could it be measured the rather, for that? For while passing, it was being extended into some space of time, so that it might be measured, since the present hath no space. If therefore then it might, then, lo, suppose another voice hath begun to sound, and still soundeth in one continued tenor without any interruption; let us measure it while it sounds; seeing when it hath left sounding, it will then be past, and nothing left to be measured; let us measure it verily, and tell how much it is. But it sounds still, nor can it be measured but from the instant it began in, unto the end it left in. For the very space between is the thing we measure, namely, from some beginning unto some end. Wherefore, a voice that is not yet ended, cannot be measured, so that it may be said how long, or short it is; nor can it be called equal to another, or double to a single, or the like. But when ended, it no longer is. How then may it be measured? And yet we measure times; but yet neither those which are not yet, nor those which no longer are, nor those which are not lengthened out by some pause, nor those which have no bounds. We measure neither times to come, nor past, nor present, nor passing; and yet we do measure times.

(translated E. B. Pusey)

6 *Paradiso*, XXX, 100–32.

7 It is hardly necessary to point out that deception, disappointment, a sense of intimate betrayal, are persistently present in Eliot's poetry at some of its moments of greatest intimacy. Apart from the 'hyacinth girl' episode in *The Waste Land* (see p. 27) we could also quote passages from such early poems as *La Figlia che Piange*:

> Clasp your flowers to you with a pained surprise —
> Fling them to the ground and turn
> With a fugitive resentment in your eyes

and *Portrait of a Lady*:

> 'Ah, my friend, you do not know, you do not know
> What life is, you who hold it in your hands';
> (Slowly twisting the lilac stalks)
> 'You let it flow from you, you let it flow,
> And youth is cruel, and has no remorse
> And smiles at situations which it cannot see.'
> I smile, of course,
> And go on drinking tea.

8 See p. 77 above.
9 *The Waste Land*, 38–41.
10 Compare, for example, the passage describing the Marabar caves which occupies a central place in *A Passage to India* (II, xii):

> They are dark caves. Even when they open towards the sun, very little light penetrates down the entrance tunnel into the circular chamber. There is little to see, and no eye to see it, until the visitor arrives for his five minutes, and strikes a match. Immediately another flame rises in the depths of the rock and moves towards the surface like an imprisoned spirit: the walls of the circular chamber have been most marvellously polished. The two flames approach and strive to unite, but cannot because one of them breathes air, the other stone. A mirror inlaid with lovely colours divides the lovers, delicate stars of pink and grey interpose, exquisite nebulae, shadings fainter than the tail of a comet or the midday moon, all the evanescent life of the granite, only here visible. Fists and fingers thrust above the advancing soil — here at last is their skin, finer than any covering acquired by the animals, smoother than windless water, more voluptuous than love. The radiance increases, the flames touch one another, kiss, expire. The cave is dark again, like all the caves.

11 Compare the following from *To The Lighthouse* (III, iv):

> 'Like a work of art', she repeated, looking from her canvas to the drawing-room steps and back again. She must rest for a moment. And resting, looking from one to the other vaguely, the old question which traversed the sky of the soul perpetually, the vast, the general question which was apt to particularize itself at such moments as these, when she released faculties that had been on the strain, stood over her, paused over her, darkened over her. What is the meaning of life? That was all — a simple question; one that tended to close in on one with years. The great revelation had never come. The great revelation perhaps never did come. Instead there were little daily miracles, illuminations, matches struck unexpectedly in the dark; here was one. This, that, and the other; herself and Charles Tansley and the breaking wave; Mrs. Ramsay bringing them together; Mrs. Ramsay saying 'Life stand still here'; Mrs. Ramsay making of the moment something permanent (as in another sphere Lily herself tried to make of the moment something permanent) — this was of the nature of a revelation. In the midst of chaos there was shape; this eternal passing and flowing (she looked at the clouds going and the leaves shaking) was struck into stability. Life stand still here, Mrs. Ramsay said. 'Mrs. Ramsay! Mrs. Ramsay!' she repeated. She owed the revelation to her.

12 Marcel Proust: *Swann's Way*, I, p. 58, translated by C. K. Scott Moncrieff, Chatto & Windus, 1922. Page 34 in the Random House edition.

13 *A la Recherche du Temps Perdu*, I, pp. 180–1, Paris, 1954.

14 *ibid.* p. 717.

15 Marcel Proust: *Time Regained*, p. 222, translated by Andreas Mayor, Chatto & Windus, 1970. This and the following passages from Proust are also to be located in Frederick Blossom's translation entitled *The Past Recaptured*, Random House edition. The equivalent page references are: 991–2, 992, 997, 998, 996, and 999.

16 *ibid.* p. 224.

17 *ibid.* p. 234.

18 It is no accident, of course, that the experience described by Eliot takes place in a garden, and that the poem speaks of 'our first world' and of passing through 'a first gate'. The whole cluster of ideas, introduced in *Burnt Norton*, is taken up again at the end of the sequence, in the final 'movement' of *Little Gidding*.

19 See *Burnt Norton*, II and p. 114 below.

20 *Time Regained* (see note 15 above), p. 234.

21 *ibid.* pp. 230–1.

22 *ibid.* p. 237.

23 We may notice, however, that Proust does use, or at least suggest, analogies of a religious kind to convey the sense of his experience. When, for example, in the passage quoted on p. 107 he speaks of the soul receiving 'la céleste nourriture qui lui est apportée', he is in fact echoing closely the language which Catholics use to describe the consecrated Host received at the communion.

24 In drawing the parallel between Proust and Eliot developed in the foregoing pages I have been much helped by Professor R. C. Zaehner's discussion of the French novelist in his *Mysticism Sacred and Profane* (Oxford, 1957), pp. 52–61.

25 Compare *Little Gidding*, III: 'United in the strife which divided them'. See p. 202 below.

26 Compare Dante, *Paradiso*, XXVIII, 41–2:

> Da quel punto
> depende il cielo e tutta la natura.

27 Here, of course, we recall the references to past and future time in the first 'movement'.

28 'And, indeed, with the end of Chapman, Middleton, Webster, Tourneur, Donne we end a period when the intellect was immediately at the tips of the senses. Sensation became word and word was sensation.' (Essay on *Philip Massinger*, *Selected Essays, 1917–1932*, p. 210)

29 Eliot seems to have taken the German word from Goethe.

30 See *The Waste Land*, I, line 62, and p. 30 above.

31 More especially in the treatises on the life of prayer entitled *The Dark Night of the Soul* and *The Ascent of Mount Carmel*.

32 The difference between these concepts, which may be said to correspond to that traditionally drawn between the realms of *nature* and

Grace respectively, can perhaps be illustrated by the following passages from St. John's writings:

This night which, as we say, is contemplation, produces in spiritual persons two kinds of darkness or purgation, corresponding to the two parts of man's nature—namely, the sensual and the spiritual. And thus the one night or purgation will be sensual, wherein the soul is purged according to sense, which is subdued to the spirit; and the other is a night or purgation which is spiritual, wherein the soul is purged and stripped according to the spirit, and subdued and made ready for the union of love with God.

(*Dark Night of the Soul*, I, viii. Translated by E. Allison Peers, New York, 1959)

The spirit feels itself here to be deeply and passionately in love, for this spiritual enkindling produces the passion of love. And inasmuch as this love is infused, it is passive rather than active, and thus it begets in the soul a strong passion of love. This love has in it something of union with God, and thus to some degree partakes of its properties, which are actions of God rather than of the soul, these being subdued within it passively. What the soul does here is to give its consent; the warmth and strength and temper and passion of love—or enkindling, as the soul here calls it—belongs only to the love of God, which enters increasingly into union with it.

(*ibid.* II, xi)

33 See notes 10 and 11, p. 226 above.
34 See p. 77 above.
35 Compare Eliot's remark in his essay on Dante, quoted in Note 48 on p. 223 above.
36 Compare *Ash Wednesday*, V:

Against the Word the unstilled world still whirled
About the centre of the silent Word.

37 I have been unable to trace the source of this quotation. It is to be found, I believe, in the writings of St. John of the Cross, and in any case expresses well the spirit of his thought.
38 See *Burnt Norton*, I, and p. 99 above.
39 Compare *Burnt Norton*, I:

. . . the leaves were full of children,
Hidden excitedly, containing laughter.

[3] East Coker

40 It is worth noting that in 1939, the year of the outbreak of war, Eliot announced that *The Criterion*, the literary review which he had edited since 1922, would cease publication. The terms of this announcement are relevant to the state of mind which finds expres-

sion in parts of *East Coker*: 'In the present state of public affairs—
which has induced in myself a depression of spirits so different from
any other experience of fifty years as to be a new emotion—I no
longer feel the enthusiasm to make a literary review what it should
be' (*Last Words. Criterion*, 18 (1939), p. 269).

41 F. O. Matthiessen, in *The Achievement of T. S. Eliot* (Oxford,
1947), states that 'Eliot listened to Bergson's lectures at the Sorbonne
in 1911 and wrote an essay then criticizing his durée réelle as "simply
not final" '.

42 See p. 125 above.

43 Compare the 'lyrical' passage which opens *Burnt Norton*, II:

> We move above the moving tree
> In light upon the figured leaf
> And hear upon the sodden floor
> Below, the boarhound and the boar
> Pursue their pattern as before. . . .

44 Compare, for a similar range of ideas, the passages from
Shakespeare's 'romances' quoted on p. 82 in connection with *Ash
Wednesday*. It is significant that Eliot is known to have given a series
of lectures at Harvard on Shakespeare's final plays, which he
subsequently judged unworthy of publication. His interest in these
plays is evident at every stage of his poetic development.

45 For a further discussion of the literary implications of this idea see
pp. 170–2 below.

46 Sir Thomas Eliot, *The Boke Named the Governour* (1531).

47 The original passage runs as follows:

> It is diligently to be noted that the associatinge of man and woman in
> daunsinge, they bothe observinge one nombre and tyme in their
> mevynges, was not begonne without a speciall consideration, as well
> for the necessarye coniunction of these two persones, as for the
> intimation of sondry vertues, whiche be by them represented. And
> for as moche as by the association of a man and a woman in
> daunsinge may be signified matrimonie, I coulde in declarynge the
> dignitie and commoditie of that sacrament make intiere volumes . . .
>
> In every daunce, of a moste auncient custome, there daunseth
> together a man and a woman, holding eche other by the hande or the
> arme, which betokeneth concorde.
> (*The Governour*, Book I, ch. xxi, first quoted in relation to *East
> Coker* by J. L. Sweeney, *East Coker: A Reading*, published in
> *The Southern Review* (1941), pp. 771–91)

48 This is what Eliot, at a later stage in his argument, will call an
'Incarnation'. See *The Dry Salvages*, V and p. 178 below.

49 This is the beginning of a line of development which will lead
finally to the vision of a city subjected to the threat of destruction
by fire in *The Dry Salvages*, II.

50 *Inferno*, I, 1-3.

51 Sir Arthur Conan Doyle's Sherlock Holmes story, *The Hound of the Baskervilles*.

52 The concept of 'evolution', or 'progress', will be the subject of further comment in *The Dry Salvages*, II. See p. 164 below.

53 *Burnt Norton*, II. See p. 112 above.

54 This, of course, is a development of the prayer originally put forward in *Ash Wednesday*: 'Teach us to sit still'. See p. 83 above.

55 It is relevant that many writers on the spiritual life, and very notably St. John of the Cross, whom Eliot doubtless has in mind here, have spoken of the Dark Night of the spirit as a necessary stage in the soul's progress towards the state of perfection. Such writers, in fact, see the Dark Night as an instrument in the hands of God, who uses it to obtain the perfection of motive necessary before the soul can advance to the fullness of life destined for it.

56 Letter of Dec. 1817 to George and Thomas Keats.

57 Compare the following from Keats' letter of October 1818 to Richard Woodhouse: 'A Poet is the most unpoetical of any thing in existence; because he has no Identity—he is continually in for— and filling some other Body.'

58 Letter of November 1817 to Benjamin Bailey.

59 Letter of December 1817 to George and Thomas Keats.

60 Letter of October 1818 to Richard Woodhouse.

61 Compare, for Wordsworth's *Immortality Ode*, such a rhetorically charged passage as this:

> Mighty Prophet! Seer blest!
> On whom those truths do rest,
> Which we are toiling all our lives to find,
> In darkness lost, the darkness of the grave;
> Thou, over whom thy Immortality
> Broods like the Day, a Master o'er a Slave,
> A Presence which is not to be put by.

The use, or abuse, of capitals, is in itself an indication of the kind of poetry involved here.

62 Letter of February 1818 to John Taylor.

63 Letter of December 1817 to George and Thomas Keats.

64 Letter of April 1818 to John Taylor.

65 Letter of May 1818 to John Hamilton Reynolds.

66 Letter of October 1818 to James Augustus Hessey.

67 'Nothing' is, in a very real sense, the key word of the whole passage. We remember that the 'funeral' referred to at the outset was 'nobody's', that there was in fact 'nobody' to bury. See p. 138 above.

68 It is interesting to compare at this point Keats' remarks in his famous 'Vale of Soul-making' letter of May 1818 to John Hamilton Reynolds.

69 The lines follow closely *The Ascent of Mount Carmel*, I, xiii:

In order to arrive at having pleasure in everything,
desire to have pleasure in nothing.

In order to arrive at possessing everything, desire to
possess nothing.

In order to arrive at being everything, choose to be
nothing.

In order to arrive at knowing everything, desire to know
nothing.

In order to arrive at that wherein thou hast pleasure,
thou must go by a way wherein thou hast no pleasure.

In order to arrive at that which thou knowest not, thou
must go by a way that thou knowest not.

In order to arrive at that which thou possessest not,
thou must go by a way in which thou possessest not.

In order to arrive at that which thou art not, thou must
go through that which thou art not.

70 It may be noted that the impression of 'heat' and 'cold', ice and
fire, are taken up once again in the opening passage, describing the
season of 'midwinter spring', of *Little Gidding*. See pp. 183–5
below.

71 See p. 133 above.

72 See *Burnt Norton*, V, and p. 122 above.

[4] The Dry Salvages

73 For an example of this tendency see Donald Davie's essay,
T. S. Eliot: the End of an Era, published in *The Twentieth Century*
(April, 1956). Mr. Davie's arguments are, in part, persuasive; but it
seems that there is a limit to what can usefully be said about poetry
in relation to the assumptions and prejudices of a particular time.
The assumptions and prejudices tend to change or to become
irrelevant, whereas the poetry, if it is at all valid, remains.

74 See pp. 181–214 below.

75 See the comment on the Mississippi quoted in Note 4, p. 224 above.

76 Joseph Conrad, *Heart of Darkness*. It is interesting to note that
Eliot had used a phrase from this story ('Mistah Kurtz—he dead')
for one of the two epigraphs for *The Hollow Men*.

77 We may remember Beatrice's question to Dante in Canto VIII, 115
of the *Paradiso*

Sarebbe il peggio
per l'uomo in terra, se non fosse cive?
Would it be the worse
for man on earth, if he were not a citizen?,

and Dante's reply accepting this truth as self-evident.

78 See, in particular, the reference to 'the perpetual Angelus' in
section IV, and p. 175 below.

79 Sir Philip Sidney, *Arcadia*, 2nd Song at Evening.

80 This could be said to be the central theme of *Ash Wednesday*, here incorporated into a different and more inclusive context. See pp. 65–7 above.

81 *East Coker*, II. See p. 134 above.

82 This theme will be taken up again, with added force, in the *terza rima* passage of *Little Gidding*, II. See p. 194 below.

83 Something similar could be said of the mood expressed through the Chorus of Women of Canterbury in *Murder in the Cathedral*, written a few years before. Compare, for example, the following:

> We have not been happy, my Lord, we have not been
>   too happy.
> We are not ignorant women, we know what we must
>   expect and not expect.
> We know of oppression and torture,
> We know of extortion and violence,
> Destitution, disease,
> The old without fire in winter,
> The child without milk in summer,
> Our labour taken away from us.
> Our sins made heavier upon us.
> We have seen the young man mutilated,
> The torn girl trembling by the mill-stream.
> And meanwhile we have gone on living,
> Living and partly living,
> Picking together the pieces,
> Gathering faggots at nightfall,
> Building a partial shelter,
> For sleeping, and eating and drinking and laughter.

84 See p. 93 above.

85 See *East Coker*, III, and p. 142 above.

86 The passages used come mainly from the Eighth Upanishad of the *Bhagavad-Gita*.

87 Quoted by Philip Wheelwright in his essay on *Eliot's Philosophical Themes*, published in *T. S. Eliot: A Study of his Writing by Several Hands*, ed. B. Rajan (London, 1967).

88 See p. 164 above.

89 *Henry IV — Part I*, V, iv.

90 Sonnet LX.

91 *ibid*.

92 *Macbeth*, I, iii.

93 *Macbeth*, I, v.

94 *Macbeth*, III, iv.

95 *Macbeth*, V, v.

96 Like the river in the first 'movement' of *The Dry Salvages*.

97 For an interesting statement of the part played by choice in human

actions as well as its limitation, we could consider the following simile from Machiavelli:

I compare fortune to one of those violent rivers which, when they are enraged, flood the plains, tear down trees and buildings, wash soil from one place to deposit it in another. Every one flees before them, everybody yields to their impetus, there is no possibility of resistance. Yet although such is their nature, it does not follow that when they are flowing quietly one cannot take precautions, constructing dykes and embankments so that when the river is in flood it runs into a canal or else its impetus is less wild and dangerous.

(*The Prince*, ch. xxv, translated by George Bull, London, 1961)

98 A comparison, especially relevant having regard to the circumstances under which these poems were written, might be provided by the attitude of a thinking man faced, in 1939, with the *choice* of accepting his part in the war which began in that year. Such a man might well have decided that resistance to the reality represented by Nazi Germany justified his acceptance of what may have seemed to him an inevitable war. He may, at the same time, have reasonably had little or no illusion about his own ability to foresee what kind of a world the war would finally bring into being, still less to judge whether or not he would, when the time came, find it desirable or attractive.

99 See p. 150 above.
100 *East Coker*, V.
101 *Paradiso*, XXXIII, 1.
102 This seems to be the direction of Donald Davie's argument in his essay, *T. S. Eliot: The End of an Era*, already quoted. Davie, in turn, draws a good deal on Hugh Kenner's essay on *Eliot's Moral Dialectic* (*Hudson Review*, 1949), later incorporated as part of the argument in his book *T. S. Eliot: the Invisible Poet* (1959).
103 *East Coker*, III, and p. 143 above.
104 See p. 161 above.

[5] Little Gidding

105 Compare Eliot's remarks on poetry and belief in the Appendix to his essay on Dante:

You are not called upon to believe what Dante believed, for your belief will not give you a groat's worth more understanding or appreciation; but you are called upon more and more to understand it. If you can read poetry as poetry, you will 'believe' in Dante's theology just as you believe in the physical reality of his journey, that is, you suspend both belief and disbelief.

106 *Acts of the Apostles*, II, iii.
107 The liturgy of Holy Saturday is closely connected with the

baptism of the new members of the Christian community, and
abounds in references to the action of the Holy Spirit.

108 *East Coker*, I.
109 *The Dry Salvages*, III.
110 *East Coker*, II.
111 *The Dry Salvages*, II and p. 165 above.
112 *Burnt Norton*, I.
113 *East Coker*, I.
114 See his own remarks on the passage and its composition in the
essay on *What Dante means to me*, reprinted in *To Criticize the
Critic* (London, 1965).
115 *Inferno*, XV.
116 In Dante, the salutation reads as follows:

> Ed io, quando il suo braccio a me distese,
> ficcai gli occhi per lo cotto aspetto
> si che il viso abbruciato non difese
> la conoscenza sua al mio intelletto:
> e chinando la mia alla sua faccia
> risposi 'Siete voi qui, ser Brunetto?'
> *Inferno*, XV, 25–30

117 The intricacy of the conception reflected in such lines as these,
and present in the whole passage, represented no doubt a technical
challenge—a challenge of expression—of a kind which Eliot seems
to have found particularly stimulating. Although the two passages
are very different, I think it possible that he may have had, at the
back of his mind whilst writing, the elaborately precise recreation of
the transformation, recorded by Dante in *Inferno*, XXV, where a
condemned soul and a serpent first coalesce into one creature and
then exchange their respective *roles* as they separate. We know from
his essay on Dante that Eliot found the passage fascinating.
118 See *The Dry Salvages*, III, and p. 173 above.
119 *East Coker*, II. See p. 136 above.
120 *The Dry Salvages*, III.
121 The line is from Mallarmé's poem *Le Tombeau d' Edgar Poe*.
122
> Considerate la vostra semenza:
> fatti non foste a viver come bruti,
> ma per seguir virtute e conoscenza.
> (*Inferno*, XXVI, 118–20)

123 *Purgatorio*, XXVI, 148. Eliot has already uséd this line in *The
Waste Land*, line 427.
124 Gerard Manley Hopkins, *The Windhover*.
125 *Ash Wednesday*, I. See p. 59 above. It may perhaps be dangerous
to try to identify the speaking voice of *Ash Wednesday*, or of any
other poem by Eliot, too directly with the poet; but perhaps it will
be agreed that there is in this case enough coincidence to make the
point here advanced valid.

NOTES

126 Published in 1920.
127 Wordsworth, *The Prelude*, XII, 277–86.
128 We have already touched upon some aspects of this problem in relation to Keats. See pp. 138–41 above.
129 'Twenty-five' is, of course, an approximation. The age of 'maturity' differs very considerably from person to person, and it is not always — in terms of creation — those who develop most quickly who show the greatest imaginative staying-power.
130 There is some reason to suppose that the final Cantos of the *Paradiso* (XXI to XXXIII) may have been written in a brief space of time and very shortly before the poet's death.
131 The First Part of *Don Quijote* was published in 1605, the second in 1615.
132 See p. 150 above.
133 See p. 211 below.
134 Juliana of Norwich, *Revelations of Divine Love*, ed. Grace Warrack (London, 1901), ch. xxvii.
135 See *East Coker*, V, and p. 148 above.
136 Andrew Marvell, *Horatian Ode upon Cromwell's Return from Ireland*:

> He nothing common did, or mean,
> Upon that memorable scene,
>   But with his keener eye,
>   The axe's edge did try;
>
> Nor called upon the gods with vulgar spite
> To vindicate his helpless right,
>   But bowed his comely head,
>   Down, as upon a bed.

137 *East Coker*, V. See p. 148 above.
138 *Acts of the Apostles*, II, iv.
139 See, for example, the distinction between 'love' and 'desire' in *Burnt Norton*, V, quoted on p. 124, and *East Coker*, II and III.
140 *Burnt Norton*, I.
141 *Burnt Norton*, V. See p. 124 above.
142 *Burnt Norton*, II. See p. 113 above.
143 *Burnt Norton*, V. See p. 122 above.
144 *East Coker*, I. See p. 126 above.
145 *Purgatorio*, XXV, 103–7.
146 *The Dry Salvages*, III. See p. 173 above.
147 *The Dry Salvages*, II. See p. 164 above.
148 *The Cloud of Unknowing*, ed. Justin McCann (London, 1924), ch. ii.
149 *See Burnt Norton*, I.
150 See *The Dry Salvages*, especially I and IV.
151 See *The Dry Salvages*, II and p. 167 above.
152 See p. 100 above.

Bibliography

The following bibliography has no claim to completeness. It is a list of books which I have found useful for formulating my own ideas, and for recommending to students. The occasional comments are designed to give orientation to the latter in their reading.

A BIBLIOGRAPHY

D. C. GALLUP, T. S. Eliot: a bibliography (London, 1969)

B WORKS BY T. S. ELIOT

T. S. ELIOT, Collected Poems, 1909–1962 (London and New York, 1963)
Selected Essays (London and New York, 1951)
    Contains most of what is valuable in Eliot's criticism.
The Use of Poetry and the Use of Criticism (London and Cambridge, Mass., 1933)
On Poetry and Poets (London and New York, 1957)
To Criticize the Critic, and Other Writings (London and New York, 1965)
    Eliot's later criticism is increasingly diffuse, sometimes to the point of confusion; but some of the ideas in these later essays can usefully be related to the poetry, and in particular to the *Four Quartets*.
Knowledge and Experience in the Philosophy of F. H. Bradley (London and New York, 1964)
    Eliot's doctoral thesis for Harvard, published for the first time in the year of his death.

C BACKGROUND

EDMUND WILSON, Axel's Castle (New York and London, 1931)
    Still probably the best general introduction to the literary ideas of the period between the two World Wars.
F. R. LEAVIS, New Bearings in English Poetry (London, 1932, New York, 1950)
    An important critical introduction to the significant poetry of the inter-war period.
E. J. GREENE, T. S. Eliot et la France (Paris, 1951)
    Useful for the influence of French poetry and ideas on Eliot's earlier work.

D COLLECTIONS OF CRITICAL STUDIES

These are collections of essays of varying value, but offering useful approaches to the poetry and bringing together in a convenient form work not otherwise easily accessible.

BIBLIOGRAPHY

JAY MARTIN, ed., Twentieth Century Interpretations: The Waste Land (New York and London, 1968)

HUGH KENNER, ed., T. S. Eliot: A Collection of Critical Essays (Englewood Cliffs, N.J., and London, 1962)
Perhaps the most useful of these general collections.

A. WALTON LITZ, ed., Eliot in his Time: Essays on the Occasion of the Fiftieth Anniversary of The Waste Land (Princeton, 1972)

B. RAJAN, ed., T. S. Eliot: A Study of his Writing by Several Hands (New York, 1949, London, 1967)
Contains useful essays by Philip Wheelwright on *Eliot's Philosophical Themes*, and by E. E. Duncan Jones on *Ash Wednesday*.

L. H. UNGER, ed., T. S. Eliot: A Selected Critique (New York, 1948)

E GENERAL CRITICAL STUDIES

VINCENT BUCKLEY, Poetry and Morality (London, 1959)
Includes a discussion of Eliot's work.

ELIZABETH DREW, T. S. Eliot: The Design of his Poetry (New York, 1949, London, 1950)
An interesting study, influenced by Jungian psychology.

NORTHROP FRYE, T. S. Eliot (London and New York, 1963)

H. L. GARDNER, The Art of T. S. Eliot (London, 1949, New York, 1950)
One of the most complete general studies of the poetry.

HUGH KENNER, T. S. Eliot: the Invisible Poet (New York, 1959, London, 1960)
Among the most perceptive American studies of Eliot's work.

F. O. MATTHIESSEN, The Achievement of T. S. Eliot (New York and London, 1947)

D. E. S. MAXWELL, The Poetry of T. S. Eliot (London, 1952)

GERTRUDE PATTERSON, T. S. Eliot: Poems in the Making (Manchester, 1971)
Chiefly valuable on the early poetry.

G. L. SMITH, T. S. Eliot's Poetry and Plays: A Study in Source and Meaning (Chicago, 1956, Cambridge, 1961)
Contains much useful material, but is concentrated to excess on the hunt for 'sources', often at the expense of the poetry.

L. H. UNGER, T. S. Eliot, Moments and Patterns (Minneapolis, 1966, London, 1967)

DAVID WARD, T. S. Eliot Between Two Worlds (London, 1973)

G. WILLIAMSON, A Reader's Guide to T. S. Eliot (London and New York, 1955)

F ON PARTICULAR POEMS

1 The Waste Land

JESSIE WESTON, From Ritual to Romance (London, 1920, New York, 1957)

SIR G. FRAZER, The Golden Bough (London, 1935)
Especially Vol. VI, Part iv: Adonis, Attis, Osiris.
The structure of *The Waste Land* rests largely on material drawn from these two books.

VALERIE ELIOT, ed., The Waste Land: Facsimile and Transcript of the Original Draft (London and New York, 1971)
   Important for the genesis of the poem, and for the changes made at the suggestion of Ezra Pound.

2 Four Quartets

HARRY BLAMIRES, Word Unheard: A Guide Through Eliot's Quartets (London, 1969)

RAYMOND PRESTON, Four Quartets Rehearsed (London and New York, 1946)